BY THE SAME AUTHOR

UNISON – the Envy of Its Competitors

*The Origins, Rise and Eventual Decline
of the UNISON Network*

Nouveaux Riches to Nouvea...

THE STORY OF THE MACALP...

Bernard

Best

Doddington

Nouveaux Riches to Nouveaux Pauvres

THE STORY OF THE MACALPINE-LENYS

Ian Macalpine-Leny

HAGGERSTON PRESS

Copies may be ordered from

Ian Macalpine-Leny,
The Old Rectory,
Doddington,
Lincs. LN6 4RU (UK)

*Price, including p & p, UK
& surface mail world wide £35.00*

or

Richard P. Gowdy II
348 Withers Larue Rd,
Berryville, VA22611 (USA)

*Price, including p & p
continental USA, $55*

FRONTISPIECE: Captain William Macalpine-Leny and his three sons. *Left to Right* Captain W. H. Macalpine-Leny, Royal Artillery; Captain J. R. Macalpine-Downie, Argyll & Sutherland Highlanders, & Major R. L. Macalpine-Leny, 16th Lancers, 14 September 1904

TITLE PAGE: the Macalpine crest – the Head of Alpin, and the Leny crest – the Cup of Hospitality

Printed in Great Britain by Martins of Berwick

ISBN 978 1 869812 26 3

For William and Jamie
in the hope
that they might keep up
the good work . . .

Contents

Author's Note

This book would not have been possible without the help and encouragement of our wider family, who have dug in their attics for photograph albums and scrap-books, answered innumerable questions about their forebears, and kindly vetted transcripts of the appropriate chapters. Most important of all, they have agreed to let me write about their families and include the entire story, warts and all. I hope that I have treated the more sensitive issues sympathetically.

Outside our family I must first and foremost thank: the Landales, the present owners of Dalswinton, who have shown me incredible kindness and encouragement; Morag Williams, the former archivist of the Crichton Hospital in Dumfries; Ian Downie and Sandy Fyfe, both of whom I met on the internet, who have painstakingly taught me how to use it to search old parish records and other online sources, and ended up unearthing much of the material themselves; Erica Johnson and the staff at the Ewart Library in Dumfries; Guy Hitchings, the archivist of the parish of Speldhurst in Kent who introduced me to a cousin that I never knew existed; and innumerable people in archives, museums and libraries up and down the UK who have cheerfully and patiently answered my countless queries. Lastly there is my good friend Javier Barcaiztegui, well known in Spain as the caricaturist 'BARCA', who did the wonderful drawings for the front and back of the cover.

Above all, I must acknowledge the great debt I owe to my father, Kenneth, who gave me my original interest in our family history. I wish he had still been here to help with this book.

And lastly, I must thank you, the reader, for picking up this book in the first place, and hope that you will not be disappointed.

Ian Macalpine-Leny
Doddington,
November 2011

1 In the Beginning

Families don't really begin – they emerge. The majority of the noble families of England emerged with grand titles and large landholdings as gifts from a grateful sovereign in return for some deed, usually on the field of battle, but occasionally between the sheets. They were mostly well documented, but the emergence of the vast majority of families in the British Isles was a matter of family folklore, which often went back no more than a generation or two. When times were hard and uncertain, parents failed to tell their offspring where they came from, and their children never thought to ask.

All this has changed with the arrival of the internet. Now anyone can start to trace their ancestry without even rising from their chair, and genealogical research has become one of the largest uses of the internet after pornography. Old parish records, censuses, wills, land transfers, military records, archive catalogues, newspapers and now even books and old maps are all to be found online, making research available to everyone with a little practice and patience. And the list continues to grow. For those families that owned land, or were in the armed forces or the Church, the task is made even easier. A whole industry has risen up to support this: classes are available for those who want to learn to do it themselves, and specialist consultants for those who do not. Research often produces some nasty surprises. Many a family has found that tales of bravery and achievement were mere inventions; still more have found illegitimacy was much more common in days gone by than it is today. Occasionally, however, epic deeds that had always been played down by those involved have come to light. All this goes to fuel the fascination of discovering our roots. The title of the popular television series says it all: 'Who do you think you are?'

For those families whose origins lie in the Scottish Highlands, there is another twist: Gaelic was never meant to be written down, and once nicknames gave way to clan names and eventually surnames, the spelling varied depending on the writer. Thus it is difficult to distinguish McAlpins from McAlpines, or Lenys from Lennys or Lennies, especially when there were several families with the same first name living in the vicinity. Every McAlpin worthy of the name claims descent from Alpin, whose son Kenneth McAlpin overthrew the Picts and then united them with the Scots to become the first king of Scotland in 843. Alpin was killed in battle around 836, and his severed head surmounting five drops of blood remains the crest of the Macalpine-Lenys to this day. With it comes the sinister legend *Cuinich Bas Alpin* – 'Remember the Death of Alpin'. Kenneth McAlpin gave rise to a long line of Scottish kings, as well as the clan that bears his name, but somewhere along the way, the lands on which every Scottish clan was based were lost, and the McAlpines ceased to exist as a clan in the traditional sense.

Our story begins in that beautiful part of Scotland where the River Forth leaves Loch Ard and meanders east through the Vale of Monteith to the city of Stirling. There an ancient fortress stands guard over the surrounding countryside and the all-important bridge over the Forth. To the south lie the striking Gargunnock and Fintry hills, with the village of Kippen standing on a promontory looking out across the Upper Forth Valley. To the north unfolds the stunning scenery of the Lower Highlands with Ben Vorlich, Ben Ledi and Ben Venue forming the skyline. To the west is the unmistakable outline of Ben Lomond. Looking out from Kippen on a bright winter's day at the snow-covered hills, it is hard not to be impressed by the sheer beauty of the whole area, and even the new wind farm to the north-east has something majestic about it.

Driving west from Stirling along the A811 through prime farmland, it is easy to forget that the countryside was very different three hundred years ago. As the sea had receded it left behind an extensive area of peat bog and marsh that formed a natural barrier to both man and beast. Apart from the natural crossing point at Stirling, guarded by the castle, the only other way across the Forth Valley, and then only with a good guide and favourable weather conditions, was the Fords of Frew.[1] These lay immediately below Kippen, along the line of the road to Thornhill and Doune. With such a natural barrier, it is hardly surprising that the Forth Valley became the boundary between the Lowlands and the Highlands of Scotland, with Kippen sitting right on the frontier.

[1] Tom Begg, *The Kingdom of Kippen*, (John Donald, 2000).

Life for the local inhabitants at the end of the seventeenth and the beginning of the eighteenth century could never be described as dull. There were constant struggles between supporters of the new Hanoverian king and the traditional Jacobite cause, not to mention the Covenanters and their religious opponents. The former were hardline Calvinist Presbyterians with the bulk of their support in the Lowlands, while their antagonists tended to be Episcopalians whose power base was the aristocracy and the Highlands. If that wasn't enough, the area suffered from a succession of raids carried out by displaced Highlanders. The Highlands were pretty much a law unto themselves at that time, and a series of crop failures towards the end of the century reduced many of the clansmen almost to the point of starvation. This increased the number of raids on the Lowlands to carry off food supplies and, typically, cattle. Motives ranged from sheer necessity, political or religious reprisals, to out-and-out theft.

The most infamous of all the cattle thieves was Rob Roy Macgregor, immortalised by Sir Walter Scott. It is pretty certain that the twenty-year-old Rob Roy was responsible for the celebrated 'Hership', or devastation, of Kippen in 1691, when two valuable herds were driven off, and the partially ruined medieval church was set on fire. Like all such stories, nothing has been lost in the telling over the years, and hard facts are difficult to come by. Whatever the case, Rob Roy went on to make a very good livelihood, using his droving expertise to steal cattle, and then being paid to 'steal' them back again or extract blackmail (protection money) from local lairds and their tenants. Based on the Aberfoyle area, by all accounts he was a thoroughly nasty piece of work, although he ended up being raised to almost legendary status first by Scott's novel and then by the 1995 film that bears his name. He died in 1734 and is buried in the Kirkyard at Balquhidder.

Henry Home, Lord Kames, was a celebrated judge and one of the founding fathers of the Scottish Enlightenment; through his interest in agriculture he was to have a profound effect on the landscape of the Upper Forth Valley. Having inherited his wife's Blair Drummond properties, he set about devising a scheme to remove the peat and drain his lands adjacent to the River Teith. This he did by constructing a waterwheel 28 feet in diameter which sent water more than half a mile over a ridge of land and into the River Forth, carrying the loose peat with it as it did so. To obtain a source of cheap labour to farm the land that was being recovered, he encouraged Highlanders by offering leases on extremely favourable terms, supplied timber so that they could construct a house, and tools so that they could dig the peat. The first arrived in 1767, and by 1774, thirteen tenants had uncovered over 100 acres between Stirling and Doune. At first all the other lairds laughed at Kames, but it wasn't long before they followed suit. This project finally came to an end in 1865 when the floating of peat down-stream was declared a public nuisance.[2]

The three families that lie at the heart of our story all came from the area and all knew each other. The exact origin of the McAlpins is uncertain, but it is probable that they came from Buchanan parish which lies about 15 miles west of Kippen on the south-east bank of Loch Lomond. There were a number of different families of McAlpins here, several of whom rather inconveniently had William as a first name, so tracing them back is not easy. According to family tradition, the family were proscribed after the 1745 rebellion and only escaped by virtue of a younger son serving as a cornet with the army of the Honourable East India Company, but although a good story, no evidence has yet been found to support this. The first reliable ancestor is one Captain William McAlpine, who did not have a regular commission but was probably part of a local militia attached to either the 71st or 78th Highlanders. He had married Jean Macpherson, who almost certainly died giving birth to their second daughter on 1 June 1787, because on 2 July of the following year, he was married to Anne Leny in the old church at Kippen, by the minister, the Rev. John Campbell. Anne was the eldest daughter of George and Elizabeth Leny who farmed at Nether Glinns, and were also tenants at Garden.

Nether Glinns Farm lies off to the west of the road from Fintry to Kippen, and about 6 miles south of Kippen. It still exists today, although the roof of part of the farmhouse was raised in the 1920s to create a second storey. It has a beautiful view over the Endrick Water to the range of hills to the south. Although the farm is actually in Balfron parish, the Lenys were regular worshippers at Kippen, and all their seven children were bap-

[2] Ibid.

tised there, so it was only natural that Anne should be married in the old church at Kippen. John Campbell was the distinguished minister of Kippen from 1783 to 1806 who contributed the Kippen section of the first *Statistical Account of Scotland 1791–1799*. He went on to become minister of the Tolbooth Church in Edinburgh, and then in 1818, Moderator of the General Assembly of the Church of Scotland. In addition to providing the first detailed account of Kippen, the *Statistical Account* included the following:

Remarkable Medical Case. It may not be improper in this place to mention the remarkable case of a boy who lost a considerable portion of brain, yet recovered, without detriment to any faculty mental or corporeal. On 1st of June 1792, William Stewart, a servant boy, about 14 years of age, was by a blow from the foot of a horse knocked to the ground, and left in a state of insensibility. From a large wound on the right side of his fore head, blood issued in considerable quantities, as well as at different times, a considerable portion of the substance of the brain. The boy not only survived the accident, but recovered, and was seen perfectly well, and was seen by the writer of this account in the month of November following. A detailed account of this case, and of the whole process of the cure, was published by Mr Robert Leny, a young gentleman, practitioner in physic, which deserves the attention of those who are curious in physiology. It is inserted in the Medical Commentaries, published by Mr Duncan of Edinburgh, for 1793, p. 301.

Robert Leny was none other than Anne's eldest brother, and he was twenty-one years old at the time. He had gone to Glasgow University in 1786 at the age of fifteen, and went on to study medicine. His account shows him to have been modest and sensible, trusting to nature for a cure rather than trying to intervene with his newly acquired medical knowledge.

Every circumstance here was unfavourable, and seemed to forebode approaching dissolution; but a desire to know the issue of so remarkable an accident, made it appear improper to desert the patient until the fatal event had actually taken place. This, and another consideration of equal importance, namely, the

THE MACALPINE-LENYS

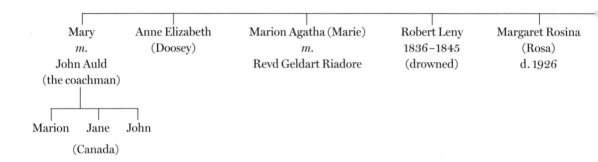

Mary	Anne Elizabeth	Marion Agatha (Marie)	Robert Leny	Margaret Rosina
m.	(Doosey)	m.	1836–1845	(Rosa)
John Auld		Revd Geldart Riadore	(drowned)	d. 1926
(the coachman)				

Marion   Jane   John
(Canada)

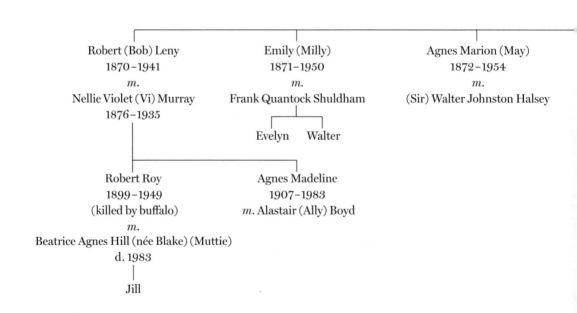

Robert (Bob) Leny	Emily (Milly)	Agnes Marion (May)
1870–1941	1871–1950	1872–1954
m.	m.	m.
Nellie Violet (Vi) Murray	Frank Quantock Shuldham	(Sir) Walter Johnston Halsey
1876–1935		

Evelyn   Walter

Robert Roy	Agnes Madeline
1899–1949	1907–1983
(killed by buffalo)	m. Alastair (Ally) Boyd
m.	
Beatrice Agnes Hill (née Blake) (Muttie)	
d. 1983	

Jill

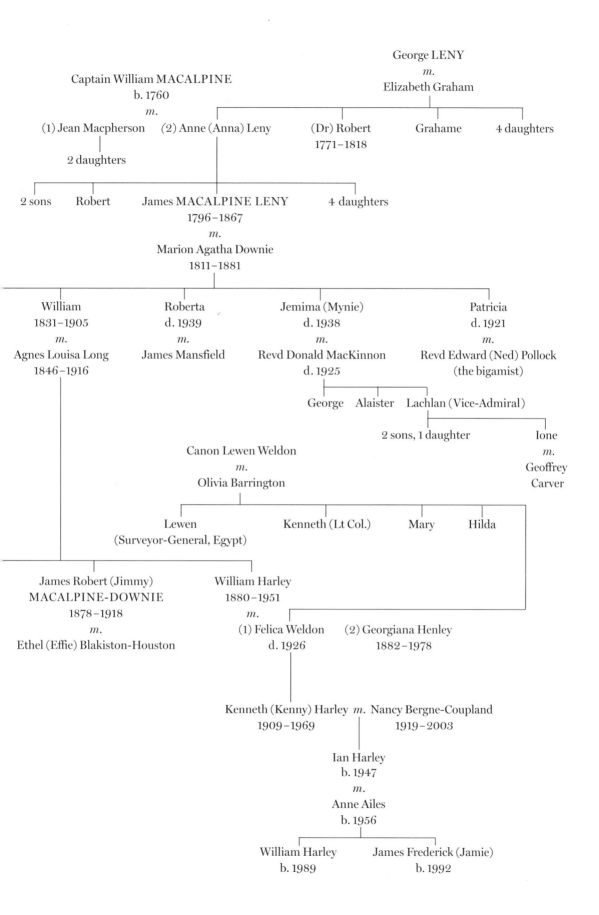

boy's low situation in life, excluding him from proper medical assistance, not the sanguine expectation of performing a cure, were the motives that induced the writer to undertake its management; and this he did, though he had hitherto been more engaged in the study than in the practice of the profession. He regulated the treatment entirely by the symptoms that presented themselves, thinking it more expedient to watch the efforts of nature, and implicitly to follow her indications, than by too active an interference upon the rules of method and system, probably to counteract her operations.[3]

He got his patient's pulse down by ordering him 'to drink moderately cordial (whiskey toddy)', and when the boy became fevered restrained himself from bloodletting – the standard treatment for many conditions at the time – long enough for a general sweat to break out and reduce the temperature. He eventually patched the hole in the boy's head with 'a piece of paste-board, lined with flannel' and sent him to stay with friends 'with strict instructions to avoid exercise'. In due course the hole hardened, the paste-board was laid aside, and he was 'found to enjoy health, strength and full exercise of all his functions, as entirely as before the accident'.

The publicity given to this case must have been a considerable help in obtaining an appointment as the surgeon on the Honourable East India Company's ship *Thetis*, on which he set sail from Portsmouth bound for India under Captain Henry Bullock on 20 June 1794. The journey to Bengal took about four months at that time, and the *Thetis* was not back in Portsmouth until November 1795. The wages of a surgeon were £3 a month in times of peace and £3.50 per month in times of war. However, following a resolution passed by the Honourable Court of Directors dated 6 March 1771, a surgeon was allowed the following stores: '14 doz Wine, Beer or other liquors; 1 cwt Cheese; 1 ditto Grocery; one and a quarter Cases of Pickles, as well as 3 tons on ships of 755 tons up wards' (*Thetis* was 850 tons). Life cannot have been that miserable. He was on board again when the ship left on her next voyage on 17 May 1796 and this time stayed in India, joining the Bengal Medical Establishment as an Assistant Surgeon on 5 November 1798. We will hear more of him later.

Robert Leny's younger brother Grahame also went to Glasgow Univer-

[3] Andrew Duncan (ed.), *Medical Commentaries*, Vol. 8, 1793.

sity, in 1789, and unlike his brother chose a career in the law, becoming a Writer to the Signet (a Scottish solicitor) in 1799. Such a move from a farming family into the professions was not at all unusual in those days, thanks to the very sound education system in Scotland. This was based on the parish, and goes back to the teaching of John Knox, who stipulated that every boy and girl should be able to read the Holy Scriptures. The initial Act of Parliament of 1633 setting up parish schools was not successful because it depended on the consent of the local parishioners; although this loophole was closed in the subsequent Act of 1646, this was overtaken by the disturbances of the time, and it was not until the 1696 Act for Settling of Schools that progress was finally made. This laid down that the heritors (landowners) should provide a school building and the annual salary of a schoolmaster in every parish that did not already have one. This resulted in an estimated male literacy of 55 per cent in 1720, rising to as high as 75 per cent in 1750, compared to only 53 per cent in England, so laying much of the foundation for the Scottish Enlightenment, and the amazing export of talented Scots to all corners of the globe.[4]

Not much is known about George Leny, the boys' father. He probably came from Drymen, about 11 miles west of Kippen. In 1767 he had married Elizabeth Graham, whose home was Over Glenny. This no longer exists, but was due north of the Lake of Menteith in the parish of Aberfoyle. George clearly was not someone to be pushed around. By 1778 the Kirk at Kippen had become somewhat overcrowded, and in September a scuffle broke out in the gallery over the scarce seating. George claimed that he had hit Andrew Lockhart of the Parks because he had pushed his mother-in-law. Lockhart maintained that he had had no option because the lady in question had stuck her hatpin into his backside since he had sat in what she considered to be her seat. Needless to say, the Kirk Sessions took a somewhat dim view of such goings on, and George Leny was fined two guineas 'for the relief of the poor'.[5]

After their marriage, Captain William and Anne (known as Anna) McAlpine went to live at Drumlean Farm to the west of Aberfoyle on the

[4] Arthur Herman, *The Scottish Enlightenment* (Harper Perennial, 2006).
[5] Stirling Council Archives, Ch. 2/390, Minutes of Kippen Kirk Session, 20 September 1778 *et seq*.

banks of Loch Ard, where he was the tacksman – a tenant, often a relative of the chief of a clan, who obtained a tack (lease) of a sizeable tract of land from the owner of an estate and sublet it to smallholders. In addition to the two daughters from his first marriage, four sons and a daughter were baptised at Aberfoyle between 1789 and 1796. Two sons probably died in infancy because we hear no more about them, but the second, Robert, and the fourth, James, born on 19 January 1796, both went out to India.

After the McAlpines and the Lenys, the third family that plays a key part in this story are the Downies. There are Downie families in various parts of Scotland, but this branch farmed at Ashentree, which still exists, in the early part of the eighteenth century. It is located on the north side of the River Forth about 4 miles north-east of Kippen, where the road north from the old crossroads (now a roundabout on the A811) forks right towards Doune. Later in the century there was a younger son, Robert Downie, who was a distiller in the district of Monteith, the farm having gone to his elder half-brother. We know very little about him, but he married Margaret Morison in Kilmadock parish in June 1758, and they produced two sons, George and Robert, and a string of nine daughters. Significantly, the Downies, Lenys and McAlpines of that generation all knew each other, and they might all have been present at the wedding of Captain William McAlpine and Anna Leny. Perhaps more importantly, at a time when so many from those parts were heading for the New World, the Downies set their sights on India.[6] It was the right decision.

---

[6] From 1759 to 1776 there was a constant flow of emigrants from the Highlands to North America. Between 1763 and 1775 alone it is estimated that more than twenty thousand Highlanders left Scotland for the New World. In 1782/3 the potato crop failed, resulting in famine across the Highlands and another wave of emigration to Canada (see Frank Adam, revised by Sir Thomas Innes of Learney, *The Clans, Septs, and Regiments of the Scottish Highlands* (Johnston & Bacon, 1970)). Any Scot who looks down on American and Canadian enthusiasm for Highland Gatherings and Scottish dress and customs had better reread his history.

2 India and Fortune

On 31 December 1600 a group of merchants obtained a Royal Charter under the name of 'Governor and Company of Merchants of London Trading with the East Indies'. Although it was originally envisaged that this company would operate in present-day Indonesia, it ended up trading with India and China. The Company struggled to gain a toehold at first due to competition from the already well-established Dutch and Portuguese, but in due course it established factories in Madras in 1639, Bombay in 1668 and Calcutta in 1690, trading in cotton, silk, indigo dye, saltpetre and tea. Saltpetre, or potassium nitrate, was a critical component in the manufacture of black powder. In 1711 a trading post was established in Canton to trade tea for silver.

By the middle of the eighteenth century, the Company's principal colonial competitor was the French, and both sides had built up a considerable military presence to defend and extend their influence. After the death of Emperor Aurangzeb in 1707, the Mughal Empire had become divided into a number of successor states, and by the end of the Seven Years War in the early 1760s, the French had lost out while the Company controlled Bengal in the north and the Carnatic, near Madras, in the south. The British Government progressively brought in a number of regulating Acts that sought to limit the Company's power and establish Parliament's sovereignty and ultimate control over it. But the opportunity remained to make a substantial fortune in a relatively short time, provided one lived to tell the tale. There was the constant threat of disease, death was an everyday occurrence, and life expectancy for many of the European arrivals was two monsoons. The average age of death was thirty for men and twenty-five for women, and in Calcutta the mortality rate in the first year approached 50 per cent. It was not only the frequency, but the suddenness of death that made such an impact on Europeans living in India. Because of the immediate onset of putrefaction, burial had to take place immediately, and it was not uncommon to breakfast with someone in the morning and go to their funeral in the evening. As one European resident put it: 'Here people die one day and are buried the next. Their furniture is sold the third and they are forgotten by the fourth.'[1]

Part of the problem was that all water in Calcutta used for domestic purposes came from the Hoogli, and most of the poorer classes disposed of their dead by simply tipping them into the river. As late as March 1864, the Sanitary Commissioner for Bengal stated in his report: 'More than 5,000 corpses have been thrown from Calcutta into the river, which supplies the greater part of its inhabitants with water for all domestic purposes, and which for several miles is covered as thickly with shipping as almost any river in the world. 1,500 corpses have actually been thrown into the river in one year from the Government Hospitals alone!'[2] But some would-be fortune-seekers never even got to India in the first place. The journey of more than 15,000 miles to Calcutta took anything up to six months, and in addition to disease on board, there was the very real possibility of shipwreck or attack by pirates or, increasingly, the French. It was not for the faint-hearted. Yet by the beginning of the 1780s, Calcutta was booming, and new arrivals from London were amazed at the palaces of the rich merchants, and the wide open streets. Not only a city of trade and business, it was also a city of staggering excess, and soon became famous for being as debauched as any port in the world. With an estimated 250 European women to 4,000 men, the young Company 'Writers' had little to do or spend their money on other than the taverns and brothels that adorned the backstreets, adding virulent sexually transmitted diseases and excessive alcohol consumption to life's other problems. But the opportunities for making large amounts of money very quickly, if you survived, drew to Calcutta in those days a constant stream of impoverished younger sons of English landed families, Scots who had lost their livelihood in one of the Jacobite uprisings, or those that just wanted to make their fortunes.

It is not entirely clear how the first member of the three families in our story came to go out to India. Few could have afforded the passage unless they had been fortunate enough to secure one of the Company's civil or military positions beforehand. We know that a Lieutenant John Downie

[1] Theon Wilkinson, *Two Monsoons* (Duckworth, 1976).
[2] Ibid.

of the Bengal European Regiment was killed at the siege of Patna in 1763,[3] but have not been able to establish any link between him and the Downies living at Ashentree Farm outside Thornhill. However, George, the elder son of Robert Downie and Margaret Morison, joined the Bengal European Regiment as a cadet in 1782 at the age of twenty-one. Interestingly, he gave the name of his uncle John at Ashentree rather than his father as his next of kin. The Bengal European Regiment had been formed in 1756, although the Company had had a military presence in Bengal for at least eighty years. The Company's principal recruiting depot was at Parkhurst in England, and subsequently Chatham, and no one was recruited in India unless they could prove that they were purely of European descent.

In the early days of the East India Company, the officers in their service were appointed by the 'Court of Directors'; their only requirements being good health, courage and common sense. The pay of the officers was little more than nominal, prize-money was plentiful; and those officers who were fortunate to render services to the Native Chiefs were handsomely, and sometimes profusely, rewarded. Cadets so appointed were not promoted to Ensigncies until they had educated themselves for their profession in the army; and in many instances they served as private soldiers in what was called the 'Cadets' Company'; or carried their muskets in the ranks, attended all drills, and took their guards in common with the privates of the Regiment. Leave to Europe was not in any case permitted. A cadet took service for his life; and if he found it necessary, on account of ill health or from some other cause, to absent himself from the country, he was deprived of his Commission. All the servants of the Company, whether civil or military, were permitted to carry on trade on their own account; which, with the advantages they possessed over the Native Traders, ensured very handsome profits.[4]

To young George, life must have seemed infinitely more exciting than back in Scotland, and he was commissioned as an ensign on 9 May 1783. He was clearly well suited to military life and made a great success of it. He was promoted to lieutenant in 1790 and captain in 1802. Some time

[3] V. C. P. Hodson, *List of the Officers of the Bengal Army, 1758–1834* (Constable, 1927).
[4] P. R. Innes, *The History of the Bengal Regiment* (Simpkin, Marshall & Co., 1885).

around 1794 he returned to Europe, and two years later, according to a Calcutta newspaper cutting of 23 October 1796, he had a somewhat unusual return journey to India:

Captain Downie, who arrived on Thursday last from Madras, with dispatches from the Hon. Court of Directors, left England in the beginning of May. He embarked at Yarmouth for Hamburgh; from thence he passed through Germany into Italy, and took shipping at Naples for Alexandria. Not withstanding the circuitous route that he had been thus obliged to pursue, he arrived in Egypt within forty days of his having left London. So far his progress was uncommonly expeditious; and had the Company's cruiser not been unluckily dispatched a few days before his arrival at Alexandria, he would have performed the journey from London to India in little more than two months.

The previous dispatch of the Company's cruiser from Suez subjected Captain Downie to much inconvenience and personal hardship. At Jidda [Jeddah] he was exposed to the rapacity and oppression of the Vizier, by whom he was imprisoned ten or twelve days. The Vizier, we understand, invariably extends a similar treatment to all travellers who are so unfortunate as to come within reach of his power. After much difficulty and delay, Captain Downie was permitted to embark on board a local Arab boat proceeding to Cochin, where he arrived after a most tedious and uncomfortable passage of twenty-seven days.

When Captain Downie was at Alexandria, the plague was prevalent in that capital. Mr Baldwin, the English Consul, was shut up in his house, from which he had not ventured to leave for some months, from the dread of the contagion.

Jeddah on the Red Sea to Cochin on the south-west coast of India was not exactly a short journey in any sort of ship, quite apart from being imprisoned. Being the good military man that he was, George took the trouble to pick up all sorts of military intelligence along the way, giving the editor of the local paper in Calcutta quite a scoop.

George went on to become deputy military auditor-general in 1798 and then, in 1800, commandant of the Calcutta Native Militia. This had been raised in 1795 and would go on to become an infantry battalion in the Bengal Army. He never married but, as was typical for Company men in those days, he had a *bibi*, an Indian mistress. She nursed him in his final illness, and after he died on 14 December 1808 at the age of forty-seven, he left her 10,000 rupees, equivalent to £60,000 today. By then only a brevet major, he was still able to leave £2,000 to each of his four surviving sisters and his nephew James Mackillop, and £500 to his brother's daughter Margaret. Nor was his uncle John at Ashentree, back in Scotland, forgotten – he was left a bequest of £100.[5]

Judging by the obituary that appeared in the local paper in Scotland in May 1809, George Downie was a highly respected officer and a much-loved member of Calcutta society:

Died at Allipore in the East Indies, on the night of Wednesday 14th December, after a short illness, Major George Downie, son of the late Robert Downie, Esq., Spittleton of Monteith, commanding the Calcutta Native Militia, highly respected as an officer, and beloved as a man. His principles were pure and independent, his friendship warm and discriminating, and his attachments steady and sincere, while his benevolence was ever receptive to the calls of distress, and active in extending relief to its proper objects. Possessed of transcendent abilities, and quick perceptions, guided by a strong judgement, he evinced himself in every situation of life, a most exemplary, a manly, and respectable character. He was endeared to his Corps, of which every individual regarded him as their Friend and Father. For nearly ten years past, Major Downie has been a member of the General Management of the Orphan Society, in which situation his benevolence has been constantly and successfully exerted to promote the comfort and happiness of the objects of the Charity, and to uphold the credit and prosperity of so laudable an institution, which has suffered a severe loss by this melancholy event. The same spirit, which distinguished the discharge of his public duties, marked his private life, and gave value to his character as a Son, a Friend and a Brother. To those friends, to his relations, and to an only brother, who shared more closely in his affections, his death comes as a heavy and irreparable affliction. Major Downie when seized with the illness which terminated in his death, was making preparations to return to his native country, where, with a competent fortune, with talents, and a mind that qualified and disposed him to do good, he would, had Providence been pleased to spare his life, have proved a blessing to his friends, and to society.

[5] Will in British Library.

Thinking this somewhat over the top, his great-great-great-nephew[6] wrote the following, 160 years later:

Died at Allipore, India, on the night of 14th of December, after a short illness, Major George Downie, son of the late Robert Downie of Spittleton of Monteith, a popular C.O. and sad loss to the Mess of the Calcutta Native Militia. He made a better friend than an enemy and, though greatly respected, made no effort to suffer fools gladly. Embarrassed, in later life, by domestic irregularities, he bought himself a seat on the Board of the local orphanage. Deeply mourned by all his creditors, it was bad luck on George dropping off the hooks like that just when he had made his pile and planned a trip to Europe. Had he managed to make it, there is little doubt that, with his undoubted talents, he would have proved a pretty slick operator.

Whatever the case, if his portrait at Doddington is anything to go by, he was a kindly chap.

None of George's letters has survived, but we can be sure that he wrote glowing accounts back home of life in Bengal, so it was only natural that his brother Robert should also come out. He was nine years younger than George, and arrived in Calcutta in 1788 at the age of seventeen. Although it would be another two years before George was promoted to Lieutenant, the very fact that he had successfully survived more than five years in Bengal would have been a great help to his newly arrived brother.

Robert probably started out as most young men did as one of the Company's writers, or clerks, but it was not long before he was trading on his own account as Downie & Co., independent merchants. Then, as business began to flourish, he went into partnership with Patrick Maitland as Downie & Maitland, with premises in Bankshall Street. Before long they were principal managing owners of a least two ships, the 250-ton *Margaret*, built at Chittagong, and the 761-ton *Porcher*, built at Calcutta in 1799. Showing the ability from early on to have his finger in any number of pies, Robert became involved with the Ganges Insurance Company. In early 1804, B. W. Page, Esq., captain of HMS *Caroline*, had captured two French cruisers which could have caused considerable havoc to shipping

[6] Kenneth Macalpine-Leny.

going in and out of Calcutta. In recognition of the considerable amount of money that he had probably saved them, grateful insurance companies presented him with a piece of silver valued at 5,000 rupees. The letter of thanks announcing this, reproduced in the *Calcutta Gazette* of 1 March 1804, was signed by Robert Downie on behalf of the Ganges Insurance Company.

In keeping with the custom of the time, Robert had taken himself a *bibi* who would have been housed in her own quarters at the back of his house. She produced at least two illegitimate children for him: Margaret, born about 1801, and Robert, born on 15 July 1803. There is no record of Margaret being baptised in Calcutta, and she was eventually to leave India for Scotland with the rest of the family. Robert was not baptised until 16 September 1808, probably rather hurriedly when it was known that he was dying. His father never forgot his *bibi*, and had paid her an allowance of 30 rupees per month after he left India, with provision in his will that this be continued for the rest of her life.

How all this went down with Mary Smith, who became Mrs Robert Downie on 8 October 1804, history does not relate, but coming from a Bengal family she would have known the form. Her father, Joseph Barnard Smith, was a senior merchant in the Company's Bengal Service, and her great-grandfather, Sir John Barnard, had been Lord Mayor of London in 1737. Her mother, Rose, was the niece of the famous French General Jean-Victor-Marie Moreau, but in part no doubt due to the anti-French feeling prevalent at the time, the family had anglicised their name to Morrow. The general beat the Austrians at Hohenlinden in 1800, but then, disliking the increasingly dictatorial behaviour of Napoleon, plotted against him. Found guilty of treason in 1804, he was allowed to go into exile in America. Mary inherited a diamond necklace from her grandmother, reputed to have been a very aristocratic lady from the French colony of Pondicherry in southern India, and this is still in the possession of the Macalpine-Leny family. All Mary's brothers went into the army: Samuel, who was a witness at their wedding along with Robert's partner Patrick Maitland, became a lieutenant-general; her eldest brother Joseph only made Lieutenant Colonel, but his son became a major-general. The youngest brother, James, was a captain in the Native Infantry when he died at sea en route for Madras aged only thirty. Of her two sisters, Amelia's husband was Lieutenant-General William Smelt, who was Commander-in-Chief, Ceylon at the time of the 1848 uprising and the highly controversial imposition of martial law, and Cordelia married Charles Corfield, who had been an army surgeon. No wonder Mary married a merchant. A string of daughters ensued – Mary Cordelia (1805), Georgina Frances (1807) and Roberta Harriet (1808) – then George in 1810.

While Robert was building his family he was also continuing to build his business and his place in Calcutta society. He sat on several grand juries from 1800 onwards, so was obviously considered of significant standing in the community. He also sat for the English painter George Chinnery, who became the most popular portrait painter of British colonial society in Calcutta. Chinnery's fame spread rapidly after he was commissioned in 1805 to paint the two children of James Achilles Kirkpatrick, the Company's Resident at the court of the Nizam of Hyderabad, and his beautiful Indian wife Khair un-Nissa. The moving account of their courtship, marriage and subsequent downfall is brilliantly told by William Dalrymple in *White Mughals*.[7]

While Robert was busily making money hand over fist, his friend Robert Leny had decided in 1797 to stay in Calcutta after his second trip out to Bengal as surgeon of the *Thetis*. He joined the Bengal medical Establishment, becoming an assistant surgeon in 1798 and surgeon in 1810. His reputation as a surgeon quickly spread, and he soon became a popular figure both with Calcutta society and the Company's military establishment. The East India Company directory of 1803 lists him as being 'with the Commander-in-Chief', and it wasn't long before he became close to General Lane. More importantly, he followed the route of so many who had amassed fortunes by working with the local nobility, in his case as physician and adviser to the Raja of Duckei, who rewarded him handsomely. Sadly, no details of this survive.

After the death of Major George Downie in 1808, his friend and brother-officer George Cruttenden resigned his commission after twenty-nine years and joined Robert Downie's firm in 1809. Clearly, the rewards for being in the Company's military service paled into insignificance com-

[7] William Dalrymple, *White Mughals* (HarperCollins, 2002).

pared to those of an independent merchant. By this time, Robert's nephew, James Mackillop, had come out from Scotland to join the firm; he was the son of his elder sister, Mary. For a short time the firm became Downie & Cruttenden, and then, after Robert left India and James joined the partnership, Cruttenden, Mackillop & Co. in 1812.

By 1810, Robert Downie had survived for twenty-two years in Calcutta, and amassed a fortune. It was time to go home. The business was in good hands and James Mackillop's younger brother George would soon join, so the family connection would continue. Robert selected the *Astell* for the return journey. She was 820 tons, launched on 9 December 1809 and left on her maiden voyage to India under Captain Robert Hay on 14 March 1810. This was pretty eventful because she was attacked by three French frigates, *Minerve, Bellone* and *Victor*, on 3 July, but managed to outsail them. However, the *Ceylon* sailing with her was captured and taken to Mauritius, where she was used as a prison ship. One cannot help wondering what happened to the passengers and crew.

The *Astell* left Calcutta for the journey home on 12 March 1811. On board were Robert and Mary Downie, their three daughters ranging from six to two-and-a-half, their precious one-year-old son George, and Robert's ten-year-old Anglo-Indian daughter Margaret. Margaret had been totally accepted by Mary, and brought up with her other daughters. Just as well, because the future for Anglo-Indian offspring in Bengal at that time was an uncertain one. But tragedy lay ahead, and baby George died at sea as they neared St Helena. He was buried there on 22 June. Mary, already heavily pregnant again, must have wondered whether another son and heir was on the way. But this was not to be; they docked on 28 August, and Marion Agatha, the future Mrs Macalpine-Leny, was born in London on 28 September.

Robert Downie had managed to achieve what many had dreamed of, but very, very few were able to accomplish: to survive in India long enough to amass a fortune, and then return home to spend it. Once home, he proved to be the very epitome of an Indian nabob – a rather coarse, larger-than-life character who might ordinarily have been a small-time merchant in Edinburgh or Glasgow. But thanks to his fabulous wealth, his quick wit and his nose for a deal, he was able to throw himself into all sorts of business ventures, join the gentry by purchasing a large landed estate in his native Scotland, and eventually buy his way into Parliament.

From a letter[8] written by Downie from London to his old friend Robert Leny back in Calcutta on 1 April 1812, we know that Leny, via his friendship with senior military figures in India, had succeeded in getting a cornetcy for his young nephew James Macalpine, the second surviving son of Captain William Macalpine and Anna Leny. Interestingly, it reveals that it had already been arranged that he would join the Company's Marine Service as a midshipman:

By a letter come in from the war-office, I observe with sincere pleasure that James Macalpine has got a cornetcy in the 8th Dragoons – this is indeed a fine provision for him. As the Sovereign sails in 3 or 4 days, I shall send him down this letter, desiring him to keep its contents entirely to himself till he reach India, for having incurred the expense of procuring his midshipman's clothes, etc, etc, he must even make the run to Bengal in that capacity, where he can be fitted out with Regimentals as well as here.

This letter, which was to be delivered by Robert Downie's nephew George Mackillop, goes on to reveal one of the principal devices he was to use in the future to encourage the electorate to nominate him – obtaining commissions for their relations in India:

Now Leny, as you have provided so handsomely for your three nephews, through General Hewett,[9] and as I was some time ago told by your friend Armstrong, that you have been most warmly mentioned to General Nugent,[10] and of whom too you will no doubt soon be a favourite, I wish you would do me the favour, to get a Cousin of mine, of the name of James Galbraith, an Ensigncy in one of the Regiments of India – the Bengal Establishment would of course be preferable [rather than Madras or Bombay]. He is a stout healthy man, has been tolerably well educated, but has been doing little good in business. He is a manufacturer, 21 years old, and having no incumberance [*sic*] whatever, wishes much to try

[8] Macalpine-Leny archives.
[9] General Sir George Hewitt, Commander-in-Chief 1807–11.
[10] General (later Field Marshal) Sir George Nugent, Commander-in-Chief 1811–13.

the Scarlet cloth in India. Do not overlook my present request, my good fellow, and write me as soon as you can, as my young friend will be naturally very anxious till I get your answer.

Bearing in mind that the very earliest that any reply could be received was eleven to twelve months, and presumably that it took even Robert Leny some time to pull a few strings, one hopes that James Galbraith's anxiety didn't get the better of him.[11]

According to family tradition, young James fell down an open hatch during the journey out, so was in need of his uncle's medical expertise when he finally arrived in Calcutta. Whether or not that was true, he certainly went to live with his uncle for some months, which would have greatly helped him to adapt to the climate and the way of life. It also fostered a strong bond between uncle and nephew, which would eventually transform his life.

By 1812 when James arrived in India, the Company had tightened its grip on large tracts of the Subcontinent. In the north, it controlled a broad swathe running north-west from Calcutta to beyond Delhi, while the kingdom of Oudh, capital Lucknow, was a 'protected state' under the Company's thumb. In the south Hyderabad and Mysore were in the same condition, while another broad swathe, running up the eastern coast from the Subcontinent's tip to Calcutta, was also directly controlled. The Hindu Maratha states of the west and centre had been subdued by Arthur Wellesley, the future Duke of Wellington, in 1803–4, and after this there was no further warfare for about ten years, while the new acquisitions were digested. But a new menace then started to rear its ugly head – the Pindaris. Originally a loosely organised body of mercenary cavalry attached to the armies of Maratha chiefs, their function was to invade neighbouring territory, plunder everything they could find and generally harass camps and villages. The Marathas then took a share of the proceeds. The Pindaris were expert horsemen who could travel large distances in a day, and relied on speed to keep them out of trouble. With the weakening of the Maratha system the Pindaris eventually began to act independently and plunder on

---

[11] It probably did; Robert Downie eventually got him a job with the Inland Revenue, so it is unlikely he ever went to India.

their own account, returning to their bases in central India during the monsoon season from June to October. Once that was over, they would set out again on highly organised *luhburs* or raiding expeditions, which involved some fairly nasty methods of torture to persuade villagers to disclose where they had hidden their valuables.

The first reported *luhbur* into British territory occurred in March 1812, and the following winter a second incursion into British territory occurred when five thousand Pindari horsemen plundered four or five villages around Surat above Bombay. Once again, by the time the Company had sent out any troops to deal with the situation, the Pindaris were all safely back at their base. When Lord Hastings took over as Governor-General in 1813, he quickly realised that the Pindaris represented an obstacle to peace and tranquillity in the area. More significantly, the local population was beginning to have serious doubts about the Company's ability to give them protection. The answer, he believed, was to wage all-out war to eliminate the Pindaris, although it was not until 1816 that the Court of Directors in London agreed to this. Behind this was Lord Hastings's vision for British supremacy over the whole of central India.

James Macalpine spent part of his active service in India engaged in the campaign against the Pindaris, but also served in the Anglo-Nepal War of 1814–16 when the Company's troops invaded Nepal to stop the incursions by the comparatively new Gurkha regime into the Indian plains. This was not the most illustrious campaign in the history of the British in India, since extreme ineptitude on behalf of the Company's forces was matched by outstanding bravery on the part of the Nepalese. However, it did result, initially through desertion, in the Gurkhas providing the nucleus for a brigade in the Company's army, and they have served with bravery and distinction with the British Army ever since.[12] There is no mention of this war in any of James's letters to his uncle, but his campaign medal complete with 'Nepaul' clasp has survived.[13]

James Macalpine was seventeen when he set out from Calcutta in Sep-

---

[12] John Pemble, *Britain's Gurkha War: The Invasion of Nepal, 1814–1816* (Frontline Books, 2008).

[13] There were only 505 issued: hardly surprising, because this didn't occur until 1851, when most of those eligible would have been dead.

tember 1813 to join his regiment. He would always be immensely grateful
for everything that his uncle had done for him while he stayed with him in
Calcutta, and his genuine concern and affection for his uncle comes out in
his letters. He was well educated, courteous, and very sensible with money,
which sadly was not going to prove a common family trait. There was no
question of accepting an offer to have his uniform made in Calcutta when
this could be done more cheaply at Cawnpore. Both uncle and nephew
were very close to the family back in Scotland, and news was always
eagerly awaited. It was clear that James was not the only recipient of his
uncle's kindness – Robert Leny had gone out of his way to help support
James's mother and sisters as well after the death of his father.

James finally joined his regiment at Cawnpore at the beginning of
December, and almost immediately set out for Meerut, between Delhi and
Nepal, which by 1813 had become a large military base. With letters from
Calcutta taking about two weeks, it was not until the middle of January
1814 that James received the letter from his uncle dated 23 December with
the sad news of the death of his elder brother Robert whilst on board ship
from Madras to China. It was clear that, like many Europeans in India at
that time, Robert Macalpine had taken to the bottle in a major way, and by
the time of his final visit to his uncle in Calcutta, Robert Leny could read
the writing on the wall. His letter to James contained an ominous warning
for the future Macalpine-Leny family; it is a pity that more of them did not
heed it:

By poor Robert's own arrival during his illness, it appears he had erred as I
always apprehended. It is now some consolation to me that I so fully apprised
him of the inevitable consequences of imprudence in his manner of living.
Indeed the tendency to the disease which has destroyed him seems so strong in
all your family, that it is only to be counteracted by the most unremitting care
and temperance. It is no doubt difficult on some occasions to adhere to very
strict rules, and the poor fellow has probably lost himself from a want of the resolution necessary for that purpose.

Life in the 8th Dragoons suited James well. He liked the regiment, and
found the climate in Meerut much better than Calcutta. There was one

nasty moment, when as a result of someone kindly recommending him to the new Commander-in-Chief, he was given a promotion to lieutenant in the 17th Dragoons. As this would have meant giving up his house in Meerut and incurring the expense of moving to Bombay, all for a mere three or four months' seniority, it seemed a thoroughly bad idea. Once again, his uncle came to the rescue, and managed to get the promotion cancelled. As it was, the document promoting him to lieutenant in the 8th was signed by the Prince Regent on 24 February 1814. One cannot help wondering when the news finally reached him.

Mr Farmer, a fellow cornet who had left Calcutta to join the regiment at the same time as James, had not been so lucky. He had started to descend the same slippery slope that had ended in disaster for James's brother Robert, and was forced to leave the regiment and go back to Calcutta. This was all the more embarrassing because he was a relation of Lady Nugent, the wife of the former Commander-in-Chief.

In his letter from Meerut of 6 October 1814, James told his uncle that three days earlier, all the troops at the camp had been put under orders to march at a moment's notice, without being told where they were going. This turned out to be the start of the first phase of the invasion of Nepal. As no letters from this period survive, we will never know what part James played in this campaign, but the 8th Dragoons took part in the failed attempt to take the fort at Kalunga when Major-General Sir Robert Rollo Gillespie, one of the more colourful soldiers in the army in India, died trying to rally his troops at the head of the storming party.[14]

There is then a gap of more than two and a half years until James's next surviving letter, which finds the 8th Dragoons in the middle of the war against the Pindaris in May 1817. These hostilities quickly turned into the Third Maratha War, since the Pindaris' employers could not prevent themselves from joining in. Besides, the Marathas were financially squeezed once they no longer received their share of the Pindaris' plunder. The first Maratha War had been from 1775 to 1782 in the days of Warren Hastings, the second, fought by Arthur Wellesley, from 1803 to 1805. The third encounter was the one that finally put paid to Maratha ambitions, as well as getting rid of the Pindari menace. Lord Hastings's strategy was simple:

[14] Sir William Thorn, *A Memoir of Major-General Sir R. R. Gillespie* (T. Egerton, 1816).

to surround the Pindaris, drive them from their bases, and slowly close the circle while preventing them from escaping. The fact that he took ninety thousand troops to overcome a force of irregulars that was never greater than thirty to forty thousand caused questions to be asked in both India and England, but by February 1818 most of the Pindari leaders had surrendered to the British authorities. James was nearby when a body of cavalry including Gardner's Horse captured all the Pindari commander Karim Khan's baggage in December 1817 as he continued to flee from the pursuing British forces. On rounding up the prisoners from that little engagement, it was found that they included Karim Khan's wife, but the chief escaped again on that occasion. At the successful conclusion of this war, which was to prove a major step in the progressive domination of the Indian Subcontinent by the British, Lord Hastings and the British Army in India received a vote of thanks in the House of Commons.[15]

In addition to describing the military manoeuvres he was involved in, James's letters made frequent reference to both his and his uncle's health, which must have been a constant topic of conversation for everyone at the time. He very much hoped that after twenty years in Calcutta, his uncle would now make plans to return to Scotland. There is also reference to his guardians back in Scotland, the fact that his sisters had moved to Stirling, and that his uncle was still pulling strings by getting young Buchanan from Ayrshire an ensigncy in the 80th Infantry.

Back in Scotland, Robert Downie was making the most of the opportunities provided by his new-found wealth, no doubt in the eyes of some, in the very worst traditions of the nouveau riche. He threw himself into various businesses, never being shy to call on his old India contacts for favours, and probably still did work for Cruttenden & Mackillop when he first arrived home. Not all of these ventures prospered, and according to family tradition, he lost a lot of money trying to launch a rival to *The Times*, but no details of this survive. One project that did seem to have promise, at least initially, was the Union Canal between Edinburgh and Falkirk.

With the opening of the Forth and Clyde Canal in 1790, it was possible for seagoing coastal ships to pass between the east and west coasts of Scotland without having to make the hazardous journey round the north of

[15] Rt Hon. George Canning, President of the Board of Control, 4 March 1819.

Scotland. In addition, it provided a good inland waterway to allow imported and locally manufactured goods to be transported from one coast to another, as well as allowing passengers to travel across the country. But goods from Glasgow destined for Edinburgh then had to be transported overland from Grangemouth, the eastern end of the canal, which was slow and expensive, and much of Edinburgh's coal came in by sea from Newcastle, incurring significant duty. The obvious solution was to build a linking canal between Edinburgh and Falkirk on the Forth and Clyde Canal. Discussions started almost immediately, but had to be broken off during the Napoleonic Wars, so it was not until 1813 that they were started up again. There was considerable opposition, and the first attempt to get a bill through Parliament in 1815 was defeated. Robert Downie was quick to see the potential and became its principal backer. By 1817 he was chairman of the Union Canal Committee, and wrote directly to Robert Dundas, 2nd Viscount Melville, on 2 April, urging him to withdraw his objection and support the bill. Lord Melville had previously been president of the Board of Control for India, but now was effectively running Scotland in addition to being First Lord of the Admiralty. Downie's lobbying was successful, and the Union Canal Bill was passed in June at the second reading. The canal was to be a contour canal, following the contours of the hills, in this case 240 feet above sea level. This had the advantage that there were no locks for the majority of its 31 miles, thereby saving water and speeding up the flow of traffic. Where the Union was to join the Forth and Clyde Canal at the village of Camelon outside Falkirk, it had to descend 110 feet through eleven locks to a basin next to Lock 16 on the latter. This was named Port Downie after Robert.[16]

Work began at the Edinburgh end on Tuesday 3 March 1818, and it was the Chairman himself who dug the first sod. He began his address:

Gentlemen, your kind partiality has conferred on me an interesting office. I have seen much of the vicissitudes of life, but I must confess the 3rd of March 1818 as one of the proudest and happiest of my days. We have, gentlemen, struggled for several years to carry this great undertaking against hosts of opposition . . . You

[16] Abandoned in 1933 and subsequently filled in. Now replaced by the Falkirk Wheel, which opened in 2002.

beheld today in the square of the Royal Exchange, the crowds of suffering men, whose eyes were fixed on us as we passed on our way here, and you see now in this field, thousands to whom you are now holding out the gratifying prospect of being able to feed their families in comfort in years to come. This is indeed, gentlemen, an ample recompence for all we have done, and we all have yet to do, before our barges pass from sea to sea. [After a short pause, Mr Downie added in a lighter tone,] I shall now convince you, Gentlemen, that some of your Committee can handle the spade as well as the pen. [He then cut a square turf from the earth, and threw it into the air, which became the signal for loud and continued cheering.][17]

The canal was opened in 1822. It had been built using the crudest methods: picks, shovels, wheelbarrows and the brute strength of several thousand Irishmen and Highlanders who had come to central Scotland looking for work. The cost was more than £600,000, and many lives were lost because of the poor working conditions. But from 1822 until the opening of the Glasgow-to-Edinburgh railway in 1841, the Union Canal played a major part in the transport of coal, wood, stone, sand and brick to the fast-growing city of Edinburgh and, at its peak in 1836, carried two hundred thousand passengers.

Robert Downie never forgot his family or the debt he owed to his parents. Shortly after yet another daughter, Rose, was born on 23 February 1813, his eldest legitimate daughter, Mary Cordelia, died at the age of seven. Robert lost no time in erecting a fitting memorial in the Kirkyard at Kincardine, about $1\frac{1}{2}$ miles west of Ashentree. In addition to Mary Cordelia, this commemorated his parents, both of whom had died while he was in India, his uncle David Downie, his sisters Robbina and Margaret, and his young nephew Robert Mackillop, youngest son of his oldest sister, Mary. It is an imposing memorial surrounded by wrought iron railings, which have somehow managed to survive.

He was always a firm supporter of the Church. In 1815 'he presented to the congregation at Norriestown, an elegant service of four silver communion cups, as a tribute of regard for that establishment, which he

[17] William Glover, *Journey through the Counties of Berwick, Roxburgh, etc.* privately printed, Edinburgh, 1818).

attended in his youth.'[18] Norriestown, which has now been absorbed by the neighbouring village of Thornhill, is about 2 miles north-east of Ashentree. With a home in Edinburgh – he was renting a house in fashionable Charlotte Square – it was only natural that Robert Downie should join a church in the city. Never one to do anything by halves, he purchased ten £20 shares issued to raise the money to build the Episcopal church of St John the Evangelist in Princes Street, which was completed in 1818. He would later purchase a family burial vault in the crypt.[19]

But it was in 1814 that two key events occurred: Mary Downie finally gave birth to another son, Robert, and Robert Downie bought the Appin Estate from the Trustees of the Marquis of Tweeddale, a substantial estate of some 37,000 acres on the west coast of Argyllshire between Oban and Ballachulish. As Appin will feature prominently later in our story, we will say no more about it now. Interestingly, Downie first bought the Dumbarrow Estate in Forfarshire some time in 1813, but apart from a passing mention in one of James Macalpine's letters, no details survive. Never a man to miss a good business opportunity, he quickly changed horses when a better one came up.

It was perhaps not surprising that towards the end of the decade Robert Downie started showing an interest in politics. He had written to the Prime Minister, Lord Liverpool, from Appin in June 1819, urging him to 'look further into the laws for the protection of the corn as well as the wool grower'. At the general election nine months later, he came forward for the venal and volatile Stirling district of burghs, of which Dunfermline was one. He was encouraged and endorsed by the Lord Advocate, Sir William Rae, who told Lord Melville, the manager of the Scottish parliamentary seats, that he 'will rather be an uncouth sort of member, but he is a sensible man and will be more easily managed than others who might be named'. He secured the votes of Dunfermline, Queensferry and Stirling, and, thus assured of victory, modestly told Melville: 'I appear to have accomplished what few men would have attempted and perhaps still fewer succeeded in, that is, destroyed for the present at least the Whig interest in

[18] *Caledonian Mercury*, 7 September 1815.
[19] Now underneath the entrance to the crypt cafeteria, which would have amused him considerably.

the Stirling district ... Three short weeks ago I certainly had not the slightest intention of appearing as a candidate for this honour.'[20]

National politics in the days before the Reform Acts of 1832 were a very different business from what they are today. The nominal 'electorate' of the Stirling burghs was the total number of councillors in the five constituent burghs: twenty-two in Dunfermline, nineteen in Culross, twenty-one in Queensferry, twenty-one in Stirling and the unusually large number of forty-two in Inverkeithing, making 125 in all.[21] Each burgh nominated a delegate who was instructed to vote in accordance with their choice in the parliamentary election. Such a procedure was easily open to corruption, and across the parliamentary system as a whole, major landowners and returning wealthy nabobs from India and the East Indies were particularly guilty of buying their seats. Robert Downie was no exception: in addition to the nineteenth-century equivalent of brown envelopes, his particular tack was to promise to get postings in India for the sons of those that had voted for him. Here he is writing from 21 Downing Street to Lord Melville after he had been successfully elected MP for the Stirling Burghs in March:

I have already taken the liberty of stating that if I could get two cadetcies for India, it would be of splendid service to my interest, and consequently to that of Government in the Stirling district of Burghs; one for Duncan Littlejohn, son of Provost Littlejohn of Stirling, and one for Robert Mitchel a near relation of Provost Wilson of Dunfermline. The sooner these could be obtained, the more shall I be obliged to your Lordship.[22]

When nothing was forthcoming, Robert Downie wrote to Melville again in rather hurt tones three weeks later:

While I have to thank you for your obliging communication of the 14th inst., I pray your Lordship may not be offended at my honestly saying, that I fear I have

[20] Dr David Fisher (ed.) *The History of Parliament: The Commons 1820–32* (Cambridge University Press, 2009).
[21] Dr David Fisher, personal communication.
[22] Dundas papers, National Archives of Scotland.

made a great mistake in coming to Parliament, for I thought that I should certainly have got a little assistance in this quarter, in paying debts of gratitude to the well disposed of the three burghs who supported my interest, and consequently that of Government, in my late severe contest; and never before having had occasion to beg, I really feel my situation most irksome. The two cadetcies as already said, are for the son of Provost Littlejohn of Stirling, and the nephew of Provost Wilson of Dunfermline, than whom, I say it with great truth, Government has not a more warm supporter in the north. Young Mitchell, the nephew in question has been encouraged to come to London by Mr Campbell some 18 months ago, and has been supported every since by his brother one of the Baillies of Dunfermline, who can indeed very ill afford such expense. The Provost's son of the Queensferry I am sending to Calcutta in the hope that the House at the head of which I was formerly, there, will give him employ: and another relation of Provost Wilson a son of Baillie Scotland also of Dunfermline I intend to have sent next season, by way of getting myself out of debt for the past. Were your Lordship to send me introductions to Mr Canning and some of the Directors, mentioning my object, I would cheerfully wait upon, in the anxious hope that I might thereby give a substantial proof to the Burghs, that I did not fight my late battle under false colours.[23]

This time Lord Melville must have taken some action, because a week later, Downie wrote to George Canning, the future prime minister, who was then President of the Board of Trade. Canning responded to Melville that if he wanted Robert Downie to have a cadetship, he could have one.[24] As so often is the case, persistence had paid off.

Back in India, James Macalpine had completely settled into the life of a lieutenant in the 8th Dragoons, and clearly enjoyed the action that the Pindari war offered. His letters to his uncle continued to enquire about his health, and express the hope that he would soon return to Scotland. Then, in April 1818, he received this from James Mackillop:

I lament extremely that our correspondence should commence on a subject so afflicting both to you and to myself, as that on which I now address you. My brother announced to you on Saturday evening the irreparable loss you had then

[23] Ibid.   [24] Ibid.

just sustained in the death of your respected uncle – Mr Leny – in him you have lost a father, and I one of my oldest and most valued friends – and society has been deprived of one of its most valuable and able members.

The manner in which it has pleased Divine Providence to remove him from amongst us is truly distressing. He felt himself a little unwell on Friday evening, and in consequence excused himself from dining with Mr Brodeswell (?) – but his indisposition must have been extremely slight, as he rode out on Saturday morning. Immediately on his return he was attacked by the prevailing fatal disease Cholera Morbus, and such was its virulence, that though Drs Cochrane, Rupell & Thomas were with him almost from the moment he was attacked, their skill and medicines were unable even for a moment to retard the progress of the fatal event. He expired at 2 o'clock. With the Army you have no doubt had too much opportunity of witnessing the effects of this fatal disease. I sincerely sympathise & condole with you on this melancholy occasion. I have just written to Mr Downie in order that he may announce the melancholy intelligence to the family in Scotland. Our respected friend was interred yesterday and it will be consoling to you to know that his remains were accompanied by all his friends.[25]

The dreaded cholera had first appeared among the immense army assembled to deal with the Pindaris in 1817 and quickly spread as it moved about India. Robert Leny was dead in a matter of hours, no doubt hastened by the efforts of the three doctors. James had a deep affection for his uncle, and the news would have come as a bitter blow. But the letter went on:

Drs Cochrane, Gillman, Williamson & myself examined his papers yesterday, & found his Will, in which he has given strong proof of his regard for you. In the course of a few days I shall give you a copy of the Will, & enter more fully into matters. Meantime I shall give you an outline of his bequests – £800 per annum to your aunt Mrs Donald, & should she leave issue by her marriage, such child or children at her death to receive £10,000, the £800 per annum then to cease. £100 per annum to each of your three sisters during their respective lives. The estate of Glins to your Uncle Graham Leny, and the remainder of the property he bequeaths to you. The whole of the property to be remitted to Britain, to be

25 Macalpine-Leny archives.

invested in the purchase of a landed Estate in Scotland, to be settled by entail on you and your heirs for ever. But which Estate to be subject to the payment of the Bequests above named, & conditioned that you take the surname of Leny. But more on this subject when I send a copy of the Will. I fancy your uncle's Estates will amount to £90,000 or £100,000 & which will consequently purchase a large landed Estate.

Now £100,000 in 1818 would have been worth more than £6 million in today's money, so at the age of twenty-two, James Macalpine had achieved the nineteenth-century equivalent of winning the Lottery. And to be required to buy a large landed estate in Scotland? No wonder he kept that letter. It is not difficult to imagine what must have gone through his head. Here at a stroke was the opportunity to leave the precarious life of an army officer in India and return to his native Scotland as a wealthy laird. And he would have had no problem with taking the name of Leny as a mark of respect to his uncle, who had become like a father to him ever since he first arrived in Calcutta five years earlier. Things happened slowly in those days, and it would probably have been at least eighteen months before he could have resigned his commission and arrived back in the United Kingdom, never to return.

The family fascination with India which had provided two fortunes would continue, and in addition to James and George Mackillop, no fewer than four of Robert Downie's nephews would go out there, three of them never to return. James Mackillop never married, and returned to Scotland a wealthy many in the early 1820s, leaving his brother George to run the business. George Mackillop married in Calcutta in 1820 at the age of thirty, and his first two sons were born there, but he was back in Edinburgh by the time his first daughter was born in 1830. His second son Charles was the last member of the family to continue the Calcutta tradition, until he in turn returned to London in 1849. He lived first in Hanover Square and then Kensington, before eventually moving with his family to Bath, where he lived in great state at 14 Royal Crescent. The spell was broken.

3 James Macalpine Leny of Dalswinton

The Dalswinton estate lies 7 miles north of Dumfries on the left bank of the River Nith, in the heart of the Scottish Lowlands. It was the Romans who first appreciated its strategic importance, and Agricola built a major fort here about AD 82 to control a ford over the river and to serve as a base from which to direct his campaigns up Nithsdale and into south-west Scotland. This was later enlarged and other forts constructed nearby before the Romans finally left Scotland and retreated south.[1]

Dalswinton rose to prominence again in the thirteenth century when the lands were held by Sir John Comyn (the 'Red Comyn'), who may have been responsible for building the castle on the site of the present mansion house which was to play a prominent part in the War of Independence. After Sir John was murdered by Robert the Bruce and Sir Roger Kirkpatrick in front of the high altar of the Greyfriars Church in Dumfries on 10 February 1306, Bruce subsequently sacked and burnt the castle around 1313. It was in the hands of the English again in 1335, but was taken by storm by Kirkpatrick in 1356, after which it was probably never fully repaired.[2] Part of the walls were still standing in 1792.[3]

After passing through several owners, Dalswinton was bought in 1624 by the Dumfries merchant John Rome, who received a crown charter incorporating his new lands into the barony of Dalswinton-Rome. It is likely that he was responsible for building Dalswinton Tower, or the 'Old House' as it was often later known. Defence being no longer a prime consideration, this was built on a more convenient site some 150 yards east of the castle. The basement and the north-west tower survive to this day. In 1649, the estate was bought by John Maxwell for 52,000 merks, and remained in the Maxwell family until 1785 when, following the collapse of Douglas, Heron and Company's bank in Ayr, it had to be put up for sale by Major William Maxwell, who was a substantial shareholder in that bank.[4]

[1] Alistair Maxwell-Irving, *The Border Towers of Scotland, Their History and Architecture* (Creedon publications, 2000).   [2] Ibid.
[3] *The New Statistical Account of Scotland*, 1841.
[4] William Fraser, *Memoirs of the Maxwells of Pollok* (privately printed, Edinburgh, 1863).

The new owner was Patrick Miller, who bought the estate without even seeing it. He was an amazing man. The third son of an Ayrshire and Kirkcudbrightshire laird, he made his fortune as a partner and director of the private banking firm of Mansfield, Ramsey & Co., and was elected Deputy Governor of the Bank of Scotland in April 1790. He was also a partner in the Carron Iron Works, which opened its first furnace in 1760 and by 1800 was the largest smelting works in Europe, with one thousand employees. He was horrified when he saw the run-down state of Dalswinton, and immediately set about improving it. He built the present mansion house on the site of the old castle, the stables and the front gates with the twin lodges; he landscaped the gardens, built the ornamental lake and circular doocot (dovecote), and laid out and built the village of Dalswinton. He was also a lifelong student of naval architecture, and it is as the designer of the first British steamboat that he is best remembered.

Miller had long been experimenting with various types of paddle wheel to drive twin- and triple-hulled boats, the motive power initially being provided by the crew. But with the improvements in engine design and technology led by James Watt, and the production of reliable engines in the 1780s after he went into partnership with Matthew Boulton, it seemed likely that a steam engine might be able reliably to provide sufficient power to drive a small boat. On the recommendation of James Taylor, who was the family tutor at Dalswinton, Patrick Miller approached William Symington, rather than Boulton and Watt, to design and build an engine to drive his small twin-hulled boat. This was 25 feet long with a 7-foot beam and was originally built on the third floor of Dalswinton House, and had to be disassembled and lowered out of the windows and then reassembled at ground level. The maiden voyage was on Dalswinton Loch on 14 October 1788, and according to Taylor, 'The vessel moved delightfully at the rate of five miles an hour.' This was probably a slight exaggeration, given the size of the engine, but Patrick Miller was completely satisfied: he had demonstrated for the first time in Britain that it was possible to drive a boat using a steam engine. His original goal was to develop a boat that could put to sea, so the following year he experimented with a 60-foot twin-hulled craft on the Forth and Clyde Canal, driven by a much bigger engine designed by Symington and built at the Carron Works. The experiment was only partially successful; on the maiden voyage on 3 December 1789 the paddle wheels broke. The second attempt with strengthened paddles on Christmas Day and Boxing Day did work, but the engine was too heavy for the boat and eventually broke down. When Miller turned to James Watt for advice, he immediately claimed that Symington had infringed the Watt steam engine patent. Disillusioned, Patrick Miller had the engine dismantled and stored at the Carron Works. The whole series of experiments had cost him a huge amount of money.

After Patrick Miller's death there was an acrimonious wrangle between Symington, who, unbeknown to Miller, had taken out a patent in 1801 and had built a stern-wheeler for Lord Dundas to tow barges along the Forth and Clyde Canal, and Henry Bell, who had introduced the first passenger service with the *Comet* on the River Clyde in 1812. Both claimed the credit for having introduced steam navigation in Britain. Patrick Miller's corner was argued by his eldest son, Captain Patrick Miller,[5] and it is abundantly clear that the accolade rests with Miller. Much less clear is the case of the carronade, which became an essential part of the armament of British naval vessels from the 1780s. The carronade was, thanks to a more accurately bored barrel, shorter and lighter than conventional guns. It could be used on upper decks and required a smaller crew, delivering a slower-moving shot which had a devastating smashing, splintering impact. Miller was certainly experimenting with improving cannons at Carron Iron Works from 1766 to 1782 and claimed in a pamphlet published in 1813, when he was eighty-five years old, that he first named the guns in question carronades. The debate was still rumbling on in the correspondence columns of the *Glasgow Herald* in 1931, but it is now generally accepted that the inventor was General Robert Melville in the West Indies during the Seven Years War, and the gun was then improved by Charles Gascoigne, the manager of the Carron Works in the 1770s. However, Miller was definitely involved in the fitting out of a privateer, the 200-ton *Spitfire*, in 1778 with sixteen light 18-pounder carronades. The success she met with led to the owners of many merchant ships placing orders for the guns, as a cheap, effective means of defence.

By 1798, Patrick Miller was running seriously short of money, so turned

[5] *Edinburgh Philosophical Journal*, July 1825 and July 1827.

his attention to improving his farms at Dalswinton so that he could get a better return from his tenants. By draining, enclosing and then clearing land of stones and every kind of rubbish, he found that after liming, the new arable land could demand twenty times the rent paid before he started work on it. He also set about a programme of establishing mixed plantations of larch and Scots fir to add to those already on the estate. He enthusiastically embraced the practice of growing fiorin grass to feed sheep and cattle in winter developed by Dr William Richardson in Ireland,[6] and was among the first to introduce the Swedish turnip or swede to Scotland. A highly intelligent, benevolent and generous laird, he was extremely popular with all his tenants.

But Patrick Miller's interests stretched still wider. He was a patron of Robert Burns – who for a short time in 1788 was a tenant of the Ellisland Farm, just across the Nith from Dalswinton – of the portrait painter Sir Henry Raeburn and of the landscape painter Alexander Nasmyth. He commissioned Nasmyth to paint a number of views of Dalswinton to hang in his new house; a pair of large canvases of the house and Dalswinton Loch from the north have survived.

But all this building, experimentation both nautical and agricultural, and patronage of the arts, had the inevitable consequence: by the time Patrick Miller died on 9 December 1815, he was bankrupt. His trustees had no alternative but to put the estate up for sale. The following appeared in the *Dumfries Courier* of 23 July 1818:

The ESTATE of DALSWINTON, lying in the Parishes of Kirkmahoe and Holywood, and Shire of Dumfries – to be SOLD by AUCTION, at Edinburgh, within the Royal Exchange Coffee House, upon WEDNESDAY, the fifth day of August next, at Two O'clock afternoon.

THIS PROPERTY extends, by Plan and Survey, to 4,039 Acres Scots, or about 5,132 Acres English statute measure; and putting a moderate value on Grounds possessed by the late Proprietor, yields a rent of £5,117. In point of compactness, beauty, soil, and climate, it is justly esteemed one of the finest and most desirable Estates in Scotland.

The Mansion House is modern, spacious, and substantial. It stands on the

[6] William Richardson, *A New Essay on Fiorin Grass* (J. Harding, 1814).

ancient site of Comyn's Castle; a situation singularly grand and beautiful, looking down upon the River Nith, which bounds the Estate by more than three miles, and commanding a most extensive and picturesque view over the adjacent country, terminating in the coast and magnificent mountains of Cumberland.

The court of offices comprehends stabling for 16 horses, subdivided into three stables, four coach-houses, extensive lofts, within harness room and accommodation for servants etc. There is an excellent garden, with walls and hot-houses, and an extensive orchard, with pleasure grounds along a beautiful sheet of water, abounding in fish. Besides a great deal of fine old timber, which surrounds and adorns the Mansion-house, there are other large and valuable woods and plantations upon the property.

This Estate lies within 7 miles of Dumfries, in an excellent neighbourhood, and enjoying the mildest and most salubrious climate in Scotland. It is in the immediate vicinity of several lime-works, which afford an inexhaustible supply of the manure best adapted to the soil. The port and market of Dumfries secure a ready demand for the produce, and all the facilities for water carriage. The Estate is bounded and intersected by good roads; the lands are laid out and sub-divided in the most approved manner; and the numerous farm-steadings are modern, commodious and substantial.

The Estate comprehends several salmon fishings in the Nith, some of which belong exclusively to the Barony of Dalswinton; and the river affords excellent angling, both for trout and salmon. To a sportsman, the property possesses the additional recommendation that it is noted for abundance and variety of game.

To the English capitalist it may not be improper to mention, that the Estate is exempted from Poors'-rates, and is subject to only a few pounds sterling per annum of land-tax, and a fixed and moderate proportion of stipend to the Parish Minister, in lieu of tithes.

This Estate, including only £10,000 for the Mansion-house, offices, garden etc, was valued in 1815 at . . . . £144,041 – 0 – 0
And the Woods and Plantations etc . . . . £26,968 – 0 – 0

£171,009 – 0 – 0

But will be exposed to sale at the reduced price of only £140,000.

Once James Macalpine, or James Macalpine Leny as he now started to call himself (the hyphen didn't appear until the next generation), had returned to Scotland, he would have lost no time in getting in touch with Robert Downie. Downie and James Mackillop were the senior trustees of Robert Leny's will, but Mackillop was still in Calcutta. Robert Downie, having bought the Appin Estate back in 1814, no doubt regarded himself as an expert on landed estates in Scotland. Thanks to his involvement with the Union Canal, he had become a well-known public figure in Scotland. But it was also a time of personal tragedy for him; his wife Mary died in childbirth at their house in Charlotte Square on 6 March 1819, aged only thirty-three.

With such a powerful adviser and supporter, it was hardly surprising that the Dalswinton Estate was discovered and eventually purchased from the trustees of the late Patrick Miller in July 1820. The price paid was £130,000, plus £1,202 to Captain Patrick Miller for the lease of Forrest Farm and the value of certain growing timber.[7] At the age of twenty-four, James Macalpine Leny found himself the laird of one of the most beautiful estates in southern Scotland. Some of the contents of the house, including the two big Nasmyth pictures, had been included in the sale, and James lost no time in moving in with his unmarried sisters.

Many a young man in that situation would have cast discretion to the winds and set out on a life of pleasure and excess, but James was not like that. He immediately set to learning about Dalswinton, agriculture and Dumfriesshire, and continuing the programme of improvements begun by his predecessor. One of the first calls on the new laird was in connection with the parish church of Kirkmahoe. The presbytery had decided that a new church needed to be built, so James, as convenor of the heritors' (land-owners') committee, called a meeting in March 1822 to carry this forward. It was agreed that this should be in the churchyard at Kirkton, about 3 miles from Dalswinton. Plans were submitted and agreed, including for 'Mr Leny's Room', which was to serve as a vestry for the new church. This was completed in June 1823, at a cost of £1,267, which was subscribed by the heritors. When it came to allocate the seating, a matter of considerable importance in those days, this was done in proportion to the total rent of

[7] Cameron Smith papers, Ewart Library, Dumfries.

the heritors' lands, and James was allocated three times that of the Duke of Buccleuch, who was the patron of the church. He chose seat numbers 19, 20, 21 and 22 for himself and his family, and a further 259 seats for his tenants, far more than anyone else.[8] After St John's, Edinburgh, this was the second church the family had been involved in building.

James also began to learn the farming business, and continued the programme of improvements started by Patrick Miller. He became very knowledgeable, and before long, a good judge of black cattle. He also inherited Miller's interest in greyhounds, and his black dog Vich Ian Vohr[9] won the Dumfriesshire Coursing Club's Spring Meeting in 1824. Building work continued, but on a more modest scale. The great thing with any Scottish house was always the approach, and the Dalswinton drive wound from the imposing front gates through the trees and then round the artificial mound before ending in the gravel sweep in front of the house. This was one thing for visiting guests, but quite another for everyday life. James built the back lodge at a cost of £100,[10] and a new, shorter drive leading up to the back of the house. While this was being constructed, a number of human bones were uncovered lying in some form of trench on the side of the mound.[11] Nor was the local community forgotten – he also built the Dalswinton School at his own expense.

For anyone who had daughters, and Robert Downie had four, marrying them off to suitable husbands was a major objective. And who could be more suitable than the laird of Dalswinton? History does not relate the lengths Robert Downie went to encourage the match, or whether there were any false starts with either of her older sisters, but on 10 June 1829, Marion Agatha, fourth daughter of Robert Downie of Appin, MP, was married in great state at St John's, Edinburgh, to James Macalpine Leny of Dalswinton. Downie had been re-elected after a struggle in the general election of 1826, and was determined to give his daughter a fitting send-off in the church he had helped to build. The marriage was performed by Dean Ramsay and among the witnesses were Robert and our old friend

---

[8] Kirkmahoe Kirk Session Records, National Archives of Scotland.
[9] Chief of Clan Ivor, a character in the Waverley Novels.
[10] Cameron Smith papers.
[11] *Dumfries & Galloway Courier*, 23 April 1833.

James Mackillop. After the service, the bride and groom left from the church door for their honeymoon in the Trossachs in their own carriage.

Two days later, there was a large public dinner in Dalswinton village to celebrate the marriage. It was remarkable for the length of the toast list. As on any such occasion, there were endless good wishes that a son and heir would soon be born, but there followed a monotonous succession of female christenings at Dalswinton: Mary in 1830, Anne Elizabeth in 1831 and Marion Agatha in 1833. It was not until 10 April 1836 that the much-hoped-for son finally arrived. Hardly surprisingly, this was fêted in royal style. As a mark of respect to the uncle who had made Dalswinton possible, he was christened Robert Leny on 10 June 1836. In those days of primogeniture, a son and heir was everything; the future laird, head of the household and carrier of the family torch on to the next generation. Everything would be focused on him first, and the rest of the family would follow. When William was born in 1839 after yet another daughter, Rosina, he would be very much the second son.

But tragedy lay ahead. At the age of nine, Robert was sent in the autumn term of 1845 to Grange Academy near Sunderland, run by a Dr Cowan, which was very popular with families from Scotland. On Wednesday 15 October, thirty-eight boys and four masters set out at midday for South Sands for their weekly bathe in the sea. As usual, strict instructions were issued about keeping together, how far out they could go, and the northern and southern limits of the swimming area. Three masters went into the sea with them, and the fourth was posted as look-out on the beach. No boy was ever allowed to swim further out than the masters. Although the sea was calm when they went into the water, it was pretty cold, and a strong swell sprang up. After five or six minutes, a number of boys got into difficulties, including sixteen-year-old Archibald Baird and his older brother Robert, neither of whom could swim. Robert Leny and another boy swam towards them to try and help, as did Mr Special, a young junior master. Tragically, Mr Special, Robert, and the two sons of Sir David Baird were all drowned. Robert was pulled out of the water immediately, but there was nothing that could be done to revive him. The other three bodies were not recovered until the evening. At the inquest the following day, the coroner was satisfied that every precaution had been taken and every effort had been made to save the boys. The jury recorded a verdict of accidental death.[12]

It is not difficult to imagine the reaction when the news reached Dalswinton. Child mortality was still high in those days, but to be drowned at school during a regular supervised swim in the sea? And Robert had only been at the school for a matter of weeks. The future course of the family had changed overnight, and with it the prospects of William, the second son, who was not quite six.

James no doubt buried himself in his work. From the beginning he had interested himself in the affairs of Dumfriesshire, and in 1832 was elected Convener of the Commissioners of Supply, a position he was to hold for thirty-five years. In the days before the advent of county councils, the Commissioners of Supply were a committee of large landowners who effectively ran the local government for their area of Scotland. James was thus one of the twelve men who ran Dumfriesshire and as Convener was a very important man in the county.

One of his other great interests was, of all things, a mental asylum. The Crichton Royal Institute for Lunatics in Dumfries became the leading centre for treatment of the insane in all Europe. It was built from the fortune amassed by Dr James Crichton, who, like Robert Leny, joined the East India Company, and ended up as physician to the Governor-General. When he returned to Scotland in 1808, he bought the Friars' Carse Estate, just across the Nith from Dalswinton, and married the thirty-one-year-old Elizabeth Grierson, some thirteen years his junior. They had no children. He would have been very interested in the new laird of Dalswinton, and would have certainly known Robert Leny in Calcutta. When he died in 1823, he left a fortune of £100,000 that 'shall be applied in such charitable purposes as may be pointed out by my said dearly beloved wife with the approbation of the majority of my said Trustees'.[13] One of his trustees was his neighbour, Captain (later Vice-Admiral) Charles Johnston of Cowhill Tower, who in 1826 married James's half-sister Lilly Macalpine, as his second wife.

[12] *Sunderland and Durham County Herald*, 17 October 1845.
[13] Morag Williams, *History of the Crichton Royal Hospital 1839–1989* (Dumfries and Galloway Health Board, 1989).

Mrs Crichton's first idea was to found a university in Dumfries, but when this was thwarted by the government, helped by lobbying from the existing under-utilised Scottish universities, she bounced back with a proposal to found a lunatic asylum. This went ahead despite a certain amount of opposition from locals and her family, who obviously thought that the money could be better spent. But she persevered, the foundation stone was laid in 1835, and the first patient admitted in 1839. Mrs Crichton's determination, an inspired building programme and above all the choice of Dr William Browne as the first physician superintendent assured the Crichton Royal of an important place in the history of mental health.

As Convener of the Commissioners of Supply, James automatically became a director of the Crichton, and when old Vice-Admiral Johnston finally died in 1856, he took over from him as one of the three trustees. Shortly afterwards there occurred a bizarre episode that indicated that, despite the so-called age of enlightenment, there was still progress to be made in some quarters. A new assistant matron had been appointed in 1858, and prior to taking up her appointment, she advised Dr Gilchrist, who had taken over as Physician Superintendent from Dr Browne, that she had become a Roman Catholic:

Dr Gilchirst was desirous to know, if that circumstance ought to enter into the agreement he had entered into with her. Mr Leny said that it was his opinion that fitness for the situation, not religious beliefs, had been the rule on which the Trustees and Directors had invariably acted; with Mrs Thomson's religious beliefs we have nothing whatever to do, and he could see no valid objection to her on these grounds; moreover, Mrs Thomson had acted most properly and honourably in acquainting Dr Gilchrist with her change of religion, in case it might be considered an objection to her . . . it would be both improper and dishonourable in us as Trustees and Directors, now to make religion a ground for disqualification, and as regards Mrs Thomson, a great act of injustice and hardship.[14]

---

[14] Hon. Marmaduke C. Maxwell, *Religious Intolerance: or a statement of facts, with reference to the appointment of a Matron to the Crichton Royal Institution, Dumfries* (Marsh & Beattie, 1859).

Mrs Thomson eventually started work, but was subjected to attempts to remove her by the husband of a patient, and threats from a minister from South Leith. Finally, on 1 March 1859, James proposed at a meeting of directors that she be officially appointed. However, Mrs Crichton's brother, Colonel Grierson, proposed an amendment that 'it was undesirable for the Institution to appoint a Roman Catholic as Matron'. The amendment was carried four votes to three, so poor Mrs Thomson had no alternative but to leave. Two of those who voted for her resigned, while 'Mr Leny, who is unable to resign in view of being a Trustee "for life", indicates his disinclination to attend the Meetings in future.'[15] As can be imagined, this whole sad saga caused quite a stir at the time.

A few years earlier there had occurred an event that was to throw James and his family into crisis, and leave an air of scandal hanging over the entire household. Sometime during the summer of 1851, Mary, the eldest and prettiest of James and Marion Agatha's seven daughters, fainted away in family prayers, and was put to bed. As she wasn't getting any better, the doctor was sent for, and rode out from Dumfries. On coming downstairs after examining the patient, he asked James if he could have a word with him in his study. 'I'm very sorry to have to tell you, Sir', began the doctor, 'your daughter is expecting a baby.' In return for his professional opinion, which proved to be absolutely correct, he was solemnly kicked down the front steps of the house.

When confronted with the truth, Mary confessed all; it was John Auld, the coachman, who was responsible. Auld, who was a Kirkmahoe man, was four or five years older than Mary, and had worked at Dalswinton for ten years. James must have been devastated, and felt terribly let down. In those days, punishment for breaking the laws of the Medes and Persians was swift and severe: they were made to get married, and were bought two single tickets to Canada via New York; Mary was given her family settlement and then written out of both James's and Marion Agatha's wills; and the family and servants were called together and told that their names should never be mentioned again. Mary was removed from the family pedigree, and no trace of her was allowed to remain.

[15] Charles Easterbrook, *The Chronicle of the Crichton Royal (1833–1936)* (Courier Press, 1940).

But scandal then as now makes the world go round, and it wasn't long before the news was out and the talk of the entire county. Thomas Carlyle even mentions it in one of his letters to his wife.[16] The choice of Canada was not entirely accidental; one of the many projects that old Robert Downie had been involved in back in 1825 was the formation of the Canada Company. This obtained 2.5 million acres of what is now Huron County in Ontario to promote its sale to prospective settlers. Robert Downie had been at the original meeting at the London Tavern when the idea of the company was suggested, and became one of its first directors. Downie Township was named after him. Mary and John Auld eventually ended up in Delaware Township, in Middlesex County, south-western Ontario. They had two daughters and a son, and Mary was still alive in 1911. Her great-grandson was in the Canadian Air Force and showed up at Courance in 1942. He said he could not understand why all the references to Dalswinton had been removed from the family album. My grandfather, Harley Macalpine-Leny (see Chapter 11) never enlightened him. The repercussions from this saga were still evident many years afterwards. When Mary's great nieces, Agatha and Simon Halsey (see Chapter 9), were growing up with horses at Gaddesden in the early 1920s, they could not understand why they were never allowed to go back to the stables and help take care of them as their friends were allowed to do. It would be another thirty years before they found out.

James continued to possess all the qualities that had made him so successful and respected in running the county: sound business habits, a good knowledge of local and general affairs, great tact, an even temper, courtesy and urbaneness. He was also bluff, open and unconventional, which came hand in hand with a kindly disposition and a warm heart. In consequence he was very popular with all his tenants on the Dalswinton Estate, and for many years would reward the occupant of the tidiest cottage with the best flower garden with a year's remission of rent.[17] It is a great pity that more of these qualities were not inherited by his second son, William.

By the autumn of 1866, James was laid low by ill health, and warned

[16] *The Collected Letters of Thomas and Jane Welsh Carlyle*, Vol. 27, 1852 (Duke, 1999), pp. 236–7.
[17] John G. Paton, *Missionary to the New Hebrides* (Hodder & Stoughton, 1891).

the Commissioners of Supply that he would not be standing for re-election as Convenor. On the afternoon of 5 January 1867, he died at Dalswinton in the presence of his butler, George Morrison, two weeks short of his seventy-first birthday.[18] He had effectively run Dumfriesshire for thirty-four years, and been on the Crichton board for twenty-six: a hard act to follow.

[18] Unusually for such a prominent local figure, he had a private funeral attended by family, close friends and his devoted tenants. He was buried alongside his eldest son under the tower of the parish church. Typical of the man, his grave was originally unmarked, but a small plaque was erected in 2010.

4 Mr W. M. Leny

William Macalpine Leny was born at Dalswinton House on 25 November 1839, and was packed off to Eton just before his thirteenth birthday. The West Coast main line had reached Carlisle by 1847 and the Glasgow, Dumfries and Carlisle Railway opened in October 1850, so in all probability William went by train with his father on that first occasion. It was a very exciting journey for a twelve-year-old, though James probably regarded it as pretty tame compared to setting out for India forty years earlier. At Eton, William was to make two great friendships that he would keep for the rest of his life: Freddy Halsey and Evan Williams. They would all go on to Oxford together, and spend much time in later life staying in each other's houses for the shooting. By the time he left Eton at the end of the Christmas term of 1857, William had played in the Field XI and rowed in *Thetis* in the Procession of Boats on the Fourth of June that year: somewhat of a coincidence, because it was as surgeon of the *Thetis* that his great-uncle Robert Leny had first set out for India in 1794.

Then it was on to Christ Church, Oxford, a snob college if ever there was one, where William joined the sons of the great and the good. Even the Prince of Wales was there for a time. If he hadn't learnt how to live the life of a gentleman by the time he left Eton, he certainly had after three years at Oxford. The amazing collection of surviving photographs from his undergraduate days shows a life of leisured ease. This was at the time that the young Christ Church mathematics lecturer, Charles Dodgson, better known as Lewis Carroll, was an active photographer. He had started in 1856, the same year that a new dean, Henry Liddell, arrived at the college with his attractive wife and three young daughters. It would be fascinating to know if, in addition to frequently photographing Alice Liddell and her two sisters, as well as many of the leading people that passed through Oxford (Dodgson was a dreadful social climber), he was responsible for any of William's photographs of members of the college.

Clearly William did take some exercise at Oxford, because he was awarded a silver-mounted rackets racket in a presentation case. Sadly, there is no inscription, and the university's sporting records do not go back that far. Despite being a good student and taking a normal course with the usual heavy emphasis on classics, he does not appear to have bothered to take a degree, not that that really mattered: he was heading for an army career, and the system of buying commissions would remain in force until 1870. So he went down from Oxford at the end of the Hilary term in 1861 and was commissioned as a cornet in the XV Hussars, a smart cavalry regiment. Although never seeing any action or foreign service, he took soldiering seriously, and his life was very much that of the young cavalry officer. In those days there was unbelievably generous leave and a good deal of high living, and knowing William, he drank a good deal more than the average man of his day. After his father died, he retired as a captain in 1868 and transferred for a time to the Dumfries Militia.

Much of our knowledge of life at Dalswinton at this time comes from the Game Book, which was started in 1864. It was more that just a record of the game killed, because members of the house party would add their comments, funny stories, occasional verse or drawings on a weekly basis. The first entry records that Mr Alex Maxwell, T. F. Halsey, W. M. Severne and W. M. Leny shot fifty-four grouse on 12 August 1864, and then:

This is Mr Alex Maxwell's 42nd season on Dalswinton Moor, Mr Halsey's 8th ditto, Dr Christison's 32nd annual visit. W. M. Leny trusts that Mr Halsey will also reach his 42nd season on Dalswinton Moor. 'What a size he will be by that time' exclaimed an envious sportsman. The 12th of August this year being on a Friday, Thomas arrived on Thursday, consequently this week had only time to break one pair of tongs and one swoggle. Besides the $15\frac{1}{2}$ brace of grouse shot at Glaisters[1] on 16th, it is worthy of remark that on that day Mr Halsey brought down a chair, severely wounded in the legs. On 16th August at Glaisters, Mr W. M. Severne brought down a lark, mistaking it for a blackcock – owing to this English habit of wearing a magnifying glass in his eye.

List of the consequences of the Lambkins' Prancing from August 11th until August 19th:

> 1 pair tongs broken
> 1 swoggle ditto

[1] Between Dumfries and Dalbeattie, and not part of the Dalswinton estate.

> 1 chair ditto
> 1 dog cart ditto
> 1 pony cart
> 1 croquet mallet ditto
> 1 powder flask crushed
> 1 carriage smashed

On 19th August Mr Halsey came down in time to hand to dinner a lady – who was envied by all the others, but he made up for that exertion next morning by not appearing till luncheon. On 31st August, Mr Halsey came down to breakfast so late that one of the ladies present asked if he had gone away.

Freddy Halsey, the butt of all these jokes who became to be known as 'the old clot' by the others, turned out to be the most successful of them all. He had ten children, became the Father of the House of Commons after a long career as a backbencher, and was knighted (see Chapter 9).

Apart from the shooting, the other great sport for the Dalswinton house parties in the summer was croquet, and it is clear that a good deal of money changed hands. There was always the problem of what to do on Sundays, apart from finding excuses for not being able to go to church.

On Sunday the 11th September, the weather being too wet to permit the XV to sit under the Sainted Hogg,[2] they found out that mallets were inexplicably missing – consequently they played at croquet with their umbrellas. On Monday 12th, Mr Leny lost £1,000 on the croquet ground: Mr Watt went out to look for them.

The keeper, James Robson, obviously had a good sense of humour:

Mr Leny remonstrated with the keeper on the want of hares in the Ladies Wood, where upon the latter worthy replied 'There's plenty of hares, Sir, but ye surely dinna think they were going to sit on the walls and look at ye'!

Then at the beginning of December that same year:

This is the second time in two weeks that Mr W. M. Leny has gone to a wedding – his family hopes he won't take the infection. He also went on a nice little trip to London, announcing that he would be away for a fortnight, but at the end of

[2] The officers of the XV Hussars staying in the house to go to Church.

three days, a south wind set in, and being certain that it would bring woodcocks, he suddenly appeared at home, much to his family's discomfiture, who had intended to profit by his absence and set off for Edinburgh, which move on their part must now be postponed, until Mr W. M. Leny sanctions their departure.

It's hard to believe. Finally on 24 December, the truth about the Game Book came out:

In July Mr W. M. Leny generously presented his father with this Game Book – rather to Mr Leny's surprise, as he is not in the habit of receiving presents from his family (indeed, quite the other way). But on Saturday, 24th December, he understood all about it and to his cost, as the bill came in addressed to himself. For *once* in his life, Mr W. M. Leny manifested no curiosity as to what was in his father's letters; indeed, he professed a desire to remain in ignorance on a subject in which as a general rule, he takes the most lively interest.

On the opening of the 1867 season, Walter Long, William's future brother-in-law, Freddy Halsey and William shot 102 grouse on the 12th, sixty on the 14th, and eighty on 16 August, a not inconsiderable feat when 'walking-up' over dogs rather than shooting driven birds. The Game Book goes on to record:

In some points Mr Halsey is greatly improved by being married, having as yet only broken *two* things. Patricia[3] hopes he won't break his wife's head. On the 12th the two Englishmen restrained themselves as well as they could, but on 14th habit proved too strong for them and so they shot with joy at two par-tridges.[4] On the 16th, the ladies took advantage of the absence of the Gentlemen at their 'Shootin Quawtaws' to finish all the wine that was out, the consequences may be more easily imagined than described . . .

And then:

Mr Halsey has become so punctual since his marriage that he even took his travelling clock to Glaisters. On his return, in an after-dinnerish condition, Mrs Long politely wished him 'Good night' – when he growled out 'Take yourself off'.

[3] William's youngest sister – see Chapter 5.
[4] The partridge shooting season doesn't open until 1 September.

Wednesday 28th is a memorable day in the annals of Dalswinton, for Mr Halsey came down into the drawing room 5 minutes before the gong rang, and actually went to table with other members of the family ... On 29th Miss Macalpine was 'dry' so she drank up a gentleman's champagne at dinner and afterwards took Cherry Brandy *from the bottle*. On the 30th Miss M. looked pale at breakfast (no wonder).

A pattern begins to emerge. Years afterwards, William's younger daughter May (afterwards Lady Halsey – see Chapter 9) was talking with her nephew who observed that she seemed to be dead against all forms of drinking. 'Well haven't I seen enough of it,' she replied. 'I've seen the whole shooting party drunk at Dalswinton.'[5] But they did have fun.

William was away in Liverpool with his regiment for the whole of October and November 1867, so did no shooting at home. His return was recorded thus in the Game Book:

On the 2nd December, Mr W. M. Leny returned to the bosom of his family, but alas! How his manners have deteriorated since going to Liverpool. The first day of his arrival, on entering the drawing room, he exclaimed, 'Surely, Rosa, you're not going to allow my mother to put coals on the fire?', at the same time throwing himself into the most comfortable chair he could find, from which resting place he surveyed the operation with complacency, and without the least trouble to himself.

Before leaving the Game Book, which was to be kept up religiously until Dalswinton was sold in 1919, we must include the following written by a house guest in 1870 after reading the many contributions that Rosa had made over the years:

> What a list of rabbits martyred
> By 'Sweet William's' deadly aim –
> Pheasants slain and patricks slaughtered,
> Make a huge array of game.

[5] Family History, Kenneth Macalpine-Leny (unpublished).

But tho' the gun has murdered many,
Yet I find the caustic pen
In the hands of Rosa Leny
Has made equal game of men.

Although Freddy Halsey married in 1865 it was not until four years later that William finally 'caught the infection'. His bride was Agnes Louisa Georgina, second daughter of Walter Jervis Long of Preshaw in Hampshire, and sister of his old Oxford friend Walter Long. Preshaw is about 7 miles south-west of Winchester, and came into the Long family in 1728. The house dates back to Jacobean times, but was extensively added to in 1810. It is set in a magnificent park and reached via an imposing avenue of mature beech trees. In 1869, Agnes's grandparents were still alive and living at Preshaw House, so her father and his family lived nearby.

Immediately after the wedding on 15 April 1869, William and Agnes set off up to London by train, and then down to Dover, accompanied by Gardiner, Agnes's lady's maid. They had a rough crossing to Calais but arrived safely in Paris at the start of their honeymoon. After a week of sightseeing they left for Brussels on 29 April and from there to Bonn, Wiesbaden, Frankfurt, Hamburg, Baden-Baden, Basle, Berne, Lausanne, Geneva and finally back to Paris on 25 May. Then it was London and the inevitable round of lunches and dinners, although William was allowed to sneak off to the Derby. Finally, it was back to Dalswinton on 29 May to be met by all the tenants at the Lodge gates.

At the age of twenty-two, it must have been somewhat intimidating taking over the running of Dalswinton, although in those days large country houses were still run by the servants, not their masters. Mrs Leny, always known as 'The Mum', had moved out with her unmarried daughters and would eventually move to London, leaving the coast clear for her new daughter-in-law. But Agnes was very practical – a large, kindly, maternal woman judging from her photographs, who would prove to be a good mother to their five children. She played the harmonium in church in Hampshire and had a strong Christian faith, which would hold her in good stead in the years to come. She also kept a diary from the year she married until the day she died. The diary was entirely factual so makes pretty dull reading, but by recording everywhere she went and the comings and goings of all the guests, it gives a very good idea of life at Dalswinton.

The first duty of every wife of that generation was to produce a son and heir, and this Agnes duly did in pretty short order – on 11 February 1870. In keeping with tradition, he was christened Robert Leny after his great-great-uncle. No doubt yet another excuse for a Dalswinton party. Robert was quickly followed by Emily (Milly) in 1871 and Agnes Marion, always known as May, in 1872. Then there was a gap of six years before James Robert in 1878 and finally William Harley in 1880. We shall meet them all in subsequent chapters.

Life at Dalswinton was a continuous round of guests coming to lunch or tea, coming to stay, or going out to lunch or dinner. Often the Dalswinton guests together with their hosts would move en masse to join a neighbouring house party, and some guests moved from one house to another, especially if they were visiting from England. The Macalpine-Lenys would typically walk over to their Johnston cousins at Cowhill, and to General and Mrs Harley Maxwell at Portrach. In the days before the telephone everyone was endlessly going to call, often finding the would-be recipient out, or occasionally on the road coming to return the compliment. The well-to-do always travelled by train, and long journeys were made overnight, so it was quite usual for guests coming from London or boys returning from school to arrive in time for breakfast. To have no one staying in the house was such a rare event that it was always remarked upon.

The highlight of the Dalswinton year was the opening of the grouse shooting on 12 August. Every year the Halseys, W. M. Severne, who was a friend from Oxford, and Agnes's brother Walter came for at least a week. Later they would be joined by brothers-in-law James Mansfield and William Barnes, and later still, when he began shooting, by Bob and his friends from Eton. Sundays presented something of a problem in such a sporting household with no shooting or salmon fishing, so after the compulsory visit to the Kirk, croquet was the major occupation. By the early 1880s, when the craze for lawn tennis swept through the smart houses, tennis parties became the fashion, with the advantage, like croquet, that

the ladies could also play. In September Freddy Halsey returned home to
Gaddesden for the partridge shooting, although substantial bags of partridges were shot at Dalswinton in certain years. Guests also had the
opportunity to fish for salmon on the River Nith where the season ran
from 25 February to 15 November, although the best fishing was always in
September, October and November. By this time Dalswinton was well into
the pheasant shooting, with large numbers of rabbits and hares also fea-
turing in the bag. By the beginning of December the loch would be frozen
over, so curling became the major occupation, with Kirkmahoe competing
against other clubs. William was very keen, and often played one of his
friends for a meal, or '£2 for the poor'. His silver-mounted curling broom
complete with inscription 'Captain Leny, Dalswinton, 1872' still resides in
the drawing room at the Old Rectory, Doddington.

Near Christmas William always had his annual shoot round the house
while Agnes had her Christmas tree party a day or two before Christmas,
to which all the tenants' children were invited. This was a pretty popular
event attended by between sixty and seventy children, with a record of
ninety-two in 1876 when the Sunday School class was also included. Then
around the turn of the year the servants had their Ball in the Barn, which
the family always went down to for a couple of hours. The butler was never
replaced after George Morrison died, but there were still seven servants in
the house, a coachman and groom, two keepers and heaven knows how
many working on the farm and in the woods, plus the gardener.

Pheasant shooting finished on 1 February, but in those days it was still
legal to shoot duck and woodcock up to the last day of February, after
which guests were reduced to shooting pigeons and crows round the house
or going ferreting for rabbits. Then there was steeplechasing, coursing and
otter hunting in June and July. May, June and July tended to be the time
for concerts and garden parties, as well as a number of private balls. There
were 150 guests at the Dalswinton party on 25 July 1891, which meant
sixty-three horses down at the stables: an interesting parking problem.
There was also plenty of tennis and croquet, the tenants' annual flower
show at Auldgirth and the Thornhill Show. Then the Halseys arrived for
12 August, and another year had passed at Dalswinton.

William's overriding passion was shooting and he was a very good shot, but then he should have been – he shot three days a week throughout the shooting season. The printed pages of the Dalswinton Game Book went from Monday to Saturday each week because someone shot every day, and if they didn't, the keeper went out. They also record some pretty spectacular bags: fifty-one brace of grouse between three guns on 12 August 1867 – not at all bad for walking up – sixty-three partridges between two guns on 6 October 1888 and 136 pheasants on 26 December 1882. The estate was clearly overrun with hares and rabbits, because bags of over 150 hares and 250 rabbits were not at all uncommon. In addition, William shot duck and woodcock, plovers, land rails, and pigeons and crows when there was nothing else. The latter were not recorded in the Game Book, nor were the rats he shot at Bankfoot Farm. On one occasion there was a bat hunt, which accounted for forty of the unfortunates in the poultry house, but the means of their demise was not recorded. On Monday 21 March 1870, Agnes wrote in her diary that 'William went out shooting rabbits and shot three of the gardener's hens.' No mention of them in the Game Book either . . .

There were an amazing number of shooting accidents on the estate. One tenant was killed when his gun exploded, and another managed to shoot himself fatally getting over a fence with a loaded gun. One shooting guest managed to shoot another in the leg, and yet another shot their host in the hand and arm, but fortunately neither were seriously hurt. Agnes's diary for 1 September 1881 reads: 'Robert [then aged ten] went shooting and unfortunately shot Tilbury [the keeper] in the foot. We had tea at Jeanie Robson's.'

Some years later, Bob and his father were walking the hill in line with other guns. They had only just started and the time could not have been later than nine o'clock in the morning, when a rabbit got up and bolted over the top of a false skyline. Bob shot it, and could just see it somersault before it disappeared over the ridge. When he walked forward to pick it up he was horrified to see his father standing in the direct line of where he had fired. If there had ever been an excuse for his father's notorious temper, that was it. But William was all smiles, and said nothing. Years afterwards, Bob was talking to his mother about old times, and said that he just could not make out how he had not shot his father that day. Agnes said, 'You did shoot him. You shot him so badly that I had to carry him to bed.' Agnes was a large woman and her strength must have been quite considerable to have been equal to the occasion, but what about William? He had been wounded at nine in the morning and walked the whole of the day without complaint. He wasn't going to say anything because it was his fault: he was out of line. And William was never in the wrong . . .[6]

Quite clearly, William always expected everything to go right, and got in a hell of a temper when it didn't. On one occasion, Milly was travelling up from London with her father. When they got to Dumfries, he found to his fury that the carriage was not waiting for them. 'Milly,' he shouted, 'get back in that train!' Back they got, complete with luggage, and just as they were pulling out of the station they saw Cameron, the coachman, trotting down the station slope with the Dalswinton carriage – he was three minutes late. Well, Cameron must have made those horses go – his very livelihood depended on it. When the train stopped at Hollywood, the next little station beyond Dumfries, there was the carriage and the horses all in a lather. William hired two 'growlers', one for himself and his daughter and the other for the luggage, and Cameron was instructed to bring up the rear of the procession. The present generation would point out that William was the loser because he had to pay for the cabs, but they did things differently in that age.[7] On another occasion, William had been persuaded to invite a certain guest for a week's shooting, who had been billed as the crack shot in all of India. The first day he never hit a thing, so that very evening William descended on his eldest daughter: 'Milly,' he screamed, 'get rid of that man!' So the unfortunate Milly had to suggest to the guest that perhaps he had other plans and his luggage would be packed in ample time to catch whichever train he fancied.

After shooting, William's other great passion was fishing, and he spent many a day fishing for salmon on the Nith, particularly in October and November. It was something of an event when a fish was caught, which Agnes always recorded in her diary, so we know that it was not at all unusual for the fish to be of between 20lbs and 30lbs in October. In 1873, William went with Major Stewart to fish in Norway for six weeks, and for several years he went with James Mansfield up beyond Inverness to the

---

[6] Family History, Kenneth Macalpine-Leny.   [7] Ibid.

River Conan for a whole month, with Agnes and Roberta Mansfield going as well. Those were the days.

Strange as it may seem, William found time for activities other than sport. He retained a keen interest in the Dumfries Militia long after he had resigned his commission, and had very much followed his father in becoming involved in Dumfriesshire affairs, being elected a Commissioner of Supply in 1861 while his father was still Convenor. He chaired the Local Authority for the County under the Contagious Diseases of Animals Act for many years, and became chairman of the Agricultural Committee of the County Council when this body took over from the Commissioners of Supply in 1890. He did actually know something about farming, and was a successful breeder and shower of Clydesdales. Like his father, he took a keen interest in the affairs of the Crichton, joining the board in 1870. This and other local business took him into Dumfries at least two days a week, when he wasn't shooting. He was a JP, and travelled up to Edinburgh for the Quarter Sessions, and became a Deputy Lieutenant of the County. At a parochial level he took his duties as the laird very seriously, and was chairman of the Schools Board and the Parochial Board for many years, as well as being an elder of the Parish Church. Politically he was every bit as staunch a Conservative as his father, and was always heavily involved with canvassing at election time. He was a pretty useful speaker because he had considerable presence, and his blunt humour won over lively audiences time and time again.

Like all Macalpine-Lenys, William had a twinkle in his eye and a good sense of humour. On one occasion he had been shooting with his Johnston cousin next door at Cowhill, and his host and two boys were standing on the front steps to see him off at the end of the day. William Johnston was loud in his praise of his eldest son Jim who had won the Tombs Prize[8] at Sandhurst, and generally been the model son of whom any father would be proud. Then there was that damned scamp Harley; always in trouble, another bad school report this half, etc., etc. William heard him out, before shaking Jim warmly by the hand and congratulating him on being an absolute paragon. He then thanked his host for the

[8] Awarded to the senior cadet of his batch in honour of Major-General Sir Harry Tombs, who won the VC at the siege of Delhi, in the Indian Mutiny.

shoot, and before getting into the dog-cart, gave Harley two sovereigns.

If Agnes had a sense of humour, it doesn't come out in her diaries. She was a kind, deeply religious woman who was very much the sheet anchor for the entire family. She knew everyone on the estate, and was always there in times of trouble, or when there was a new addition to the family. In those days infant mortality was still quite high, and the laird's wife was one of the first to visit at a time of family tragedy. She had taken an ambulance course in Dumfries, so was able to administer simple first aid when necessary. When the gardener's wife was extremely ill after giving birth, Agnes sat up all night with her. Mrs Brown died the next day. Agnes was then asked to go down and pray for her before the lid was closed on her coffin, which she found pretty daunting. When the old retired keeper James Robson lost his hand in the sawmill at the age of seventy-eight, Agnes was there at his bedside at Douganstyle every day. Much to the joy of all, he recovered. He had worked at Dalswinton for more than forty years, and was almost one of the family.

Apart from looking after the welfare of her own family and everyone else on the estate, Agnes took a keen interest in the farm and garden. She had her own pig, and the number of piglets that it produced on a regular basis was faithfully recorded. She had a poultry yard up near Douganstyle which, judging by the number of house guests that were taken to inspect it, was obviously a thing of pride. She treated the hens for gapes, and helped to fumigate the hen house. She also had her own cows. Her diary of 28 March 1889 reads: 'Sat up with Mr Carroll till 2.30 am when she calved.' Then the following day: 'I went down to the byre morning and afternoon. Lilly [cow] ill.' But it was through improving the garden that William and Agnes left their greatest mark on Dalswinton. Trees and shrubs were planted round the house, a tennis court was laid, and flowers from the gardens were always being sent to friends and local hospitals. Every year, hundreds of bunches of snowdrops were sent by train to friends and deserving causes in London. And they both worked alongside the men when it came to cutting, chopping and clearing the banks along the front drive.

Agnes introduced penny readings[9] to Dalswinton and, being very

---

[9] Originally instigated by Charles Dickens so that anyone could have the benefit of hearing his work. Agnes sang and provided accompaniment on her harmonium.

musical, sang and played the harmonium at concerts she arranged in the Barn. She was also pretty handy with her Singer sewing machine, covering sofas and chairs and making baby clothes. She even took ladies work classes in the village to teach them the necessary skills, as well as teaching at Sunday School. When it came to cutting up another bullock, it was Agnes rather than William who supervised the work. But it was to be the Barony Church that would be her lasting legacy at Dalswinton.

Coming from a good Christian family in England where the Church was an important part of her life, Agnes was horrified to find that there was not even any music in the parish church at Kirkton, let alone a choir. As she had her own portable harmonium, she started to canvass members of the parish in early 1872 to see if they would welcome the introduction of singing. The answers were favourable, so at the evening service on 8 December that year, music was introduced for the first time on an experimental basis, with Agnes playing her own harmonium. This seemed to have been accepted, because early the following year she was busily going about the parish collecting subscriptions to buy an organette. This was ordered from a Mr Bell of Guelph in Ontario, Canada, who had originally emigrated from Kirkmahoe, and had made a name for himself as a builder of such instruments.[10] It duly arrived, and a space was cut in the western-most pew at the belfry door to make way for it. It was first used at the evening service on Sunday, 16 November 1873, with Agnes playing and Mr Hamilton leading the choir. The minutes of the Kirk session on 23 November 1873 read: 'Mr Helm moved that the organette be introduced in support of the psalmody at the regular service, which was seconded by Mr Smith and agreed by Mr McKie. Mr Walker objected. The session authorised therefore the use of instrumental music in the public worship of God.'[11]

Every attempt to modernise church services brings out reactionaries, and Walker was soon joined by a young Dumfries solicitor named John Corrie.[12] The next Kirk Session was on 22 January 1874:

[10] Cameron Smith papers.
[11] Kirkmahoe Kirk Session Minutes CH2/431/3.
[12] No doubt due to divine retribution, he died on 27 July 1881 aged only thirty-three.

A petition has been received from 'members of the Established Church in Kirkmahoe' requesting the session to disallow the use of the organette in the Psalmody of the Church and to remove it. Mr Helm moved that the petitioners be not granted and that their former decision be adhered to, which was seconded by Mr McKie and acquiesced in by the moderator. Mr Walker protested against this decision as being *ultra vires* of themselves to introduce instrumental music, took instruments in the clerk's hands and craved extracts.

Finally, on 26 April 1874: 'The session considering the number and violence of the objectors order the discontinuance of the organette, its removal out of view, and the cut seat to be restored to its former condition.' Although, typically, there was no mention of her feelings in her diary, Agnes must have been bitterly disappointed. The only small consolation was that the subscribers presented her with the organette.

It was about now that Agnes resolved to build a church at Dalswinton. These things take time, and it was not until 1 April 1879 that a planning committee was formed. Later that year Maxwell Hutchinson, who was to become a good friend of the Macalpine-Leny family, was ordained Minister of Kirkmahoe, and he was to prove an enthusiastic supporter of the project. The following year Agnes started to receive donations from friends and parishioners, and by the beginning of 1881, enough money had been collected for work to start. A site was selected on the road between Dalswinton village and the gates to Dalswinton House, with William granting to the Church Committee the 'free use of ground on which the church stands as long as the church lasts'. The foundations were laid in April and the prefabricated church duly arrived as a flat pack, and was erected very quickly. The total cost, including preparing the site and laying the foundations, was £415 18s 11d.[13] This was far more than had been raised, so a loan of £200 was taken out. This was eventually repaid three years later thanks to the proceeds of a bazaar in Dumfries organised by Agnes.

The first service in what had become known as the Iron Church was held on Sunday, 7 August 1881, with Agnes playing the organette. It was attended by nearly three hundred people. Once the church debts had been

[13] Dalswinton Barony Church Minute Book.

paid off, the organette was replaced by a new harmonium and the French governess at Dalswinton House employed to play it for a fee of £2 a quarter. Finally Agnes's dream of having a choir and music in the church had been realised; it wouldn't be until 1894 that this monumental step would be taken by the parish church.[14] One can't help wondering what she would have thought of the performance of *Joseph and the Amazing Technicolour Dreamcoat* which took place in the Parish Church on 3 November 2006, with Sarah Landale in the title role.[15] The Church was rocked to its very foundations, and the original objectors to the organette must have been quaking in their graves outside. Where so many of the old 'tin tabernacles' have fallen into disrepair over the years, the Dalswinton Barony Church still goes strong to this day, thanks to generous financial support from the Landale family. Agnes would have been thrilled.

Although William was a larger-than-life character well known throughout the county as a great sportsman and raconteur, he was not a well man. A fairly heavy alcohol consumption could not have helped. He had a succession of nasty abscesses that had to be cut out of his neck and back, and on two occasions had fainting fits. As the years went by he suffered increasingly from rheumatic gout in both his feet and one hand, and by the end of 1892, when he was still only fifty-three, he was spending an increasing amount of time in bed. With the birth of children, their numerous ailments and Agnes's neuralgia and diabetes, Dr Thomson and Dr Borthwick before him were frequent visitors, often staying overnight if the situation warranted it. They also became family friends, and were included in shooting and other sporting parties.

According to family tradition, most of Dalswinton went down William's throat. Although some of it certainly did, that is not entirely fair. As many a family found in the nineteenth century and subsequently, the economics of running a landed estate in Scotland without any alternative source of income simply did not make sense. Also, from the 1870s onwards, really until the Second World War, British agriculture was depressed, reeling under the impact of cheap food imports as the American railroads drove westwards, opening up the prairie wheat lands, and

[14] Kirmahoe Kirk Session Minutes, 29 April 1894.
[15] She stepped in at a week's notice. Peter Landale was Pharaoh.

refrigerated ships brought meat from there and from Australia. It was not as if William would have gone into what was then rather unkindly called trade – he was a cavalry man, dammit. But he didn't only have to contend with an expensive lifestyle and hopeless grasp of business; on top of everything else, Dalswinton suffered three significant natural disasters.

The first occurred in 1881. The first week of March saw very heavy snowfalls. This was followed by more snow and rain then rapidly rising temperatures as a warm wind blew from the south-west. The resulting massive snow melt saw the River Nith rise alarmingly until parts of Dumfries were flooded. This continued until the flood was within 3 or 4 inches of the height reached in 1848, and then it suddenly stopped. It was not long before the reason became apparent – the Nith had burst its banks at Dalswinton. There was a substantial breach in the embankment at Sandbed about a quarter of a mile downstream from the Portrack Bridge, resulting in severe flooding downstream. The village of Kirkton was completely cut off on all sides, and one man was drowned trying to get home. An eyewitness estimated that to repair the main breach alone would have cost several hundred pounds. For the first time ever, rail traffic was disrupted because the northernmost pier of the Portrack Bridge had given way. Passenger trains from Glasgow stopped just north of the bridge and passengers had to walk across before embarking on another train to take them on to Dumfries.[16]

The second occurred on the night of 11 December 1883, when a hurricane did widespread damage throughout Dumfries and Galloway, destroying all the best trees around the house and ruining much of the plantations at both Dalswinton and Carnsalloch.[17] There was another severe storm on the night of 22 December 1894 which, coming at the end of a very poor year for farming, dealt a further financial blow to the estate.[18]

William, as the only nephew of the fabulously wealthy Miss Downie of Appin, thought his long-term financial future was secure. Then, when she finally fell off her perch on 12 May 1881 and her will came to be read, it

[16] *Dumfries and Galloway Standard*, 12 March 1881.
[17] *Dumfries and Galloway Standard*, 12 December 1883.
[18] A 'water cloud' on 23 July 1904 did great damage to the mill dam and elsewhere.

turned out that she had left Appin and the balance of her fortune to William's and Agnes's three-year-old second son James, in trust until he was twenty-one (see Chapter 10). William's response was unprintable. By April 1893 he had decided that the only thing to do was to move abroad to economise. Agnes gave notice to all the indoor staff except the faithful Jessie Laing, the family's long-time nanny; the silver was packed up and sent to the bank in Dumfries; the house was shut up, and in May the family moved to a rented house in Guernsey. Not normally one for showing her feelings in her diary, Agnes admitted that she cried all the way through her last service in the parish church.

William and Agnes already knew a lot of people in Guernsey – even their Johnston cousins from Cowhill lived there for a time, so they were soon very much part of the social scene: parties at Government House, watching tennis and football, and the endless round of people coming to tea. Sisters, cousins and aunts came to stay in a never-ending stream, and Jimmy and Harley came for the school holidays. Agnes immediately busied herself in the life of the church, and went to read in the hospital every Wednesday, often accompanied by May. At that age May was very athletic, and was always playing in tennis tournaments. Then after three years, William and Agnes moved to London just before May's wedding to Walter Halsey, the eldest son of William's life-long friend Freddy (see chapter 9).

Meanwhile, Dalswinton House and the shooting had been let, first to Mr Walker and then in 1897 to Mr Davidson. The Davidsons gave up their lease in May 1899, enabling William and Agnes to move back in October after their usual two months in Guernsey over the summer. So after an absence of six and a half years, William was able to spend his sixtieth birthday at Dalswinton. Despite increasing problems of gout in both feet, he was able to go out shooting a few times, though he had not picked up a gun since he went to Guernsey. He even managed to get out on the ice again, but fell heavily and broke a rib, so that was the end of his curling career. Their stay witnessed another sad milestone in the life of Dalswinton when Brown, the gardener for twenty-three years, died suddenly of a heart attack on 4 January.

There had been a good deal of sprucing up of the house during their stay, with Agnes busily organising new curtains and carpets ready for the next lot of tenants. When they finally left on 6 April 1900 for Wennington, the house they had rented near Marble Hill in Twickenham, it was the last time that William saw Dalswinton. The Ranken family took the house later that year, and remained as excellent tenants until the estate was sold in 1919.[19]

Life for William had become increasingly difficult. He had recurring attacks of rheumatic gout in his feet and right hand, sciatica down his left side, and now walked with two sticks. But he was still able to get up to town occasionally to have lunch at 'the Rag'.[20] Agnes also had her problems: she had diabetes, was increasingly blind and deaf, and underwent a cataract operation in the autumn of 1904. But she never complained, kept open house for all her friends and family, and continued her good works – not to mention entertaining for tea what William called 'all the old frumps'.

Somehow William managed to retain his sense of humour in spite of all. In his last letter to his youngest son, telling him that he had to go into a nursing home in four days time to have an abscess cut out of his palate, he warned him: 'Oh, Harley, when you have a house of your own, *never* allow spring cleaning, or if you do, take my advice and take unto yourself the wings of the morning and get anywhere you like, but get . . .' He survived the operation, but died from heart failure four days afterwards, at the age of sixty-five. The service at Richmond Presbyterian Church was packed.

Like so many of his generation who had had a privileged upbringing, William was an upright, public-spirited and generous man. He was immensely popular with friends and tenants alike, and hugely enthusiastic about everything he did. And he was very good company. But he became increasingly out of touch with a changing world, and paid the consequence. It was a strange coincidence that on the day the laird died, Sunday 4 June 1905, so did the oldest tenant on the Dalswinton estate. James

[19] Robert Burt Ranken, WS, was a distinguished and prosperous Edinburgh solicitor. After his death in 1902, his eldest son, Tom, took over the tenancy. The third son, William (1881–1961), was the well-known painter. Louis, the youngest, kept up the Game Book.
[20] Army and Navy Club.

Weir had farmed at Clonfeckle for more than thirty years. It really was the end of an era.

Agnes moved down to Hove on the south coast with her unmarried sister Emily, and continued to keep open house for her family, surrounded by numerous Long relations. She had been the perfect loving wife, and still missed William enormously. When she finally died in 1916, she joined him in Twickenham cemetery.

5 The Great Aunts and their Surprising Husbands

We have already seen that Mary, the eldest and prettiest of the Miss Macalpine-Lenys, was made to marry John Auld, the coachman, before they were both shipped off to the New World in disgrace. She must have been made of pretty strong stuff, because settling in Canada in the 1850s was no picnic, especially coming from such a privileged background. They had originally gone to New York, but had moved to Canada by 1857 and eventually settled near Delaware in western Ontario. They had three children: Marion, the cause of all the trouble, Jane and finally John born in 1861. By 1881, Mary was widowed, but still farming, and she was still alive in 1911. Perhaps one day the full story of the Aulds will be known.

The second sister, Anne Elizabeth, known as Doosey in the family, was only eighteen months younger than Mary, so the whole saga must have had quite an effect on her. Perhaps that was one reason why she never married. If the Dalswinton Game Book is anything to go by, she had also inherited the family thirst, which may explain why she died a few days short of her forty-second birthday.

In those days one of the principal concerns of any father was to marry off his daughters to suitable husbands. Eldest sons with landed estates were top of the list, followed by men of the cloth, the latter considered highly respectable, if somewhat impoverished. An army officer came a poor third. Thus it was that no fewer than three Miss Macalpine-Lenys married Church of England clergymen.

The first was Marion Agatha, known as Marie, who was two years younger than Doosey. She met Geldart Riadore when he was domestic chaplain to the 5th Duke of Buccleuch, and they were married at St John's, Edinburgh, in 1862 when he was a respectable thirty-four. He then became rector of All Saints in Chichester, retiring at the gentlemanly age of forty-four to the village of Lavant, just north of the town. They both just about made ninety.

The second was Jemima, always known as Mynie. Mynie was very bright, and not afraid to take on roles normally in those days reserved for men. Hardly surprisingly, she married a very interesting man. If Geldart Riadore appears in retrospect to have been a bit dull, Donald Hilaro Ouseley Dimsdale MacKinnon certainly wasn't. The eldest son of a major-general, he met Mynie when as a young curate he came to Mrs Macalpine Leny's house in London to see about her coachman's children going to school. He subsequently baptised all five McSwineys at the same time with Mynie acting as godmother. Having first asked Mrs Leny's permission, he proposed to Mynie, and they were married on 29 June 1875 at St Mary's Bryanston Square. Donald took his new bride on an expedition to Lapland for their honeymoon, and subsequently published an account of the trip.[1] This would be a fairly unusual destination today, let alone in 1875.

The MacKinnons are an interesting family. In 1785 Donald's great-grandfather lived in the French province of the Dauphiné on account of the ill health of his eldest son. His youngest son, who was to go on to become Major-General Henry MacKinnon, was placed in the Military College of Tournon. Here he struck up a remarkable friendship with an ambitious character called Napoleon Bonaparte who was then a subaltern of a regiment stationed in the neighbouring garrison, and who became a frequent visitor to the MacKinnon home. Napoleon eventually proposed to Eliza, the youngest MacKinnon daughter and so Donald's great aunt. She turned him down. When she died, a chestful of letters from the young Napoleon were all burnt in accordance with her wishes. She never married.[2]

Donald's great-great-great-uncle on his mother's side was the eminent physician Dr Thomas Dimsdale, who along with Dr Edward Jenner worked on perfecting an inoculation for smallpox, the scourge of the eighteenth century. In 1767 he published a pamphlet on the subject. This impressed Empress Catherine II of Russia at a time when an epidemic of smallpox was sweeping through her country, and she invited Dr Dimsdale to go out to inoculate herself and her son, Grand Duke Paul. He went with his son Nathaniel the following year, and having successfully demonstrated the procedure on one of her pages, went ahead and inoculated the

---

[1] *Lapland Life, or Summer Adventures in Arctic Regions* (Kerby & Endean, 1878).
[2] D. D. MacKinnon, *Memoirs of Clan Fingon* (Hepworth, 1899).

empress, the Grand Duke and other members of her family. As a measure of her gratitude, she showered him with gifts and made him a baron of the Russian Empire.

In 1879, Donald MacKinnon became curate of Speldhurst in Kent, and he and Mynie, together with Rosa her unmarried older sister, moved into the rectory. Thus began the MacKinnons' involvement with Speldhurst, which was to last for thirty-two years. With his characteristic enthusiasm Donald tackled every aspect of church and parish life, and after taking over as rector in 1889, effectively became the squire of Speldhurst as well. He organised the choir, the maintenance of the churchyard, wrote the parish magazine, was president of the cricket club and ensured that the rectory was always open to anyone in the parish who was in need in any way. In this he was assisted by Mynie and Rosa, who both worked endlessly for the good of the parish. Mynie played the organ in church, while Rosa became involved with the bell-ringers and herself became a very enthusiastic hand bell-ringer. Together they organised countless concerts, outings, choirboys' treats, Christmas parties, mothers' meetings and rector's parties, and were always there to visit the sick or anyone in the parish who had fallen on hard times. Mynie gave a number of lectures on subjects of topical interest to ladies' groups and became a governor of the village school in an age when it was most unusual for a woman to do such a thing.

Such was the esteem in which Rosa was held by the parish that they gave her a party for her fiftieth birthday. More than three hundred people contributed to the presents she received. She responded by putting on a sit-down dinner followed by games and dancing in the rectory garden for some 280 invited guests, and repeated the performance for her sixtieth birthday. Nor was her hospitality confined to the parish. On one occasion, she invited the off-duty booking clerks, ticket collectors and porters from Tunbridge Wells station to dine at the rectory. That same afternoon she had fifty children after school for chestnuts roasted in the stable yard on a brazier borrowed from the watchman on the local drainage works. Later on, the young people from Mynie's Bible class arrived to play every imaginable indoor game from 7 to 9 pm, which they were allowed to do every Wednesday evening in the winter months. So life at the rectory was never dull.

This was immediately apparent to everyone who stayed. There was much fun and laughter, and they all hoped to be asked again. Guests were expected to join in with whatever was going on: cutting down trees in the churchyard, playing tennis, golf and whist, and even singing in the choir. There were frequent organ recitals and plays in the village, with many of the participants staying in the house. Often there were total strangers, who were in Speldhurst to preach, give lectures or had just turned up for one reason or another. All were given a tremendous welcome and made to feel at home. The Highland hospitality was legendary, and as the house was not exactly teetotal, the conversation after dinner often went on into the wee small hours. There were great discussions, much storytelling and practical joking and a decided weakness for punning.

One of the things immediately noticeable to every guest was the number of animals in the house. In addition to the usual collection of dogs and cats there were two mongooses, a parrot (until it was eaten by one of the mongooses), and somewhat unusually, a black-backed jackal called Jack. The rector had brought Jack home from South Africa during the winter of 1892–3. He quickly became acclimatised, and was soon a well-known feature of life at the rectory. Jack had various escapades: he once escaped from the zoo where he always went when the rector was on his annual holiday to Germany, and having evaded capture by a number of keepers, he swam the River Medway complete with 4 feet of chain and returned home via Tunbridge Wells. On another occasion he had the misfortune to be set upon by a pack of hounds being exercised near Eridge and was brought home in a very sorry state. The local vet patched him up as best he could, and everyone was delighted when Jack was fully fit again in six weeks. He lived to the considerable age of fourteen, and was then honoured with a well-deserved obituary in the parish magazine.

Donald MacKinnon was very fond of Wagner, and always went to Germany for two months every summer so that he could take in a number of Wagnerian occasions. When their three boys were small, Mynie stayed behind and took the boys to Folkestone, and Rosa went off to Germany with Donald. In a later age this would have been considered highly irregular and been all over the press, but the MacKinnon household was the very epitome of propriety. Besides, Rosa was no oil painting, poor thing.

The eldest son, George, went into the Navy and retired as a commander. The second son, Alaister, was almost a remittance man, and lived in Canada. The youngest son, Lachlan, had a brilliant naval career and retired in January 1939 as a vice-admiral. Then, with war looming, he became a commodore in the Merchant Marine. On 18 October 1940, his convoy bound for the UK from Nova Scotia sailed into a trap set by five of the latest U-boats. After valiantly trying to ram one, his flagship, the twenty-six-year-old *Assyrian*, was torpedoed.[3] Lachlan spent some considerable time in the freezing waters of the North Atlantic but, in part thanks to the surgeon on board his rescuing destroyer having a trial consignment of penicillin, he survived, at the age of fifty-seven. The naval tradition continued into the next generation. Tragically, both Lachlan's two Fleet Air Arm sons were killed in independent flying accidents after the war. His second daughter, Ione, married Geoffrey Carver, who as the torpedo officer of HMS *Dorsetshire* fired the three torpedoes on 27 May 1941 which at the time were thought to have finally put an end to the *Bismarck*. Recent underwater analysis of the wreck indicates that the inner hull was not breached, and she was probably scuttled.

At the end of 1911, Donald MacKinnon retired as rector of Speldhurst and he, Mynie and Rosa moved to Speldhurst Close in Sevenoaks. He actually died in Wiesbaden on his final trip to Germany in 1925. Rosa died in 1926 and Mynie in 1938, aged almost ninety. Perhaps the best epitaph was that written in the Speldhurst Rectory visitors' book more than thirty-five years earlier: 'A remarkable man, with two very remarkable wives.'

Roberta was only born a couple of years before Mynie, but was very different. Although endowed with a generous helping of shrewdness and a good judge of character, she didn't have Mynie's intellect, and unusually for a Macalpine-Leny, had no sense of humour. She married James Mansfield, a wealthy Edinburgh advocate, just before her twenty-first birthday. The Mansfields lived very close to the Macalpine-Lenys' Edinburgh house, so Roberta didn't have to look too far afield for a husband. James was a very keen shooting and fishing man, and the Mansfields were regular guests at Dalswinton. He was also an extremely good golfer, and the club and ball with which he won the Honourable Company of Edinburgh

[3] Doddy Hay, *War under the Red Ensign – the Merchant Navy 1939–1945* (Jane's, 1982).

Golfers' Gold Medal in 1877 were proudly displayed in the hall at 8 Chester Street. He went on to play in the first Amateur Championship in 1885, but was knocked out in the first round. He died at the relatively early age of forty-seven after being thrown from his horse outside his own front door.

As a wealthy widow with no children, Aunt Roberta was able to maintain an Edwardian lifestyle long after such things had been swept away by the First World War and the subsequent stock market crash. Her highly regulated daily life was not to be disturbed by anything, and woe betide an unpunctual great-nephew who was not washed, changed and ready to leave at the appointed hour. Having always been used to getting her own way, anything that prevented this was met by an uncontrollable fit of temper. Although an object of fascination for younger members of the family, she could never be described as charming, and had a tendency to control other people's lives.

Her ample staff was dominated by the chauffeur, an unlikely fellow called Paterson, who had charge of an enormous Daimler Double Six. As Aunt Roberta didn't appear at breakfast, guests were able to enjoy *The Scotsman*, which always arrived early. About ten o'clock, the parlour maid would come in to remove it, saying that Mr Paterson had come in and wanted it. He was always installed in the study with the paper while Aunt Roberta completed her plans for the day. Every one of her expeditions took an incredible amount of time. No one had ever seen Aunt Roberta in a hurry; nor was she ever late. Each trip was planned in meticulous detail in the comfort of the study. The route and time having been decided upon, the car arrived on time. So did Aunt Roberta. The parlour maid held the front door, the luggage had been long packed and stowed on the roof by Paterson; the lady's maid carried the jewel case and sat in front, and Aunt Roberta sat behind Paterson with a carriage rug or two over her knees. One of the key elements in the planning of every expedition was where to stop for the picnic lunch. This was an elaborate affair with a table being set up and laid with a white tablecloth, silver and glasses, exactly as if she was at home. Suggestions for an alternative lunching spot were always rejected by Paterson with, 'Oh, Mrs Mansfield wouldn't like that.' Being a creature of habit, she always wanted to know exactly which bush she could go behind to spend a penny.

Major George Downie, 1762–1808, commandant of the Calcutta Native Militia

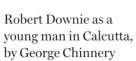

Robert Downie as a young man in Calcutta, by George Chinnery

Robert Downie of Appin, MP, 1771–1841, by J. Graham, 1829. Appin House and the island of Shuna can be seen through the window

Letter from James Mackillop to Lieutenant James Macalpine, 23 March 1818, informing him that his uncle Dr Robert Leny has died, leaving him his fortune

Dalswinton, by
Alexander Nasmyth,
one of a pair

James Macalpine
Leny of Dalswinton,
1796–1867

Dalswinton House, Dumfriesshire

Dalswinton Tower, all that remains of the Old House

Marion Agatha Macalpine-Leny,
née Downie, 1811–81

William, 'Mynie'
and Roberta
Macalpine-Leny,
c.1852

William Macalpine-Leny at
Christ Church, Oxford

XVth Hussars on manoeuvres

William Macalpine-Leny, cornet in the XVth Hussars

Left to right: Agnes Macalpine-Leny, Jimmy, Milly, Harley, May and Bob

The Dalswinton keepers

The Dalswinton indoor staff:
the governess on the left
and Jessie Laing (nanny) on
the right

The Macalpine-Lenys by Dalswinton's front door. *Back row*: Bob, William, Agnes and Milly; *front row*: May, Jimmy and Harley

William and Agnes Macalpine-Leny, 14 September 1904

The Revd Donald MacKinnon

James Mansfield, Rosa
Macalpine-Leny, Mynie
MacKinnon and Roberta
Mansfield

Patricia Pollock, *née* Macalpine-Leny

Edie and Charlie Severne

Bob Macalpine-Leny, cornet in the 16th Lancers

Captain Bob Macalpine-Leny on Duchess, about to leave India for South Africa in 1900

Major Bob Macalpine-Leny on his return from the Boer War

Bob Macalpine-Leny with Roy, c.1907

Roy and Madeline, *c.*1907

Mogera House, Kenya, 1926

Roy Macalpine-Leny serving with the King's African Rifles during the Second World War

Two safaris meeting up. Roy's Bedford truck is second from left

The penultimate safari, 1949: Roy Macalpine-Leny (in trilby hat) and two German clients with village children

Muttie Macalpine-Leny in her greenhouse at Nanyuki, Kenya, 1972

When still a schoolboy, her great-nephew Archie Macalpine-Downie (see Chapter 10) was with her in the drawing room of 8 Chester Street when Aunt Roberta suddenly let out an enormous sneeze, and her false teeth flew across the drawing room carpet. Completely undaunted, she said hurriedly, 'Well, come on boy, pick them up.' When she died in 1939 at the age of ninety-one, she was the last survivor of that generation.

The youngest sister, Patricia, was the third Miss Macalpine-Leny to marry a Church of England clergyman. Edward Downing Pollock, always known as Ned, was the fourth son of James Edward Pollock, vice-president of the Royal College of Physicians and Physician Extraordinary to Queen Victoria. They did not have a happy marriage, had no children, and Ned was always away a lot. Patricia had a great sense of humour, but she needed one. She died in 1921 and Ned a year or so afterwards. Only after he had died and the last screw turned in the lid of his coffin was it discovered that he was a bigamist, and had another wife and family. Not bad for a Church of England minister, even in those days. Poor Patricia had smelt a rat long before. Her will, drawn up in 1909, contained the following astonishing instruction to her executors:

I also desire that the packet of papers in the custody of Mr Henry Gordon addressed to me be handed to Major Macalpine of Dalswinton. In the event of my husband after my death marrying a lady therein named that he shall in honour be called upon to renounce all interest in his Marriage Settlement with me dated July 13 1881 and also hand over to Major Macalpine Leny all goods and chattels of every description which he had the use of in consequence of the said marriage with me, and I call on the Trustees to demand this with the assistance of my Executors.

Pretty strong stuff.

We can't leave the great-aunts without mentioning Aunt Edie. Edith Chica Sophia Long was the third daughter of Walter Jarvis Long of Preshaw and so Agnes Macalpine-Leny's younger sister. She was the most appalling snob, whose principal mission in life was Aunt Edie. At the age of twenty-six she had married a charming chap eighteen years her senior called Charlie Severne, who had more money than he knew what to do with. They lived in great state at Hove on the south coast, but always decamped to Menton on the French Riviera for the winter. When Charlie died in 1909, Aunt Edie was sixty. They had no children.

Three years later, Aunt Edie announced her engagement to Harry Vicars, who was nine years her junior. Reading of their engagement in *The Times*, Bob Macalpine-Leny wrote to his sister Milly: 'I suppose the silly old fool thinks he is in love with her.' Milly duly read out the letter at the breakfast table. Unfortunately, their aunt was staying in the house at the time and was not amused, and promptly wrote Bob out of her will.

On the face of it, Major William Harry Vicars was the height of respectability. Formerly of the Scottish Rifles and York and Lancashire Regiment, he was the eldest son of the late Colonel W. H. Vicars of the 61st Regiment. After an engagement of only six weeks, they were married in the parish church at Hove by the Bishop of Lewes, who was Harry's cousin. Perhaps one thing Harry didn't mention was that his younger brother was Sir Arthur Vicars, who had lost his job as Ulster King of Arms four years earlier over the scandal surrounding the theft of the Irish Crown Jewels. Who stole the Irish Crown Jewels and what became of them remains one of the great unsolved mysteries of Ireland, and bears all the hallmarks of the classic scandal. It involved very well-connected people, a possible homosexual ring, a less than satisfactory police investigation, considerable royal interest, and an official cover-up. And the Jewels have never been found.

The Irish Crown Jewels were nothing like the English Crown Jewels that are kept securely in the Tower of London; they were the regalia or insignia of the Order of St Patrick. This was an order of chivalry founded by the government in 1783, designed to be the Irish equivalent of the British Order of the Garter. The Jewels were presented to the Order by King William IV in 1831 and were supposed to have been made up from diamonds belonging to his mother, Queen Charlotte. They consisted of a star and a badge composed of rubies, emeralds and Brazilian diamonds mounted in silver, which were worn by the Lord Lieutenant as Grand Master on formal occasions. The Ulster King of Arms, who had been Sir Arthur Vicars since 1893, was responsible for registering the Order's membership and the safe custody of the Jewels,[4] kept in a locked safe in the Office of Arms, which had recently been moved to the Bedford Tower of Dublin Castle. After the move it was found that the safe was too large to go through the door of the strongroom, so it resided in the library outside Sir Arthur's office. On the afternoon of Saturday, 6 July 1907, it was found that the door of the safe was unlocked and the Jewels were missing. The police were immediately called, and it was established that the lock had not been tampered with, and the safe had been opened with a key. There were only two, and both were held by Sir Arthur.[5]

The government was particularly embarrassed because a few days later King Edward VII was due to visit Dublin and invest a new knight of the Order of St Patrick, which he now promptly cancelled. Lord Aberdeen, the Lord Lieutenant, decided to appoint a Viceregal Commission in an endeavour to find the culprit and establish whether Sir Arthur had taken all necessary steps to ensure the safety of the Jewels. Unfortunately it did not have the power to compel witnesses to attend and give evidence under oath. Sir Arthur, the most important witness, refused to attend, but it did interview the other prime suspects who reported to him – the three unpaid assistant heralds. These were his nephew Pierce Gun Mahony, Cork Herald; Francis Shackleton, the brother of the polar explorer Sir Ernest Shackleton, Dublin Herald, with whom Sir Arthur shared a house; and Francis Bennett Goldney, sometime mayor of Canterbury, Athlone Pursuivant. When the Viceregal Commission reported in January 1908 it was not able to say who had taken the Jewels, but concluded that Sir Arthur 'did not exercise due vigilance or proper care as the custodian of the Regalia.' Five days later he lost his job.[6]

Rumours continued to abound, with Shackleton appearing to be the prime suspect, but surprisingly he had been completely exonerated by Chief Inspector Kane of Scotland Yard, who led the police inquiry. Unfortunately, Kane's report on the case is one of several documents that have disappeared. Stories emerged thanks to an article in the Irish-American nationalist newspaper *Gaelic American* of drunken goings-on and worse

[4] Sean J. Murphy, *A Centenary Report on the Theft of the Irish Crown Jewels in 1907* (Centre for Irish Genealogical and Historical Studies, 2008).
[5] Ibid.   [6] Ibid.

at the castle involving Lord Aberdeen's son, Lord Haddo, and a disreputable friend of Shackleton's, Captain Richard Gorges. Francis Bennett Goldney also came in for considerable suspicion when it was discovered after his death in a motor accident in 1918 that there were a number of ancient charters and documents belonging to the City of Canterbury among his possessions. But no one was ever charged, and the Jewels were never recovered. Hardly surprisingly, theories abound to this day to explain what became of them: they were supposedly stolen by insiders, or by Unionist conspirators eager to derail Home Rule, or by Republican plotters seeking to embarrass the British government.[7]

Back in Hove, it soon became clear even to Aunt Edie that Harry Vicars was nothing more than a well-bred adventurer who had married her for her money. He was also a crook. He was always taking jewellery off to the jewellers to be cleaned; things started to disappear and he seemed to spend a lot of time away on business. They eventually agreed to separate, and Harry Vicars was swept under the carpet. When Aunt Edie died in 1921, her nephew Harley was her executor. Travelling down to Brighton, he was greeted by a badly shaken lawyer who had had a new will on his desk for six months waiting to be signed, which left everything to Harley. Unfortunately Aunt Edie had slipped into a coma and never been able to sign it. Her old will split everything up among the many nephews and nieces. When Harry Vicars learnt that he had been left nothing he called at her solicitor's office, and producing a pistol, suggested that the will be changed. But old Woolley, her solicitor, called his bluff, and Harry was never seen again.

When the jewellery was divided up, Milly's tiara was valued by Collingwoods at some £700, and May's at 17s. 8d. Harry Vicars had got there first and substituted paste for May's diamonds. There was never any doubt in the minds of the Macalpine-Lenys of the identity of at least one person who had been involved in the theft of the Irish Crown Jewels . . .

---

[7] *Ibid.*

6 Robert Leny Macalpine-Leny

Nine months after William and Agnes returned from their honeymoon in Europe, a son and heir arrived in 1870, which in those days would have been considered a highly satisfactory state of affairs. In keeping with family tradition, he was christened Robert Leny in memory of old Dr Leny.

Young Robert, who would inevitably become Bob as he grew up, was very much brought up as the future laird. Tilbury, the keeper, taught him to shoot, and he learnt to ride and fish from an early age. When he was eight he was packed off to Cargilfield, the fashionable prep school outside Edinburgh. One of his good friends there was David Landale, the son of the minister at Applegarth, who would come to stay at Dalswinton in the holidays. While Landale would go on to Fettes, Bob was inevitably sent to Eton. The photographs of the day show rather an aloof young man, but perhaps that was the pose considered appropriate at the time. When David Landale sensibly went into business after school and joined Jardine Matheson, Bob went to Sandhurst. There was no question of any of William's sons going into 'trade'. On 8 October 1890 he was commissioned in the 16th Lancers, one of the smartest cavalry regiments of the day.

On the following 11 February, when there was a huge bonfire and party on the Mulloch Hill overlooking Dalswinton and Mr Hattersley waxed lyrical proposing the health of the young laird at his coming of age, Bob was several thousand miles away in India. He had arrived in Bombay at the beginning of January and travelled by train to Lucknow to join his regiment. It was the beginning of a new life. The second week he was there, there was a large party in the mess on 22 January 1891 when the regiment entertained the future Tsar Nicholas of Russia and his cousin, Prince George of Greece, to dinner.[1] They were all introduced.

It would have been impossible to join the 16th Lancers without a

---

[1] The Tsarevitch and Prince George were on the Grand Tour, and visited the regiment because the 16th had provided an escort for the Tsarina on her visit to London in 1889. The silver tankard that he presented at the dinner is a prized part of the 16th Lancers' regimental silver.

private income, and Bob was soon to find that his quarterly allowance of £100 wasn't enough. How he wished his father could afford £600 a year. One of the greatest expenses was servants, and then there were the mess bills and the horses, quite apart from travel while on leave. But it was not exactly a hard life: there was polo or cricket every day, football and hockey matches, tennis and golf, and of course riding. There were point-to-points, jackal hunts, race meetings, and the occasional bit of pig sticking thrown in for good measure. On the rare occasions that the regiment went on manoeuvres, the officers seemed to spend every morning and evening shooting, mainly snipe and duck, but also quail and partridges. Someone gave a dance at least once a week and there was the endless round of lunch and dinner parties, and the all-important teas. People from other regiments were always passing through, and Bob invariably knew someone from home or Eton or Sandhurst. It was like one continuous party.

Bob struggled in the riding school initially, especially when they were made to ride without stirrups, and every time he fell off there was a £1 fine to pay, which focused the mind considerably. But he was a natural sportsman, and soon improved. He was a very good cricketer and usually opened for the regiment as well as bowled, and was even known to keep wicket. When not playing visiting regiments, there would be games between the various squadrons, scratch sides, and on one occasion even men against women, with the men playing left-handed. They still won. The last game of 1898 was Old Etonians and Old Harrovians versus the Rest of the World. Bob's other all-consuming passion became polo, and by the time he left India, he was playing for the regiment. He also played an extremely good game of tennis.

The efforts of a succession of Dalswinton governesses were not entirely in vain because Bob spoke fluent German and pretty acceptable French. He also played the piano. Being brought up in an age when amateur theatricals were all the rage in country houses, he was always keen to act. In his first six months in Lucknow he breathed new life into the regimental theatrical society, taking it over and running it very successfully. In time he also became an accomplished photographer, and out of necessity did all his own developing and printing.

It wasn't long before he fell prey to that all too common complaint afflicting those recently arrived from Europe – too much sun. After he had been confined to bed for a couple of weeks the colonel prescribed the usual cure – two months in Kashmir. This enabled Bob to look up friends from home in Srinagar, and go on his first real hunting expedition. He initially found it pretty difficult to hit a moving target with a rifle, but was eventually successful in shooting both a red and a black bear. Needless to say, the cure was successful.

Bob's first home leave came three years after arriving in India. The ship docked at Marseilles, and he and a fellow-officer went by train to Paris. After dinner, they amused themselves by going to the Moulin Rouge 'to see some girls dancing', he recorded in his diary. 'They hold their petticoats over their heads whilst doing so. It rather surprised me, I must say, and I should not think it would improve the morals of the country.'[2] He returned home to find his parents moved from Dalswinton and living in Guernsey. In view of the unsatisfactory state of his father's affairs he even offered to resign from the 16th Lancers. But nothing came of this, and at the end of his three months' leave, he was back in Lucknow.

By this time he was courting Nellie Violet, the younger daughter of Colonel and Mrs Murray. They had met the year before on the tennis court and were soon riding out together. Vi was pretty athletic: she was a good horsewomen, played a good game of golf and was a keen competitive rower. She also played the violin. Almost two years after they first met Bob proposed, and was accepted. They could not afford to get married, so there then began an engagement with its inevitable ups and downs which was to last over two and a half years. The Murrays, especially Vi's father who was now a major-general, proved pretty difficult and didn't seem to entirely approve of their future son-in-law. For a time Bob was not allowed to visit until tea time, and Mrs Murray would never let them leave the drawing room together after dinner. The Murray family finally moved back to England in November 1896, but it was not until 28 September the following year that Bob and Vi were married in Brighton by his uncle Geldart Riadore on Bob's next home leave. For their honeymoon, they spent a week staying with friends in Dumfriesshire, which enabled Bob to introduce Vi

[2] R. L. Macalpine-Leny, unpublished diaries, 1891–1902.

to all the Dalswinton tenants, and have lunch in the house. It was probably her only visit.

For the journey back out to India, they took the Dover–Ostend crossing, and then the train to Trieste via Cologne and Vienna. Trieste to Bombay took twenty days by sea, and then it was thirty-six hours in the train to Lahore, and another seven and a half to Umballa,[3] where the regiment was now stationed. The trains in India ran all through the night, so it was not at all unusual to catch and leave trains in the small hours. Including a twenty-four hour stopover at Lahore, the entire journey had taken twenty-five days – quite a proportion of three months' home leave.

The move from Lucknow to Umballa in 1896 had not been entirely popular because the game shooting and pig sticking had been particularly good around Lucknow, but Umballa was closer to Kashmir. This was where Bob headed with Vi for his six months' leave in April 1898. They went first to Srinagar and then on a ten-week trip under canvas right up to the snow line. At one point they were at 12,000 feet. They were accompanied by two *shikaris* who acted as trackers and guides, and a team of coolies who carried all the baggage and ensured that everyday life continued as if they were at home. When on the march the coolies went on ahead and pitched the tent, and if everything went to plan, dinner would be well on the way by the time the rest of the party arrived at the chosen campsite. The coolies would also clear any snow off the tent in the morning. A key member of the team was the post coolie, who ensured that the regular flow of mail to and from Srinagar continued uninterrupted on an almost daily basis, wherever they were.

The principal objective of the trip was to shoot bears. Bob discovered that initially he was shooting 2 feet above everything, which could not have gone down too well with the *shikaris*, but he eventually got the measure of it and ended up with eight. Each bear was carefully skinned and the pelt preserved so that it could be sold at the end of the expedition. The party also came across the tracks of a snow leopard, but although they came very close, Bob never managed to get a shot at one. The other great prize of hunting in Kashmir, the Himalayan ibex, was seen on several occasions, but none was shot. Bob had succeeded in shooting two on his

[3] Now Ambala

previous trip. Vi was clearly made of strong stuff because she managed the walking well, and even had her first lesson in rifle shooting. When they got back to Srinagar, she went down with a very bad attack of fever, but it was not enteric, so all was eventually well.

Although Bob was never selected to do any active service – he was the regiment's acting paymaster by 1897 – there was always a succession of officers on the station going to or from the north-west frontier, where there always seemed to be fighting going on. This included his friend Fin in the 16th, better known as Lieutenant Viscount Fincastle, who was awarded the Victoria Cross during the Tirah Campaign. The citation read:

During the fighting at Nawa Bali, in Upper Swat, on 17th August, 1897, Lieutenant Colonel R. B. Adams proceeded with Lieutenants H. L. S. MacLean and Viscount Fincastle, and five men of the Guides, under a very heavy and close fire, to the rescue of Lieutent R. T. Greaves, Lancashire Fusiliers, who was lying disabled by a bullet wound and surrounded by the enemy's swordsmen. In bringing him under cover he [Lieutenant Greaves] was struck by a bullet and killed – Lieutenant MacLean was mortally wounded – whilst the horses of Lieutenant Colonel Adams and Lieutenant Viscount Fincastle were shot, as well as two troop horses.

Active service was not the only occasion for loss of life. There were still outbreaks of cholera, and enteric fever (typhoid) continued to claim the occasional victim. Then an officer in the Rifle Brigade fractured his skull playing polo, and Bob's great friend Lieutenant MacNaughten was drowned while out fishing. In addition, regimental life in India did not suit everyone: there were three suicides in the regiment between 1891 and 1899.

By the time the weather began to get hot in March, Vi was expecting a baby, and very sensibly went to stay with friends in Simla – a hill station where it was much cooler. Robert Roy was born in the small hours of 2 November 1899. He weighed 6 pounds. As further good news, Bob's promotion to captain came through the following day.

By the beginning of June that year, the papers were full of the news of the failure of the Bloemfontein Conference between Sir Alfred Milner, the ardently imperialistic British High Commissioner of the Cape Colony, and President Kruger of the Boer Transvaal, and war seemed inevitable. There was a sense of excitement throughout the regiment, because if war was declared, it seemed certain that they would be sent to South Africa. War was finally declared on 11 October, but it was not until 24 December that the regiment received orders to go on active service, by which time Lady-smith, Mafeking and Kimberley were under siege and the British had suffered some serious reversals. It sailed from Bombay on 6 January 1900, the same day that Vi and two-month-old Roy left for England. Bob wondered if he would ever see them again. Fifteen days later, the ship carrying the regiment and all their horses and equipment arrived off Durban, but immediately had orders to proceed up the coast to Port Elizabeth, where they disembarked. Here they had a few days' rest to recover from the journey and get organised. With Bob's friend Major Hubert Gough on secondment to Lord Dundonald as part of his force to relieve Ladysmith, Bob was given temporary command of D Squadron. Shortly afterwards they received orders to go by train and join General Babington's brigade at the Modder River.

On 15 February the 16th Lancers took part in one of the very few true cavalry charges of the war. General French realised that the Boers were holding the *kopjes* to the left of his division to prevent them reaching Kimberley and those on the right to prevent them turning towards Bloem-fontein. If they rushed the ridge in the middle, they might be able to get through, so he ordered Colonel Gordon to do just that. Gordon selected the 16th, but as A Squadron was on the far side of the Modder River and would not have time to get back, he ordered a squadron of 9th Lancers to take the right flank. C were on the left and Bob with D Squadron in the middle. If the Boers had protected the top of the ridge with barbed wire, the whole thing might end in disaster, so Lieutenant Hesketh and Sergeant Hale and ten men from C Squadron were issued with wire cutters and ordered to precede the charge and go forward to give due warning of wire.

As soon as the squadron commanders returned to their squadrons after receiving their orders, they began to advance. Bob was in front of his squadron, so could see Hesketh racing forwards with his patrol about 500 yards in front of the Regiment. They charged for about 1,000 yards under a shower of screeching bullets which was most unpleasant but, at the same time, very exciting. Once they reached the top of the ridge, the Boers stopped firing, jumped on their horses, and bolted. Those whose horses had galloped away continued firing until the squadron was 100 yards off, then slung their rifles and came forward laughing, waving a little white rag in the hope that their lives would be spared. But after the hail of bullets that they had been through, the men were having none of it, and ran them all through with their lances. One trooper of the 9th missed his man and lanced his horse instead, whereupon his lance broke. Not to be outdone, the trooper pulled the Boer off his skewered horse and shot him with his own rifle. Once at the top of the ridge, Bob took twenty men and left in search of the Boer guns, but in typical fashion, they had vanished.

Bob's squadron accounted for twelve Boers lanced or shot, in return for six men wounded, two severely. One of Bob's men had a very lucky escape. He was concussed by a bullet which just grazed his temple without breaking the skin, and he fell, bringing his horse down with him. When he came to, his horse was still there, so he remounted without knowing he had been hit. Seven horses were killed and about twelve wounded, and another eleven were so exhausted that they had to be shot afterwards. Regimental Sergeant-Major Callaghan had two horses killed under him. Poor Hesketh was killed along with two men from the forward patrol, and another two wounded. A Boer waited until he was 6 yards away, then jumped up and shot him through the forehead. Neither Bob nor Duchess, the charger he brought from Umballa, was hit, but as he wrote to his sister Milly, 'Even so, I do not wish to do that sort of thing again.' Fortunately, the Boers on that occasion were pretty poor marksmen. If it had been British infantry instead of Boers on that ridge, it might have been a very different story. But the strategy worked, and Kimberley was relieved later that day.

Twelve days later, the 16th took part in the battle of Paardeberg, which ended with the surrender of General Cronje and four thousand men. The following day, Hubert Gough led a cavalry column into Ladysmith. In the space of two weeks, the Boers had lost two of their siege towns and a major part of their army in the west. Bloemfontein would follow, and eventually Mafeking would be relieved too.

The following year saw the war enter its most controversial phase. The brilliant Boer General Christiaan De Wet realised that he couldn't hope to take on the vastly larger British forces in set-piece actions, so resorted to commando tactics with great effect. The British answer was to burn the Boer farms on which they depended for supplies, kill all their livestock, and take their women and children into what were called at the time refugee camps – in effect some of the first concentration camps. This provoked questions in Parliament – not the least of which was why it took an army of 425,000 to subdue a Boer army of never more than 35,000 fighting men. Bob was heavily involved with the depressing activity of burning farms, and wondered at the time if it wouldn't have been better to simply cull all the ponies on which the Boers depended rather than drag their women off to refugee camps. His diary entries illustrate the emotions involved:

We went out at 9.00 am and cleared some farms west and south of this. They were all burned for harbouring Boers. In the evening we reached a farm called S. The people were well to do and were very upset when I told them they had to move. We only had time to move their heavy baggage this evening. The General [then] decided at 8 pm that these people were not to be moved. I rode out at 9.00 am to tell [them] that they would not be moved, and all the ladies fell on me and made me feel such a fool. They clasped me round the legs and covered my hands with kisses. It was most embarrassing as I had nothing to do with the order allowing them to stay on their farm. One of the girls gave me a Kruger penny and an Orange Free State rosette to send to my darling. Charles (Campbell) and I went to have tea with them in the evening and they played to us on the piano.

After a spell as acting adjutant, Bob was now assistant provost marshal on General Babington's staff. He was a thoughtful, popular officer with a good sense of humour who always tried to make the best of everything. This included coping with increasing deafness and endless trouble with his teeth – the latter culminating in a set of South African false teeth. One morning the water in which his teeth had been languishing overnight froze in his tent. He was justifiably critical in his diary of the shortcomings in the tactics of some of the generals, but was always quick to acknowledge when things were done well. He was a student of both history and warfare, and was reading the *Life of Stonewall Jackson* at the time. He was also a good judge of character. Later, while intelligence officer on General Bruce Hamilton's staff, he noted in his diary, 'Allenby seems a nice man and has a remarkably strong face. He looks like a man who would do well.' He would prove to have considerable influence on Bob's future career.

Like members of his family both before and since, Bob was always having problems with money, and had arrived in South Africa leaving debts behind in India. Slowly, he managed to pay these off, but it made him think about his future, and he toyed with joining the South African police. This was greeted by a wail from home, not least from Vi, and he eventually dropped the idea. By the end of 1901, Bob was made assistant provost marshal at East London. Things had eased considerably and he was able to ask Vi to come out and bring Roy. When they arrived at Port Elizabeth on 11 January 1902, he hadn't seen them for two years.

By the time the proclamation of peace was read out in all churches on 1 June, Bob's work had begun to wind down and he was studying hard for the Staff College exam, which he failed first time round. On 14 November the Military Office at East London was closed, and Vi and Roy left for England at the beginning of December. When Bob left a week later he had some black game for dinner on board ship 'which brought sad remembrances of dear old Dalswinton. What a happy time we had in those jolly days, and how little did we know what was before us.'[4] When he arrived at Southampton on 27 December 1902, he had only spent twelve weeks in England in the previous twelve years.

At the end of four months' leave Bob's promotion to major came through, together with orders to take a draft out to Cape Town on 1 June. So it was back to South Africa again. The good news was that this gave him time to study for the Staff College exam, and this time he passed. He lost no time in taking up his place when he got home at the beginning of the following year. Two years later saw him appointed as a company commander at the Royal Military College, Sandhurst, so Bob and Vi moved to Camberley. It was here that their daughter was born on 11 March 1907, and christened Agnes Madeline in the RMC chapel.

After several years of staff appointments, on 31 August 1910 Bob

[4] R. L. Macalpine-Leny, unpublished diaries.

rejoined his regiment. By now Gough was the commanding officer of the 16th Lancers, and wrote on his old friend's annual confidential report:

This officer has only returned to regimental duty after several years on the Staff, but he at once took over command of a Squadron at the Cavalry Division and the Army Manoeuvres, and did it very well. He is very keen, reads and studies and is determined to pick up all details of Regimental training that his absence on the Staff may have caused him to forget. He is a very cheery disposition, gets on very well with the junior officers but maintains a strong and excellent influence. He suffers slightly from deafness which at times is a little handicap to him in the Field.[5]

The regiment was based in Norwich but in 1911 was moved to Liverpool and Manchester. This was the year that Winston Churchill mobilised the Somerset Light Infantry amid great controversy at the time of the Welsh miners' strike. The following year, the 16th were sent to Wigan to deal with the miners' riots – a slight change from active service in South Africa. In October they were posted to the Curragh outside Dublin and, with Bob in command, embarked at Holyhead on 1 October. Here in Ireland was to occur one of the most unusual events in the history of the British Army.

In the spring of 1912, the Liberal government under Prime Minister Herbert Asquith introduced the Third Home Rule Bill to repeal the Act of Union between Great Britain and Ireland and propose Parliament for the whole of Ireland in Dublin. The large number of Protestant Unionists in the north objected to rule from Dublin, and founded the Ulster Volunteers paramilitary group to fight, if necessary, against the British government. By the spring of 1914, the Ulster Volunteers had amassed a considerable arsenal of rifles and ammunition, principally from Germany, keen to encourage unrest.

To deal with the potential threat of violence from the Ulster Volunteers in the event of the Home Rule Bill being passed, the General Officer Commanding Ireland, Lieutenant-General Sir Arthur Paget, was summoned to London. Paget had seen service in Burma, the Sudan and South Africa and was now sixty-three years old, and his personality was one of the

[5] Agnes Macalpine-Leny, unpublished diaries, 1869–1916.

causes of what followed. He was considered 'too out of date, too casual, and intellectually too shallow . . . He could be genial and amusing, and was a great ladies' man, but his old-fashioned pomposity was a standing joke. He talked as if he was thinking aloud, and his rambling and often highly coloured language portrayed the romantic and even melodramatic current of his thoughts, besides a deep-rooted egotism.'[6] He was instructed at the War Office to move eight hundred men into Ulster to reinforce depots and arms stores there. On expressing concern about the possible response of his officers, he was told that officers ordered to act in support of the civil power should not be permitted to resign their commissions but must, if they refused to obey orders, be dismissed from the army. Officers domiciled in Ulster might be allowed to resign.

On his return, he summoned his unit commanders, who included Hubert Gough, now brigadier-general commanding the 3rd Cavalry Brigade who, though brought up in London, always considered himself to be Irish. The brigade consisted of the 16th Lancers, the IVth Hussars, the 5th Royal Irish Lancers and two batteries of Royal Horse Artillery. When giving his orders, rather unwisely Paget added on his own initiative that officers could resign. The commanding officers of the units concerned in turn briefed their officers. As a result, fifty-seven of the seventy officers based in the Curragh, including Bob and all sixteen other officers of the 16th Lancers and their brigade commander opted for dismissal rather than be involved in active military operations in Ulster. When news of this reached London, Gough and his commanding officers were summoned to the War Office. Faced with what had happened, the government climbed down, claiming there had been a genuine misunderstanding. Gough returned to Dublin with a guarantee that all officers would be reinstated and their troops would not be called upon to enforce the present Home Rule Bill in Ulster; he was proclaimed a hero by the Irish press. Four months later, all this was forgotten when Germany declared war and the regiments concerned found themselves among the first into action.

The regiment went direct to France from Dublin in August 1914. At the same time, Bob was appointed to the headquarters staff of the 1st Cavalry Division under General Allenby as deputy assistant adjutant and quarter-

[6] The Curragh 'Mutiny' 1914 website.

master general (DAA&QMG). In Allenby he had a born leader but a difficult man, and it would take time for him to win the respect and admiration of his staff. He was also not popular with many of his brigade commanders, particularly Gough. This didn't help matters at a critical time. By the end of August things were not going well for the British Expeditionary Force. The Imperial German 1st Army under General von Kluck poured through Belgium and into France in one vast sweeping flanking movement: the Schlieffen Plan. The great retreat began. By the evening of 25 August, the Second Corps under General Sir Horace Smith-Dorrien had been marching for three days and nights and was completely exhausted, and von Kluck was pressing hard on their heels. What followed was one of the most interesting battles of the war, and one that would be the subject of recriminations and counter recriminations after it: Le Cateau.

Allenby went to Smith-Dorrien's HQ at Le Cateau and warned him that if he continued to retreat, the cavalry would not be in a position to give full support because part of his division had become separated.[7] Smith-Dorrien immediately called a conference of his divisional commanders in the early hours of 26 August. Bob was present, but quite why he should have been included in such a crucial meeting is not clear; perhaps he had key information which Allenby needed. He also spoke fluent German, which may have been a factor. The general consensus was that the men would not be fit or able to move again until daylight, and several of the commanders believed that their troops would be better off fighting than marching. With Allenby agreeing to come under his orders and protect his right flank, Smith-Dorrien took the decision to stand and fight, against the orders of the Commander-in-Chief, Sir John French, rather than risk annihilation by continuing to retreat in broad daylight. It was a costly decision in terms of casualties, but by halting the German advance, almost certainly saved the British Expeditionary Force from complete rout. French never forgave Smith-Dorrien for countermanding his orders, and ultimately forced his resignation in 1915. But history eventually came down on the side of Smith-Dorrien and he was able to clear his name.[8]

[7] Brian Gardner, *Allenby* (Cassell, 1965).
[8] Ian F. W. Beckett, *The Judgement of History: Sir Horace Smith-Dorrien, Lord French and 1914* (Tom Donovan Publishing, 1993).

Bob continued on the HQ staff of the 1st Cavalry Division until the spring of 1916 when he returned to England to instruct on the Second Staff Course at Clare College, Cambridge. His next assignment was something totally different again – to join the future 75th Division of the Egyptian Expeditionary Force as assistant adjutant and quartermaster general. He left Marseilles on 28 December 1916 aboard the 14,000-ton *Ivernia*, a Cunard liner hired by the government as a troop transport, which was taking 2,400 troops to Alexandria.

Unknown to the *Ivernia* or her destroyer escort, HMS *Rifleman*, the German submarine UB47 commanded by Kapitan-Leutenant Steinbauer was lying in wait some 50 miles south-east of Cape Matapan in Greece. At 10.12 am on 1 January 1917 there was an enormous explosion as one of UB47's torpedoes struck home. Within an hour, the *Ivernia* had sunk, and three officers and eighty-two other ranks were drowned, together with the ship's surgeon, chief engineer, and thirty-four of the crew. The captain, who survived, was none other than Captain William Turner, who had been captain of the *Lusitania* when she was torpedoed and sunk nineteen months earlier. Survivors were picked up by the *Rifleman* and two armed trawlers, which took the lifeboats in tow to Suda Bay in Crete. Bob managed to scramble aboard one of the trawlers, and always claimed to have been torpedoed again while sat on the aft rail with his backside over the side, because the trawler was a bit light on plumbing, but no damage was done. There cannot have been many cavalry officers who were torpedoed twice . . . When he finally arrived in Alexandria, he was given a chitty by the assistant provost marshal in Cairo which read: 'Major R. L. Macalpine-Leny, 16th Queen's Lancers, a survivor of the transport 'Ivernia', has no clothes, but has permission to walk about the streets.' Needless to say, he kept it.

When Allenby strode into GHQ Cairo on 28 June 1917 as the newly appointed Commander-in-Chief, Egypt, it didn't take him long to shake the Egyptian Expeditionary Force out of the lethargic sleep into which it had fallen under his predecessor. He lost no time in moving his headquarters from Cairo into Palestine so that he could be near his troops, and a number of staff officers who had spent much time propping up the bar at Shepheard's Hotel in Cairo found themselves on the boat home. He then set about preparing in minute detail for his force to go on the offensive. By now Bob was a temporary Lieutenant Colonel.

After a complicated deception leading the Turks to believe that the main attack would come at Gaza, the advance started with an attack on Beersheba during the final week of October, followed by a secondary attack on Gaza. Anxious to capitalise on the initial success, Allenby drove his army forward relentlessly. The fighting around Jerusalem in which Bob's 75th Division were heavily involved was particularly bitter, but on the 9 December 1917, forty days after the start of the offensive at Beersheba, the city surrendered. It had been four centuries and one year since Turkish rule of the city of Jerusalem had begun. Two days later, Allenby made his official entry into the city on foot.[9]

Bob was awarded the DSO on 1 January 1918 for 'services in military operations leading to the capture of Jerusalem'. Unfortunately, the full citation has been lost. This was three years after his youngest brother, Harley (Chapter 11), won his immediate DSO, which must have caused some interesting exchanges between the brothers at the time. Ten days later Bob was mentioned in despatches for the second time. That year there was an Old Etonian dinner in Jerusalem on the 4 June. Some ninety old Etonians including Bob, Reggie Halsey (Chapter 9) and Arthur Kavanagh (Chapter 10) sat down to *hors d'œuvres, consommé, mayonnaise de poisson, bœuf à la paysanne, asperges, gateaux,* and *œufs aux anchoies.*

Bob spent the rest of the war in Palestine, was mentioned in despatches again in October 1918 and promoted to brevet Lieutenant Colonel in May 1919. By the time he retired the following year, he had spent twenty of his thirty years in the army outside Great Britain. This was the time when the British government was anxious to encourage more white settlers to go out to what was then Kenya Colony, and devised the ex-soldier settlement scheme. Approved applicants could apply to purchase farms in a ballot at preferential terms, and 1,031 farms were allocated under the scheme.[10] Bob knew nothing about farming, but the prospect seemed very appealing, as it must have done to a number of his fellow-officers. Land was

[9] Brian Gardner, *Allenby.*
[10] Elspeth Huxley, *White Man's Country: Lord Delamere and the making of Kenya* (Macmillan, 1935).

cheap, it was a wonderful climate, there was excellent big game hunting, and the national sport of the white settlers seemed to be polo. Besides, while he was still based at Ismailia in Egypt, his father's trustees had put Dalswinton up for sale in the autumn of 1919. The estate was heavily in debt, and largely owned by the bank, so there was no alternative. Purely coincidentally, it was bought for £70,000 by his old prep school friend David Landale, who had made a fortune with Jardine Matheson in Hong Kong.[11] By the time he returned to Camberley the following year, Bob had been successful in the ballot, and had purchased a farm in Kenya. Sad though it was in many ways, he turned his back on the past, and looked forward to an exciting colonial future.

[11] The Landale family have taken wonderful care of Dalswinton. The house is in perfect order, and the estate, which is still the same size as when they bought it, goes from strength to strength.

7 Kenya

Of all the countries of Africa, Kenya in the 1920s offered the perfect life for the British settler. Land was cheap, and servants even cheaper; the climate, particularly in the highlands, was very pleasant – on the Equator but you needed a fire at night; polo was the all-consuming passion, and big game hunting provided that element of excitement that so many needed. It also acted like a magnet for many wealthy would-be sportsmen from overseas. In Nairobi, a social circuit sprang up centred on the Muthaiga Club which rivalled anything in London, Newport or St Moritz. It was not by accident that Elspeth Huxley titled her book on Lord Delamere and the making of Kenya *White Man's Country*.

But it hadn't always been that way. Life for the early settlers was extremely tough. Clearing land for farms and fighting disease among sheep and cattle, not to mention having to deal with lions and black rhino took a lot of hard graft, and not everyone came through unscathed. By the beginning of the First World War, when Kenya had the unusual distinction of being the only part of the British Empire to be invaded by the enemy, when a handful of German soldiers ventured over the unguarded border with their colony of Tanganyika, life was still pretty rudimentary. But all this was to change with the ending of the war and the sudden influx of ex-servicemen to claim farms which totalled 12,000 square miles in a country of 240,000 square miles. Many knew nothing about farming, and some of the allocated land was totally unsuited to farming of any sort. What they lacked in experience they made up for in enthusiasm, although many had to clear a road to their future farms, which must have come as a bit of a shock.

Bob Macalpine-Leny's farm was Mogera in the highlands near Thika. Although completely ignorant about growing coffee he knew a lot about logistics, so with plenty of help he started to clear the land and plant coffee bushes. As a retired Lieutenant Colonel with a good war record and a DSO to boot, not to mention the right sort of pedigree, he slipped effortlessly into Kenya society. As soon as he started to build a house, Vi came out to join him together with Madeline, who was now a young teenager. Roy by this time had left Marlborough where he excelled in all sports, particularly squash, and was at Sandhurst. He was commissioned as a 2nd lieutenant in the Argyll and Sutherland Highlanders, the regiment of his Macalpine-Downie cousins (Chapter 10), in 1918 and posted to Dublin at the height of the Troubles. Here he decided with a brother-officer to conduct an intelligence exercise to gather information about infiltration by spies. They persuaded their batmen to lend them their uniforms and, thus adorned, went to the 'Other Ranks' ball. True to form, they had too much to drink and got found out. Roy had to resign, and went to Kenya to join his parents.

The surviving photograph of Mogera taken in 1926 shows a spacious house by Kenya standards with a lovely flower garden in front, so the Macalpine-Lenys started life in Kenya in considerable style. But things did not go well for long. Bob did not know one end of a coffee bean from another, and clearly did not bother to learn. There were a couple of disastrous harvests, and then in 1927, Mogera was completely gutted by fire. This was an all too common occurrence in those days because the roofs of the early houses were thatched, and at an altitude of over 5,000 feet, there always needed to be a fire at night. Everything was lost. Totally unabashed, Bob had it rebuilt, and brought more furniture out from England.

A letter to his brother-in-law Sir Walter Halsey at Gaddesden (Chapter 9) dated 9 November 1930 finds Bob teetering on the verge of bankruptcy, and gambling all on the next coffee crop. But the price of coffee crashed. Finally in 1931, his creditors moved in: all his possessions were hurriedly parcelled out to friends to prevent them being seized, and Mogera was sold to pay his debts. The family moved to Nanyuki at the foot of Mount Kenya and bought a 40-acre plot down Lunatic Lane on which they built a much more modest house.

Madeline meanwhile had developed a wonderful gift for riding horses, and one or two other things besides. When still only nineteen she married Ally Boyd, who had won the Military Cross in the Scots Guards during the war, but that did not last long. Back in Kenya, she proceeded to develop almost every vice known to men and women, and a few more besides, so the less said about her the better. Even in old age, and absolutely destitute, she still possessed the Macalpine charm that had taken in so many people in days gone by, and was very good company.

Bob was to succeed in burning down the house at Nanyuki as well, and with it the rest of the Macalpine-Leny possessions, including his full-length portrait, and the hearth rug with the Macalpine-Leny crest complete with five drops of blood. The only thing that survived was a pewter tankard that was being repaired in the village, and a silver mustard pot, both of which are at Doddington to this day. Vi died on 17 May 1935 aged only fifty-eight, probably of a broken heart, and is buried in the graveyard at Nanyuki. Bob was devastated, and incredibly lonely. About this time he made his last trip back to England to stay with his sister May at Gaddesden. By then he was a slovenly old man, smelling of whisky, and rejoicing in a large brown stain down the front of his trousers. His young nephew, Kenny (Chapter 12), a product of Marlborough in the 1920s who was very particular about his dress, was horrified. By the end he was living in the Sportsman's Arms at Nanyuki, and was eventually run over by an army lorry on 11 Feb 1941 while staggering home, almost completely blind by this time. It was a sad end for a man who had been a very good soldier, an excellent sportsman and extremely good company. He was buried next to Vi, but no one could afford a headstone, and anyway, by this time there was a war on.

At this point we should introduce the Hills. Beatrice Agnes Blake didn't like either of her Christian names, so at an early age took the name of her pet cat – 'Muttie'. In 1921 she went out to India to marry Major Sydney Hill, who had served with the Royal Engineers during the war and had got a job as an engineer working on the Indian Railways. They were married in Bombay Cathedral. Muttie hated India, but fortunately for her Sydney's job came to an end after three years and they returned to England. Not long afterwards they met Mervyn Ridley, an old family friend of the Blakes, in the Burlington Arcade. On hearing that Sydney had no job, he immediately proposed that he should go out to Kenya and run his coffee factory, as he knew he was a very good engineer. 'Where on earth is that?' they both asked. So it was that Sydney went out to run the Ridleys' coffee factory near Thika in 1924 for the princely sum of £10 per month, and Muttie followed after a few months.

She went by rail from Nairobi to Thika where she was met by a Model T Ford, and her heavy leather steamer trunks with all her best dresses were left at the station to be picked up by bullock cart the next day. Unfortunately it rained during the night, and her precious dresses eventually arrived all sopping wet. On arriving at the Ridleys' farm at Makuyu, Muttie was alarmed to come across a cheetah at the side of the road, which she subsequently discovered was Mrs Ridley's pet. Such was her introduction to Africa.

The Ridleys turned out to be neighbours of the Macalpine-Lenys, and Muttie went on to establish a firm friendship with Roy. Elspeth Huxley's parents, the Grants, were also neighbours, and Sydney helped them with running their coffee factory as well. Life in those days for the European settlers was pretty good. There was polo at Makuyu every Saturday and Sunday, and this along with gymkhanas and amateur racing became the hub of the social circle. Sydney Hill was extremely adept on a horse, and a very good polo player and amateur jockey. Roy was very good-looking, an extremely good sportsman and a wonderful rider, so was instantly at home becoming one of the best polo players in the whole of Kenya. But he needed to earn his living, especially after his father went bankrupt. He shot elephants and sold the ivory, and for a time also caught animals for various zoos. The problem was not catching them but keeping them alive afterwards. Eventually he obtained his professional hunter's licence and joined the leading company of Safariland Ltd to take clients on hunting safaris.

Meanwhile, in 1928/9, the Hills had moved from Makuyu to Kitale where Sydney ran a tea factory for the Hoey family. Their daughter Jill was born at Eldoret in 1934. Then in 1937 they moved to Nairobi, where Sydney ran the office of Mitchell Cotts, the shipping firm. He had suffered from angina for some time and died suddenly in 1939, leaving Muttie with a large establishment and a five-year-old daughter. But she was nothing if not resourceful, and soon arranged for friends whose husbands had volunteered for the war to come and be her paying guests, assisted by her Sudanese major-domo, Sadi.

The white settlers lost no time in either joining up to meet the threat from the Italians, taking part in the invasion of Italian-occupied Ethiopia in 1941, or going back to England to enlist. Roy became a Major in the 23rd King's African Rifles (KAR), who were based in Nanyuki, and immediately became involved in the Ethiopian campaign. In the meantime, he and Muttie were married on 21 February 1942, and moved to Nanyuki. The old house down Lunatic Lane was still a complete wreck, so they set about building a new one. There was a large Italian prisoner-of-war camp at Nanyuki, and with the help of five 'trusties', three of whom were stonemasons, a new house was completed by the end of the war.

The only anecdote to survive about Roy's war was the time he was driving down the road up on the Ethiopian border when an Italian aeroplane came over, then tipped sideways as they had to, in order for the rear gunner to fire at him. He leapt into the ditch clasping his rifle, and waited. When the plane came round again, Roy took careful aim and fired at the gunner, and as he did not fire the third time round, presumably hit him. The 23rd KAR, whose soldiers all came from Nyasaland, was posted to Mogadishu, and marched all the way there, a distance of some 1,000 miles. Roy and Muttie rented a flat in Mogadishu, cooked for by Wachira, who had started working for the family as a kitchen *mtoto* at Mogera, before becoming Roy's safari cook and then bearer during the war. Jill, who was then at school in Thomson's Falls, remembers being driven for three days in a staff car to Mogadishu, and Wachira going to the Italian ice-cream parlour across from the flat twice a day to fetch ice creams.

At the end of the war, the 23rd KAR marched for two and a half weeks back to Nanyuki. Roy then took the soldiers back to Nyasaland. After that it was a question of finding a job, so he went back to work for Safariland. This involved the considerable expense of buying a new Bedford truck, and getting kitted out to take clients on safari again. In those days safaris would last anything from one to two months, during which time he would be completely out of communication. While on safari Roy earned £5 per day plus 50 shillings[1] for his truck. In the school holidays, he would often take time off to take Jill and one of her schoolfriends on a photographic safari. By then Roy had a Leica camera, and had become a very good photographer.

As a child, Muttie had suffered from corneal ulcers and missed a lot of

[1] There were 100 shillings to the Kenya pound.

schooling, and these started to cause problems again during the war. By 1949 they had become so bad that the only hope of saving her sight was to have treatment at Moorfields Eye Hospital in London. In May 1949 she left by flying boat from Lake Navasha, Jill went back to boarding school in Nairobi, and Roy left on his last fateful safari. His clients were the Fishers – a young American doctor and his wife, who arrived on 30 March. The following day when Roy went to buy their ammunition, the doctor insisted that he wanted to use his own .30 rifle. Roy warned him that it was not heavy enough for big game, but in the end let him have his way. They left Nairobi on 1 June, and after a couple of problems with the Bedford lorry, spent the night at Narok. They left at 10 am the following day and continued down towards the Mara river on the way to the Tanganyika border. They saw plenty of game, but the doctor was not a very good shot. On about the third day he had a shot at a wildebeest at 50 yards and succeeded in missing it twice, and then two shots at a Grant's gazelle, both missed. After tea, he managed to have three shots at wildebeest and three at Grant's gazelle without a single hit. Roy recorded in his safari diary that he hoped he would get another chance tomorrow. That was the last entry.

The following day, Monday, Dr Fisher had his first chance at a buffalo, and using his .30 only succeeded in wounding it. The buffalo disappeared into long grass and, instructing him to keep back, which he didn't like, Roy took his double-barrelled .450 rifle and went forward with his gun bearer to find the wounded animal and finish it off. As every professional hunter knows, a wounded buffalo can be more dangerous than anything else – they tend to circle round and attack from the side. It will never be known exactly what happened – Roy had new shoes and Muttie thinks he might have slipped, but in a flash the buffalo was on him, goring him severely and then kneading him with its sharp hooves. At the same time his gun bearer was knocked down but fortunately not hurt. Quickly the doctor came in and fired several shots, killing the buffalo, but the damage was done. It was only with the greatest difficulty that they got Roy into the car.[2] The journey from the Mara back to Nairobi took three days, by which time gas gangrene had set in, and there was nothing that could be done.

[2] From the account written by the Safariland storekeeper, Wally King, transcribed by Tony Dyer, the last president of the East African Professional Hunters' Association.

Jill heard the news when she was in a chemistry lesson, but by the time she reached the hospital it was too late – he had died at 9am with the faithful Wachira still at the hospital.

In those days there was no question of postponing the funeral until Muttie could have got back from England, which would have been impossible anyway as she was still undergoing treatment at Moorfields, so it went ahead, arranged by one of her close friends, Tassie Rowe. It was taken by the Scottish Minister in Nairobi who was the father of David Steele, the future leader of the Liberal Party, and Roy was buried in Nairobi. An indication of how different things were in those days: Jill – by then fifteen – was not allowed to go to the funeral. Roy has no headstone – Muttie hated such things – but instead she donated money to build a water trough for camels in Wajir, a small town in the north-east of the country which Roy often used to go through on his safaris.

When Muttie came out of hospital she went to convalesce with her brother at Wellingborough, and with the Halseys at Gaddesden. Bob's younger brother Harley invited her to stay at Courance in Dumfriesshire but, fearful that he might turn out to be a younger version of Bob, she declined. She returned to Kenya in October; she had tremendous pluck, and a great many friends, and was determined that life must go on. She started a thriving nursery garden business. After Jill left school in 1952, Muttie took her to England to go to Reading University.

Back in Kenya the Emergency, as the Mau Mau rebellion was called, had begun, after which life in Kenya would never be the same again. All Kikuyu, including poor Wachira, were rounded up and detained until they had been cleared, and many Europeans carried revolvers at all times, and slept with them under their pillows. Muttie was fortunate that her house was made of stone and had cedar-bark shingles on the roof. The poor old Lydfords, who occupied the last house (Muttie's was the second-to-last house) down Lunatic Lane, had a thatched roof, and Jill remembers being woken at 2am by their house boy to say that their house had been set on fire.

Everyone closed up their houses at 6.30pm before it got dark (Nanyuki is on the equator, so it gets dark at the same time all year round), with all the servants locked outside. They, being equally vulnerable, had to lock themselves in their houses. Muttie told many a story of her escapades at that time, but the only time she used her revolver was to shoot through the back door. When she opened it she discovered a badly shaken Wachira, fortunately unharmed. All the revolvers ended up down the outside loo, the 'long drop'.

Jill had returned from Reading early, probably because she could not stand the English cold any longer, and her mother got her a job in the Standard Bank in Nanyuki. Here she met Sebert Lewis, who was stationed in Nanyuki with No. 1 (Independent) East African Armoured Car Squadron from 1954 to 1957. They were married in Nanyuki Church in 1956, when Jill was only twenty-two. It rained, which was considered by the Africans to be extremely lucky.

While I was still at university an uncle, Gerald Moyers, was staying with an old friend of his in Nanyuki, and sent me a postcard to say there was a Mrs Macalpine-Leny living nearby: 'I think she must be a relation.' I tried to write to her care of the Muthaiga Club in Nairobi, little knowing that she had not been a member for years. Then out of the blue came a large registered package from her containing all the old family letters that had somehow managed to survive the various fires,[3] followed eventually by a letter. When Muttie made her next annual trip to the UK in 1971, I arranged to take her out to dinner, and went to the Regent Palace Hotel ('my common little pub') to pick her up. Out of the lift came a small, determined-looking lady with a stick. 'Come up to my room for a drink,' was the second thing she said. Once there, she rummaged in her suitcase and produced a bottle of sherry and two tooth mugs. I knew we were going to get on immediately, and made her an honorary aunt on the spot. I had recently become a member of the Travellers Club, so there was no question of where I would take her to dinner. She was hypnotised by the fact that the lift went through the middle of the gents' loo on the way up to the first-floor dining room, and with wire-caged sides, left nothing to the imagination. 'You must come out to Kenya,' she said, so, taking four weeks' holiday, I did just that.

[3] They had been stored in the Dalswinton safe, and were only given to Muttie when she came to stay at Gaddesden in 1949.

I arrived in Nairobi at 8am on Saturday, 30 September 1972, to find Aunt Muttie waiting to meet me, complete with stick, large hat and the enormous brown handbag that she never went anywhere without. I later discovered that among other things, it contained a large ball of plasticene. This was apparently in case the petrol tank should get holed when travelling over particularly rough ground. We squeezed into her small white Peugeot (I soon discovered that all cars in East Africa were white to reflect the heat) and were soon hurtling through the outskirts of Nairobi. Considering that to all intents and purposes she only had one functioning eye, she drove with considerable confidence. As soon as the outskirts of the city had been left behind, she pulled into the side of the road and told me to drive, which I did for the rest of my stay. Ten minutes or so later, I was told to stop in the middle of nowhere. 'I need a widdle' – and with that she disappeared into the bush, only to reappear all of forty-five seconds later. 'No good – prickles.' I began to have some inkling what I was in for.

Thus began the most wonderful four-week stay, during which my ancient honorary Aunt called in no end of favours, and pulled out all the stops. No doubt all her friends were equally curious to see what this real live Macalpine-Leny relation was like. The only person to be disappointed was old Wachira – because I was not dark like Uncle Bob and Roy, he did not consider me a Macalpine-Leny at all.

The day started when the house boy brought my early-morning tea and shaving water, which came in a gleaming brass kettle, at 6.30am. I would then go out and get an hour and a half's birdwatching in before breakfast. Standing in the porch of my aunt's house you could see the snow-covered twin peaks of Mount Kenya between the trees. This was a sight of which I would never tire. Aunt Muttie always had breakfast in her room, so I breakfasted in solitary state on fresh pawpaw, mango or pineapple, followed by bacon and eggs and toast and marmalade, waited on by the house boy. I was just polishing off the last of the toast and marmalade on my first morning, when my aunt came in. 'Good morning, Aunt Muttie,' I said, getting up politely, 'did you sleep well?' 'Sleep well?' came back the reply. 'Of course I slept well. I always sleep well. If I hadn't slept well you would have heard all about it by now!'

We were sitting at the dining-room table one lunchtime when the house boy passed in front of the window, on his way to clean my outside guest bedroom. On his head was a large new bush hat with a smart leopard-skin band. Shaking with indignation, my aunt ambushed him on his return journey. 'What's that on your head?' 'A hat,' he said, which clearly did not do much for his career prospects. I had earlier naively remarked on the attractive lattice-work on the windows, little realising that this was an anti Mau Mau precaution, along with the sirens in the roof.

On Monday morning my aunt took me into Nanyuki (the 'village') to meet the bank manager, so I put on a jacket and tie. 'I say,' said some old codger we met in the street, 'is that an Uppingham tie?' Kenya in those days was still exactly as I had imagined. We travelled all over, visiting and staying with my aunt's friends, because having been in Kenya for over fifty years, she knew one or two people. They were all both fascinating and hospitable and lived in some amazing houses. The really old houses all tended to lead on from one room to another, because they were extended as and when funds became available. As a prelude to such expeditions, Wachira packed the car with enough provisions to feed a small regiment, and always included a folding entrenching tool, in case we got stuck in the mud. Needless to say, when *White Mischief* (by James Fox, about the murder of Lord Errol in Kenya in 1941) was published in the 1980s, I recognised quite a number of the names, although the Macalpine-Lenys, along with the vast majority of the white settlers, were never involved with the Happy Valley set.

Aunt Muttie sold up and moved back to England in 1976, and died at her daughter Jill's home at Askerswell in Dorset in 1983. Before she left Kenya, she made over half of her 40 acre plot to Wachira, for all the faithful service he had given the family. In accordance with her wishes, her ashes were scattered over the Northern Frontier Province by her granddaughter Julia, from Tony Dyer's plane.

8 The Quantock Shuldhams of Norton

The Shuldhams are a family of great antiquity. The first known ancestor was one William Shuldham of Shuldham in Norfolk, who was mentioned in a deed about land there in 1373.[1] The family continued to live in East Anglia until the end of the seventeenth century, but then moved to Ireland. Arthur Lemuel Shuldham, who was born in 1752, had properties in both Ireland and Devon, but as his eldest grandson never married, the Irish properties passed to a cousin and the family line continued through his third son, Molyneux.

Molyneux Shuldham was named after his cousin and godfather, Vice-Admiral Molyneux Shuldham, who became governor of Newfoundland and then, in 1775, Commander-in-Chief on the coast of North America from the St Lawrence river to Cape Florida. The naval force at his disposal was insufficient to patrol 1,000 miles of seaboard effectively, and the number of rebel American vessels was able to multiply until they were virtually unopposed along the length of the entire eastern seaboard. Finally, in July 1776, Molyneux Shuldham was replaced by Admiral Lord Howe. Early the following year he was back in England and had been given a peerage, having failed to succeed where success was impossible. He died in Lisbon in 1798 and the title became extinct.[2]

With such an illustrious godfather, it was hardly surprising that the young Molyneux should also decide on a naval career. He joined in 1793 and served in the *Veteran* during the attack on the island of Santo Domingo in 1795. He was promoted to lieutenant in 1799, having managed to survive a shipwreck off the coast of Ireland. He was 3rd lieutenant of the *Edgar* during the bombardment of Copenhagen in 1801 when the 2nd lieutenant was killed and the 1st wounded, so came out of the action as acting 1st lieutenant. In 1806 he was appointed to command the *Adder* gun brig. She had the misfortune to be driven on shore and captured near

[1] *Burke's Landed Gentry*, 18th Edition, Vol. III (Burke's Peerage, 1972).
[2] Robert Neeser (ed.), *The Despatches of Molyneux Shuldham, January–July 1776* (The Naval History Society, New York, 1913).

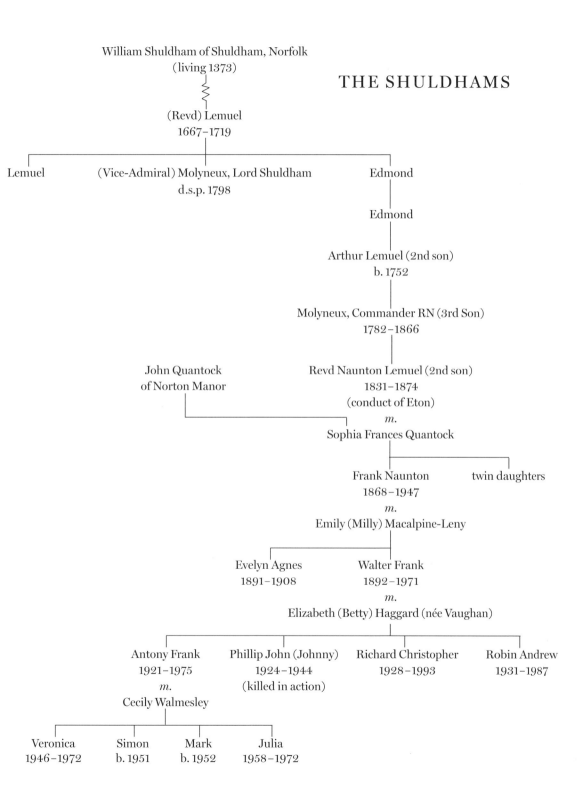

William Shuldham of Shuldham, Norfolk
(living 1373)

THE SHULDHAMS

(Revd) Lemuel
1667–1719

Lemuel | (Vice-Admiral) Molyneux, Lord Shuldham | Edmond
d.s.p. 1798

Edmond

Arthur Lemuel (2nd son)
b. 1752

Molyneux, Commander RN (3rd Son)
1782–1866

John Quantock
of Norton Manor

Revd Naunton Lemuel (2nd son)
1831–1874
(conduct of Eton)
m.
Sophia Frances Quantock

Frank Naunton   twin daughters
1868–1947
m.
Emily (Milly) Macalpine-Leny

Evelyn Agnes   Walter Frank
1891–1908   1892–1971
m.
Elizabeth (Betty) Haggard (née Vaughan)

Antony Frank   Phillip John (Johnny)   Richard Christopher   Robin Andrew
1921–1975   1924–1944   1928–1993   1931–1987
m.   (killed in action)
Cecily Walmesley

Veronica   Simon   Mark   Julia
1946–1972   b. 1951   b. 1952   1958–1972

Abreval on the French coast, and Molyneux Shuldham was taken prisoner. It was while in captivity at Verdun for the next eight years that he developed a land yacht that could be adapted for use on the ice. After his release in 1814 he continued to work on naval projects. He received one gold and two silver medals from the Society of Arts for his improved pulleys and blocks and improvements in working a capstan, as well as his 'New Method of Ballasting Vessels'. He was the original inventor of the revolving rig, which enabled him to beat any sailing vessel that came against him. One of the many inventions he proposed to the Admiralty was some kind of torpedo, but this was rejected on the grounds of being too cruel an instrument of war. He was made a commander on retirement in 1843, and lived to the ripe old age of eighty-four.

Molyneux Shuldham's eldest son retired as a Lieutenant Colonel in the 108th Regiment, but in spite of producing eleven children with the help of two wives, was succeeded as head of the family by his younger brother, the Reverend Naunton Lemuel Shuldham. Naunton was very bright, and an extremely good preacher. A fellow of Magdalen College, Oxford, he was appointed conduct (chaplain) of Eton and assistant-master at Eton College in 1862. While there, he was classics tutor to the young Prince Leopold for three years when the court was in residence at Windsor. On his marriage to Sophia Frances Quantock at Eton College Chapel, Queen Victoria gave them a magnificent silver inkstand, which the family has to this day. His new wife was the daughter and heiress of John Quantock of Norton Manor, which brought the Norton estate and the Quantock name into the Shuldham family. The year after he was married, Naunton left Eton after five years' service and was appointed vicar of Scawby in north Lincolnshire. Here his only son, Frank, was born in 1868, and two twin daughters, who died in infancy. Then when Frank was only six, both his parents died within three months of each other and he had to be brought up by uncles and aunts.

Naturally, Frank was sent to Eton. Here he met Bob Macalpine-Leny, who was two years his junior. Bob left in July 1886 and Frank in December, and Bob invited him to stay at Dalswinton for a couple of weeks at the end of August. He obviously made quite a hit, because when he left, Bob's mother wrote in her diary: 'We were so sorry to say goodbye to Shuldham.'

Emily Macalpine-Leny, always known as Milly, was sixteen months younger than Bob and would have been only just fifteen when Frank first came to stay. With her younger sister May, she had been brought up to the ordered and rather unexciting life typical of privileged girls in those days. They had never gone away to school, but been educated at Dalswinton by a series of governesses. They could both ride well, play the piano and play tennis, and had been subjected to that horror of all children of a certain age, going to dancing classes. Unlike the Miss Macalpine-Lenys of the previous generation, they were both very attractive, which would hold them in good stead when it came to finding husbands. Like Aunt Mynie, May seemed to have had a monopoly of the brains, but what Milly lacked in mental agility she made up for in sheer exuberance. In short, the Macalpine-Leny girls were both very good fun.

The arrival of Frank Shuldham at Dalswinton must have caused quite a stir with the two sisters, as the male friends of an elder brother always did. He was tall, dark and very good-looking, and rumoured to be the sole heir to a country estate – quite a catch for any young girl. So it cannot have been entirely by accident that when the two sisters were invited to stay with Aunt Mynie in Kent the following March, Frank found himself invited too. 'Have spent a very pleasant week,' he wrote in the rectory guest book at the end of his stay, 'and am quite entranced with a charming and accomplished lady.'

Frank's invitations to shoot at Dalswinton became increasingly frequent, and at Milly's coming-out dance when her father pulled out all the stops and imported the Blue Hungarian Band from London, he danced with virtually no one else. 'Why does Frank always dance with those Leny girls?' said old Mrs Steel. 'Why doesn't he ever dance with my daughters?' 'Well,' replied Bob, obviously after dinner, 'everyone has their likes and dislikes.'[3] On 1 February 1889 they became engaged, and were married at St John's, Dumfries, on 8 April the following year. Milly was eighteen and Frank, now a lieutenant in the XIII Hussars, twenty-two. Having succeeded in marrying off his eldest daughter to the lord of a Somerset manor with a private income, and knowing the increasingly precarious state of his own finances, William must have been well pleased. The newly-weds

[3] Kenneth Macalpine-Leny, unpublished Family History.

immediately moved into the manor at Norton, which like the entire village is built of the beautiful golden stone from nearby Ham Hill. It is essentially a Tudor house with an early Georgian west wing, but facing the wrong way, so it was rather dark and gloomy. However, it had a lovely garden complete with a fine Georgian summer house and an impressive coach house across the road.

No house that Milly lived in could be dark and gloomy for long. She just loved life, and was never happier than when throwing some huge party. She managed to get to most of the parties in the county by hook or by crook – she did not really mind whose hook or crook very much, the important thing was to get there. Her energy was proverbial, and she died without a grey hair in her head having given it a hundred strokes every night. She was the soul of unpunctuality and incredibly stupid – the complete opposite of her younger sister. The best picture of life at the manor in Frank and Milly's day is painted by their nephew Kenny (Chapter 12), who used to stay at Norton in the school holidays when his parents were in India after the war:

Frank was a punctilious soldier and a double first classical scholar who could have harangued an Athenian mob. He was always on time, correctly dressed and with a great awareness of the fitness of things. Aunt Milly was as mad as a hatter and never known to be on time for anything. She always entered the breakfast room as the rest of the household were leaving. When dinner was announced, it was generally found that she had decided to take another snip off the rockery and hadn't even dressed yet. She used to drive poor Frank mad; I can see him now, standing in the hall with his watch out. 'Kenny, if I had breakfast at eleven o'clock in the morning, your Aunt would be religiously twenty minutes late for it.'

It was the funniest thing to hear Aunt Milly posing as an intellectual and misquoting Latin tags: 'Have you read *Nudus Veritas*?' '*Nuda Veritas*' gasped Uncle Frank with a scholar's shudder, '*Veritas*, I think you'll find, is feminine.' 'Very well, then, Frank says it's *Nudo Veritas*.' 'Oh my hat!' Poor Uncle Frank – he spent half his life laying down correct procedures and was the soul of rectitude himself; the other half was fully occupied apologising for his wife's shortcomings. I have known Aunt Milly think for five minutes before playing a card. When the rubber was over, it was found that she had led out king, queen, and knave of trumps, the ace having been discarded – and I have yet to learn what on earth she was thinking about.

Aunt Milly dearly loved entertaining and had great social 'flair'. She was a wonderful hostess, but extremely haphazard. She seemed to have no head for figures, and numbers meant nothing to her. Uncle Frank boasted but one grass court and a croquet lawn. When Aunt Milly organised a tennis party she would invite anything up to twenty players to compete for her one court. If they were not asked to play they could play croquet, or if things got too sticky she was not above organising a game of rounders in the field. The whole thing was run on the lines of amateur theatricals – 'it will be alright on the night.' In spite of all this, I never remember a dull party at Norton.

The nicest room in the house was the dining room, with its lovely bay windows looking out on the rose garden. Famous for its fruit, there was never a meal at Norton without apples, peaches, nectarines, grapes and raspberries right through the season. What a pity that Aunt Milly always sailed in just as everyone else was leaving. Uncle Frank always kept a barrel of cider in the house, and for some astonishing reason, served his port in sherry glasses. He disliked all forms of change; his 'Blue Vinnie' cheese was imported from Dorset, and he had been known to complain that there was no cake on the luncheon table.[4]

After the old Macalpine-Leny parents moved from Dalswinton to Guernsey, it was only natural that Norton should take over as the family hub, and May would be married from there three years later. Nothing suited Milly better than keeping open house to all and sundry, and she was very good at it. Frank had transferred to the Reserve of Officers shortly after they were married. This was more in keeping with his new life as a country squire and gave him ample time to play cricket, go shooting, and hunt with the Cattistock and Blackmore Vale. Evelyn had been born in 1891 and Walter a year later. After that, Milly had some fairly serious problems with her female plumbing, which put an end to the hope of any more children.

Evelyn grew up to be a bright, attractive girl, but tragedy lay ahead. She was taken ill in Paris, where she had gone to study in the spring of 1908,

[4] Ibid.

and it was confirmed as typhoid. Milly rushed over and when things continued to deteriorate, she was joined by Frank and her brother Jimmy. But it was all in vain, and in ten days Evelyn was dead. She was seventeen.

Frank and Milly now concentrated all their affection on Walter. He was already turning out to be a star pupil and would go on to be one of those maddening people who were good at everything. Breaking the Eton tradition, he had been sent to Marlborough where he proceeded to excel in every sport. He was in the 1st rugby XV, the hockey XI and the cricket XI, the last for three years. In his final summer term, he won every single track and field event to become athletics champion by the largest margin ever recorded. He would go on to play cricket for Somerset.

When the order came to mobilise on 4 August 1914, Frank was a major and second-in-command of the West Somerset Yeomanry. By October he had been promoted to Lieutenant Colonel and had taken over command. There then followed a rather frustrating ten months while the regiment trained in England, after which he was offered the opportunity to go to the Mediterranean as dismounted infantry, so hurriedly had to retrain again. Finally they left for the Dardanelles aboard HMT *Olympic* on 23 September as part of the 2nd Mounted Division, with Frank in command, and Walter, by now a lieutenant in the same regiment. By the time the West Somerset Yeomanry landed at Sulva Bay on the Gallipoli peninsula on 9 October 1915, the worst fighting in that ill-fated campaign was over. But the Somersets had their share, and also had to contend with the dramatic change in the weather. After the withering heat of the summer, there was a tremendous rainstorm on 27 November that lasted three days. Water swept down from the high ground occupied by the Turks and flooded the British and ANZAC trenches, many of which collapsed, burying their occupants. Then at the beginning of December came snow, and many of the men died of exposure or suffered from frostbite.

When General Sir Charles Munro replaced General Sir Ian Hamilton, who had been dismissed and recalled to London, his assessment of the situation was that it was untenable. Kitchener made a personal visit, and reluctantly agreed. From 7 December the evacuation began, right under the noses of the Turks. What had been predicted to be a very costly withdrawal proved to be the saving grace of the whole disastrous campaign, and by 9 January, fourteen divisions had been evacuated with hardly the loss of a man. The Somersets left on 19 December, exactly ten weeks after they had landed. Out of an initial muster of twenty-five officers and 477 other ranks, only ten officers and 148 other ranks were still fit for duty.[5]

The regiment returned to Egypt for regrouping and retraining, and after seeing action in the Senussi campaign,[6] eventually became part of the Egyptian Expeditionary Force as the 12th Battalion, Somerset Light Infantry. This enabled Frank to meet up with his old friend and brother-in-law, Bob Macalpine-Leny, who had by now arrived in Egypt. Frank was slightly wounded in the hand by a shell in April 1917, but had otherwise come through unscathed. Then on 17 October, just as Allenby's campaign was getting under way with the run-up to the battle of Beersheba, he was admitted to hospital and ended up being invalided home, so that was the end of his war. Walter, now a captain, had transferred to the Indian Army earlier in the year.

Back at Norton, anxious to do her bit for the war effort, Milly had turned the manor into a Voluntary Aid Detachment (VAD) hospital. These had been set up so volunteers could help the medical units of the Territorial Force (later Territorial Army). With the help of the Red Cross and St John's Ambulance, women were trained as nurses and men as orderlies, all on a voluntary basis. Once wounded started to arrive daily from the Western Front, VADs sprang up all over the country. The Manor began as a twenty-bed Red Cross hospital and initially accepted wounded Belgian soldiers, but as they were considered to be foreigners, the War Office would not provide funding or equipment. Nothing daunted, Milly set about providing furniture and facilities herself with the help of her friends and the local community – she could be very persuasive when necessary. The 'Justice House' in the manor garden was converted into a chapel, and a Belgian priest came weekly to say mass. By April 1915 the first British wounded arrived and the War Office miraculously started to provide money and supplies. The number of beds increased to thirty-five,

---

[5] Capt R. C. Boyle, MC, *A Record of the West Somerset Yeomanry 1914–1919* (St Catherine's Press, 1920).

[6] The Senussi were a religious sect based in Libya, who had been persuaded by the Ottoman Empire to attack the British in Egypt.

and then to fifty, with tents erected in the grounds to cater for the additional numbers. The gardener's cottage was converted to serve as a hostel for the nursing staff, and Milly was in her element as commandant of the hospital. By the time the hospital closed on 1 February 1919, it had treated 412 wounded servicemen, one of whom had sadly died and is buried in the churchyard.[7] One can not help wondering what state the house was in afterwards. Poor Frank . . .

Meanwhile, Walter had transferred from the Indian Army to the Indian Political Service and by the time he retired in 1933, was State Secretary to the Maharajah of Jaipur. For two years he had been the trusted and confidential adviser to the young Maharajah, from the time he was first invested with ruling powers. There was no better country for someone so passionate about cricket, and Walter continued his First Class career playing for Rajputana. He played in two matches against an MCC touring side alongside the Maharajah of Dungarpore, but despite such an illustrious personage at No. 3, the tourists were victorious.

When Walter returned to England he rather hoped that his parents would have been prepared to move from the manor and downsize, but nothing doing – they resolutely refused to leave. As he had married Betty, the widow of Capt. Mark Haggard, in 1920 and now had four sons, he needed somewhere to live. Eventually he found East Stoke House, a much nicer house than the Manor, on the edge of Stoke sub Hamdon, only 3 miles from Norton. Predominantly Georgian with a Victorian wing superimposed on a much older sixteenth-century wing, it had been owned by the Chaffey family since the seventeenth century. When they sold in 1927 it was bought by the Petters, who sold it to Walter and Betty in 1936 for the princely sum of £4,000, including all its 150 acres of land.

It is for the fruit farm rather than the hospital that Norton and the Shuldhams are best remembered. Charlie Sweet, the first foreman, came to work on the estate in 1901, but it was not until about 1911 that Frank experimented with the first fruit trees. Then there was the long interlude of the war, so it was the early 1920s before the experiment was taken fur-

---

[7] John Jones, *Voluntary Aid Detachments in Norton sub Hamdon during the First World War*, Somerset Archaeological and Natural History Society Newsletter No. 66, Autumn 2002.

ther. The original planting had been only 4 acres, but the results were very encouraging, and in 1928 a further 29 acres were added, all under the watchful eye of Charlie Sweet. Packing was originally carried out in the east end of the manor coach house, but this soon proved inadequate for the ever-growing quantities of apples, so in 1936, the packing shed was built. This contained machinery and cold stores as modern as any that could be found in the UK. All the fruit was sized, graded and packed before being despatched to the leading markets in Bradford, Leeds, Bristol, Manchester, Liverpool and Cardiff.[8]

By the time Walter returned from India in 1933 his father was sixty-five, so it was the perfect time to take over the business. He was joined by his first cousin Bill Halsey (Chapter 9), who after leaving the navy had spent time with an electrical company involved with refrigeration, which was very timely for the building of the packing shed and the extensive cold storage facilities. Under Walter's careful direction the fruit farm continued to expand and prosper, and included a large acreage of soft fruit. At its height there were 150 acres of blackcurrants contracted to Beecham for the manufacture of Ribena and 6 acres of strawberries grown under polythene to catch the early market. All went well until a fox pursued by the local hunt ran across the polythene. In addition there were loganberries and raspberries, and of all things, 10 acres of rhubarb, which was frozen and processed the moment it was pulled. All this was very labour-intensive; there were some twenty employees year-round, increasing to seventy or eighty in the picking season, with pickers being bussed in daily from nearby Yeovil. Everyone in Norton had some connection with the Fruit Farm. In December 1951, after being employed by the Shuldhams for fifty years, Charlie Sweet reluctantly agreed to retire at the age of seventy-six. He was succeeded as foreman by George, one of his two sons.

Of Walter and Betty's four sons, Johnny had been killed in Italy in 1944 while serving as a lieutenant in the Coldstream Guards, and Christopher and Robin never married. Tony, the eldest, had married his childhood sweetheart Cecily, the eldest of the four vivacious Walmesley sisters when he was a twenty-year-old lieutenant serving in the Welsh Guards and she was twenty-one. Any concerns about their being too young were soon

[8] George Sweet, 'The Norton Fruit Farm', *The Nortonian*, No. 1, 1993.

dispelled and they had the happiest of all marriages. While Tony was on active service in North Africa, Cecily gave up nursing and went to help on the fruit farm. Every day she and her father-in-law would have tea with Frank and Milly, who by now were getting pretty ancient. Milly's eyesight was going and a few other things besides, so Walter and Cecily had carefully to scrape the mould off the scones before eating them. When Veronica was born in 1946, Tony and Cecily proudly took her down to the manor in a carry-cot to show her off to Frank and Milly. 'I never thought I would see my great-granddaughter in a cardboard box', was the old man's response. A year later, Frank died at the age of seventy-nine. He had been a very good soldier, a caring employer, and a much-loved squire. After he died the manor was sold and poor Milly went pretty batty and sold most of the family silver. Walter bought a lot of it back, but much of it was beyond his means. She died in 1950.

Tony took over the running of the fruit farm from his father Walter, and turned it into a limited company with outside shareholders. However, ill health forced him to give up, and with no one to take over, it was sold as a going concern in 1970. Unfortunately the new owner was killed in a car crash six months later, and the farm was broken up and sold. The village of Norton has never got over it.

In addition to Veronica, Tony and Cecily had Simon born in 1951, Mark in 1952 and Julia in 1958. But tragedy lay ahead. In April 1972, Veronica, then a very attractive twenty-six-year-old air hostess with BOAC,[9] took her thirteen-year-old sister on a three-week holiday to Kenya. On the return journey they had to give up their BOAC seats and fly back on East African Airways. After a stop to refuel at Addis Ababa, the plane crashed on take-off and both girls were killed. Their father never recovered. But as always, life must and does go on. Today, when the sun rises over Ham Hill and touches the golden Ham stone of East Stoke House, the Shuldham flag is flying as firmly as ever.

[9] British Overseas Aircraft Corporation, which later merged with BEA, British European Airways, to form British Airways in 1974.

9 The Halseys of Gaddesden

There have been Halseys at Gaddesden for ever. No one knows where the family originally came from, but they have lived on the hilly ridge between Hemel Hempstead and the Chiltern escarpment in Hertfordshire since the Middle Ages. The earliest legal document in the family archives dates from 1458 and records that one Richard Halsey, together with other parishioners, covenanted with the prior of the Dominican priory of King's Langley to pay ten shillings (50p) to the poor of Great Gaddesden – a payment that is still made annually to the vicar to this day.[1]

By 1520, John Halsey was the tenant of the rectory lands of Great Gaddesden, centred on the Golden Parsonage, so named according to family tradition because of the sea of wild daffodils in which it once stood, but 'Golden' may have been an early misprint of 'Gaddesden'. The land belonged to the prioress of Dartford, the only Dominican convent in England, who held it 'to the use of' the prior of King's Langley, because being a mendicant (begging) order like the Franciscans, Dominican friars were not permitted to hold land in their own right, while nuns could do so. When Henry VIII dissolved the monasteries, King's Langley Priory was closed in 1539. Five years later, John's son William Halsey purchased about 200 acres from the Crown at a cost of £174 13s 4d.[2]

It is supposed that the Thomas Halsey who sailed with his family to Boston was the son of William's grandson, Robert, and was brought up at the Golden Parsonage. What is certain is that by 1637 he was living at Lynn in Massachusetts, but after unrest among the new settlers, he moved with his family to Long Island where he became one of the founders of the town of Southampton. The house that he and his sons built about 1650 is thought to be one of the oldest surviving timber-framed houses in New York State, and is now a museum. It opened in August 1958 to coincide with a visit by John Halsey to represent the Gaddesden Halseys, bringing with him a Breeches Bible as a gift from the Golden Parsonage. The house

[1] *A Brief History of the Halsey Family of Great Gaddesden* (Gaddesden Estate, 2008).
[2] Ibid.

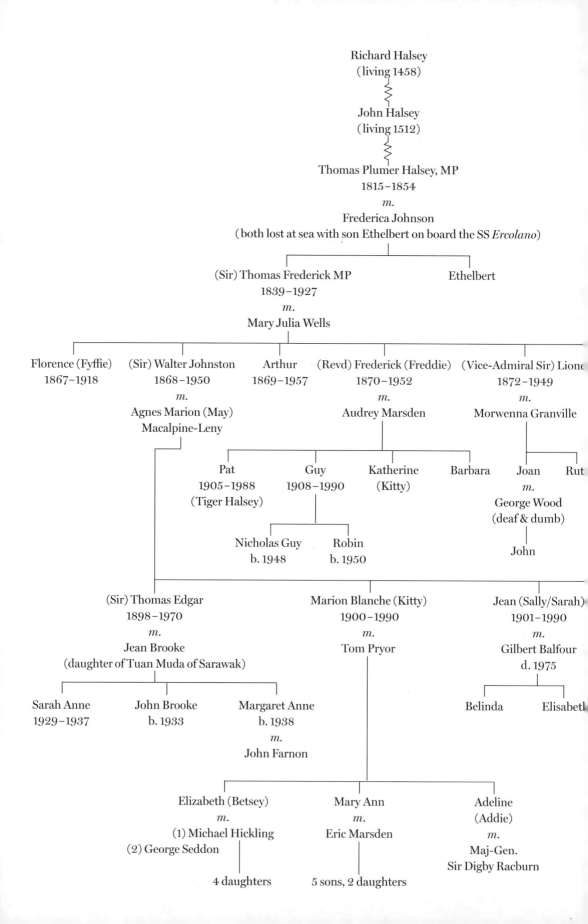

Richard Halsey
(living 1458)

John Halsey
(living 1512)

Thomas Plumer Halsey, MP
1815–1854
m.
Frederica Johnson
(both lost at sea with son Ethelbert on board the SS *Ercolano*)

(Sir) Thomas Frederick MP   Ethelbert
1839–1927
m.
Mary Julia Wells

Florence (Fyffie)   (Sir) Walter Johnston   Arthur   (Revd) Frederick (Freddie)   (Vice-Admiral Sir) Lione
1867–1918   1868–1950   1869–1957   1870–1952   1872–1949
                    m.   m.   m.
                 Agnes Marion (May)   Audrey Marsden   Morwenna Granville
                 Macalpine-Leny

                        Pat   Guy   Katherine   Barbara   Joan   Rut
                     1905–1988   1908–1990   (Kitty)   m.
                    (Tiger Halsey)   George Wood
                                                                            (deaf & dumb)
                        Nicholas Guy   Robin   John
                          b. 1948   b. 1950

(Sir) Thomas Edgar   Marion Blanche (Kitty)   Jean (Sally/Sarah)
1898–1970   1900–1990   1901–1990
m.   m.   m.
Jean Brooke   Tom Pryor   Gilbert Balfour
(daughter of Tuan Muda of Sarawak)   d. 1975

Sarah Anne   John Brooke   Margaret Anne   Belinda   Elisabeth
1929–1937   b. 1933   b. 1938
                              m.
                              John Farnon

Elizabeth (Betsey)   Mary Ann   Adeline
m.   m.   (Addie)
(1) Michael Hickling   Eric Marsden   m.
(2) George Seddon   Maj-Gen.
                                                            Sir Digby Racburn

4 daughters   5 sons, 2 daughters

THE HALSEYS

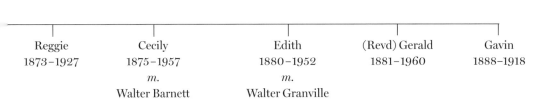

Reggie	Cecily	Edith	(Revd) Gerald	Gavin
1873–1927	1875–1957	1880–1952	1881–1960	1888–1918
	m.	*m.*		
	Walter Barnett	Walter Granville		

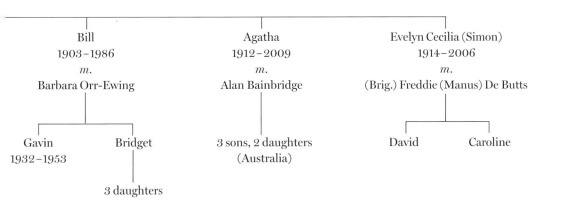

Bill	Agatha	Evelyn Cecilia (Simon)
1903–1986	1912–2009	1914–2006
m.	*m.*	*m.*
Barbara Orr-Ewing	Alan Bainbridge	(Brig.) Freddie (Manus) De Butts

Gavin	Bridget	3 sons, 2 daughters	David	Caroline
1932–1953		(Australia)		

3 daughters

was supposed to be haunted by Phoebe, Thomas Halsey's wife, who had been murdered by the Indians, so no one was ever prepared to stay there. John insisted on spending the night there with a friend, armed with a bottle of gin to fortify them, in the hope of meeting Phoebe. But either she didn't show up, or they missed her. Like many of the early settler families, the American Halseys have prospered over the years and spread the length and breadth of the USA. One of the most high-profile members was Five Star Admiral William F. 'Bull' Halsey, Jr, commander of the United States Third Fleet during part of the Pacific War against Japan. He was present when Japan formally surrendered on the deck of his flagship, USS *Missouri*, on 2 September 1945.

Back at Gaddesden, Robert's grandson John went to school at Winchester, followed by New College, Oxford. During the Civil War when Charles I had his headquarters at Oxford, the colleges of the university were encouraged to donate their silver to the royalist cause so that it could be melted down and minted into shillings and half crowns to pay the royalist forces. To this day, however, New College boasts a very fine collection of pre-Civil War silver since the college fellows entrusted it to John Halsey, and it was probably hidden at the Golden Parsonage. He went into the law, became a Master in Chancery and a junior judge, and ended up being knighted by Charles II.[3]

Sir John's son Thomas became a Member of Parliament for Hertfordshire in 1688, a position held by various members of the family off and on until 1906. He made substantial changes to the Golden Parsonage, and is responsible for the house as it stands today. The original house was very substantial in his father's day, and Sir John Halsey is recorded as paying tax on fifteen hearths. The present main block completed in 1705 is thought to be the west wing of a much larger house that was never built. Thomas's eldest son died unmarried, but his second son Charles established a trading company in Hamburg with the Hanbury family and moved his family there. His two sons served as Commissionaries-General to the British forces in Germany, which must have further helped the family fortunes, and the eldest, Frederick, was also ADC to the Prince of Brunswick. By the time his younger brother Thomas returned to England,

[3] Ibid.

the Golden Parsonage seemed sadly dated, so he set about using some of his fortune to build a residence more in keeping with his new circumstances.[4] His choice of James Wyatt as architect was inspired. At the age of twenty-two, Wyatt had just returned from six years in Italy, and was about to embark on his hugely successful career as the leading architect of the day. The resulting Gaddesden Place is an imposing Palladian villa perched on the top of a hill in open parkland looking down to the River Gade. On its completion in 1773, the family moved from the Golden Parsonage, and all but the new modern wing was pulled down.

Thomas Halsey went on to become MP for Hertfordshire in three successive parliaments, as did his grandson, Thomas Plumer Halsey. While in his third term in 1854, Thomas Plumer took a Mediterranean cruise with his wife and younger son. The eldest son, Thomas Frederick, had been behaving abominably at Eton at the age of fourteen, and was gated,[5] so couldn't go on the family holiday. Sometime during the night of 24 April, their Italian steamship, SS *Ercolano*, was hit by an unknown ship off Cape Antibes. The following account was sent by the British Consul in Nice to Thomas Plumer's brother-in-law:

It is with grief and regret that I have to confirm the melancholy intelligence which has reached you of the death of Mr T Halsey, his wife, youngest son, and two servants – one a man he brought with him from England, the other a lady's maid Mrs Halsey engaged at Nice. The particulars of this sad event will no doubt ere this have reached you from other quarters, however in compliance with your request I will communicate all that has come to my knowledge on the subject, as related to me by Mr Charles Lansom, travelling companion of Sir Robert Peel, one of the few passengers who were enabled to escape from the wreck.

The *Ercolano* left Genoa on Monday afternoon the 24th April. In the evening at 7 o'clock Mr Lansom was on deck when the steward came to ask him if he would go down to dinner, but he declined as the weather was rough, and dining below would be disagreeable. He told the steward however that if the weather became calm he would go down to supper. Soon after this he went to his cabin and fell asleep until past 10 o'clock when the steward came to him. He ordered

[4] Ibid.
[5] In later life TFH invented the story that he had been gated for being caught smoking.

supper, and sent to his friend Sir Robert Peel, who was in his carriage on deck suffering from sea sickness, and to Mr Halsey who was in his cabin, inviting them to join him. Sir Robert Peel declined, but Mr Halsey accepted.

After supper, Mr Halsey returned to his cabin and Mr Lansom lighted a cigar and went on deck again – this was at about half past 11 o'clock. He was looking towards the land when he perceived a light at no great distance, and cried out in French to the helmsman to be on his guard, but received no answer. Soon after there was a second (blue) light, and he was then certain that a vessel was near. He called again, but met with no answer and he saw no one on deck except the man at the helm. He heard however the bell strike four times. Soon after the bow of the *Sicilia* struck the *Ercolano* mainly at the place where his cabin was situated – he saw the collision distinctly. He then ran to the carriage of Sir Robert Peel calling to him frantically and also to Mr Halsey, when he was struck down by the boom of the *Ercolano*. Immediately afterwards the mast and rigging fell upon him, but almost miraculously he remained unhurt and after crawling out on his hands and knees, he ran towards the helm with the intention of jumping overboard and swim for his life, when he saw two sailors lowering one of the boats to make their escape. He jumped into it before it reached the water, and so rapidly was the *Ercolano* sinking that the waters had nearly touched the deck before he got into the boat. After great exertions and peril they reached Antibes at 3 o'clock in the morning.

Mr Lansom never saw any of the Halseys again after the collision – they probably could not leave their cabin. Sir Robert Peel's carriage having been broken in two by the falling of some spar, he immediately jumped into the sea and swam to the other vessel, where he was picked up by the Engineer. You will have heard the names of the few who escaped this fearful wreck. I have been to Antibes and left instructions along the coast in case of any of the bodies in a state to be identified being washed ashore, but as yet not a vestige of the wreck has been seen. The eldest son was not on board with his parents. He is now at Gaddesden Park [sic], at the Rev G. J. . . . Halsey's.[6]

So Freddy Halsey was orphaned at the age of fourteen, and was brought up by his maternal grandfather, General Frederick Johnson of Hilton. Getting gated for bad behaviour at school can never have had a

[6] Letter to M. W. Tyrwhitt-Drake Esq., Halsey archive.

more significant outcome. It was at Eton that Freddy's great friendship with William Macalpine-Leny began, a friendship that would not only last a lifetime, but lead to the Macalpine-Lenys marrying into the Halseys. Both boys went on to Christ Church, Oxford, where Freddy outshone William; not only did he actually succeed in taking a degree, but he also rowed in the Oxford boat in 1860. Cambridge won by a length that year.

Freddy first went to shoot grouse at Dalswinton when he was seventeen, and would go up every August for the next thirty-five years. Judging by the comments in the Game Book, he was very much the butt of all the jokes and pranks, but would go on to do better than any of that close-knit group of friends. He was the first to get married, to Mary Julia Wells when he was twenty-five and she twenty-two. They were very happily married for fifty-seven years and had ten children, seven sons and three daughters. They first went to live at the Golden Parsonage, but moved into Gaddesden Place when Freddy's grandmother died in 1869. He greatly improved the estate by building the Home Farm and many of the cottages, added the billiard room to the Golden Parsonage and the front portico and the splendid conservatory (known to successive generations as 'Granny's little porch') at Gaddesden Place.

TFH, as he was known to the family, gave a lifetime of public service. He was elected Conservative MP for Hertfordshire in 1874 and returned unopposed in 1880. Following constituency boundary changes he represented West Hertfordshire from 1885 until he lost the seat to the Liberals in 1906. By 1899 he had become chairman of the all-important Commons Standing Orders Committee, before which all bills to be introduced to the House had to come, and chairman of the Committee of Selection, which chose all the committees on private members' bills and many other bills. For this he was appointed to the Privy Council in 1901. By the time he left parliament, he was Father of the House of Commons.[7]

TFH had been a JP and chairman of the Quarter Sessions long before these were replaced by the county councils in 1888, and he then chaired Hertfordshire County Council for fifteen years. He was also heavily involved with the masons, and became Deputy Grand Master of England. Having undergone military training while still at Oxford, he became a

[7] An honorary title for the longest-serving MP.

major in the Hertfordshire Yeomanry, retiring in 1889 as an honorary Lieutenant Colonel. A life of public service was summed up by his biographer thus: 'Loyalty to conscience before loyalty to party is in brief the verdict to be passed on the public life of Mr T. F. Halsey.' By then the Grand Old Man of Hertfordshire politics, he was made a baronet in the 1920 Birthday Honours. Not bad for someone who was always referred to by the rest of the Dalswinton shooting party as 'the old clot'.

The eldest of his seven boys was Walter, who first went to shoot grouse at Dalswinton with his parents when he was sixteen. Agnes Marion Macalpine-Leny, always known as May, was a year younger than her sister Milly and would have been twelve at the time. Both sisters were very attractive, but very different, May more serious and highly intelligent. As a young girl she was a good tennis player and won many a local tournament. While still at Dalswinton she would go out with the otter hounds, became an excellent horsewoman and caught her first salmon on the Nith. She was also very musical, and organised all the music in the Iron Church for several years, playing the organette at the services.

After May moved to Guernsey with her parents in 1893, Walter's visits became more frequent, and eventually a marriage was arranged for 28 July 1896. With a Dalswinton wedding no longer an option, her mother hoped that they might be able to use Preshaw, but when this proved impossible, Frank and Milly Shuldham readily offered Norton. It was a great occasion: the village and front of the manor were decorated, and a flag flew from the church tower. The Halsey family always travelled en masse, and this was no exception. Walter's brother Arthur, a lieutenant in the Royal Navy, was best man, and Freddie, who was then domestic chaplain to the Archbishop of Canterbury, married them. Lionel, the next brother down, also a lieutenant in the Royal Navy, was at sea, but Reggie, Gerald and Gavin were all there. Walter's three sisters, Fyffie, Cecily and Edith, were bridesmaids, together with one of the Long cousins, and Milly's two children Evelyn and Walter were the train bearers. The only Macalpine-Leny missing from the official photograph on the manor lawn was Bob, who was with his regiment in India.

So began May's membership of the Halsey family. Anyone else would have been intimidated by joining such a large, noisy family who were constantly playing practical jokes on each other. But May had a quick wit and was never lost for a word, so felt instantly at home. She also earned a lot of marks by producing a son and heir, Thomas Edgar, in fairly short order. A daughter followed after another couple of years, christened Marion Blanche, but always known as Kitty. For others, marrying into the Halsey family came as something of a shock. When Walter's sister Cecily married Walter Barnett, the Barnetts were horrified when all the Halseys threw buns at each other at the dinner the night before.

Walter was a solicitor, and soon became a partner in his firm, which was a great help to the family finances. In 1897 his brother Lionel was appointed to the new cruiser HMS *Powerful* for service on the China Station. On her return voyage to the United Kingdom *Powerful* was diverted to South Africa to help cope with the rapidly deteriorating situation in the Boer War. Following a series of tactical blunders towards the end of October 1899, General Sir George White found himself confined to Ladysmith with a strong force of Boers rapidly approaching. Realising that he was going to be in serious trouble because the Boers outgunned him, he urgently asked for naval guns to redress the balance. *Powerful* docked at Durban and disembarked two 4.7-inch guns, four 12-pounders and four Maxims. A hurriedly constituted Naval Brigade consisting of Lionel and three other lieutenants, a fleet paymaster to act as transport officer, two engineers, a surgeon, a gunner, seven midshipmen and 259 men under the command of Captain Lambton left Durban for Pietermaritzburg with the guns in two trains. It was going to be touch and go whether the trains would get there before the Boers. By the time they reached Ladysmith the bombardment had already begun, but the Boers had not yet cut the railway line.

Once offloaded, the guns had to be hauled into position. The following conversation was overheard between an able seaman and a petty officer between the blasts of exploding shells and the roar of gunfire from the town's perimeter.

Jack, with one horny hand resting on a 12 pounder, to PO: 'Now we've got this bastard ashore, how do you propose we get it into action?'
PO to Jack, pointing at the waiting herd of oxen: 'See them fucking cows over

there? Catch some of the bastards and hitch 'em on!'
Later.
Jack to oxen: 'That's got you lot fast; now fucking cows, start fucking pulling!'[8]

The arrival of the naval guns did much to restore calm and raise morale in the town, that had been in a state of near-panic. They were manoeuvred into strategic positions on the surrounding hills, and started to return the Boers' fire with encouraging effect. On the third day a shell from one of the Boer 6-inch guns came through the parapet and hit Lieutenant Egerton, shattering one leg and the other foot. He didn't lose consciousness, and as they put him on the stretcher simply said 'I'm afraid that will put an end to my cricket.' He tried to make the men think he was not bad, and lit a cigarette on the stretcher on the way to hospital, where they had to amputate both his legs. He regained consciousness after the operation but died quietly twelve hours after he was hit. On the same day, the Boers cut the railway and the telegraph wires.[9]

Lionel had charge of one 4.7-inch gun and one 12-pounder that had been dragged 500 feet above the town to what became known as Princess Victoria Battery on Cove Redoubt. Although a fairly conspicuous target for the Boer guns, he had a clear arc of fire and an excellent vantage point. From here the Navy were able to shell the Boer positions at a range of between 9,000 and 12,000 yards, far beyond the range of White's artillery. He and his seventeen men were completely self-contained and able to filter and boil all their own water, which would prove a godsend in the fight against disease. Apart from being under pretty constant bombardment, the other real scourge was the flies, which covered everything and contested every mouthful of food. As if that wasn't enough, there was always the threat of snakes, not a particularly pleasant thought when sleeping on the ground on a mackintosh sheet covered by a blanket and greatcoat. As the weeks dragged on and Sir Redvers Buller's relieving force never came any closer, things began to deteriorate: food and forage for the horses became scarce; supplies of alcohol and tobacco became exhausted; ammunition began to run low, and enteric fever and dysentery took an

[8] Tony Bridgland, *Field Gun Jack versus the Boers* (Osprey Publishing, 1998).
[9] Lionel Halsey, unpublished letters from Ladysmith, 1899–1900.

ever-increasing toll on the beleaguered garrison. What Lionel longed for more than anything else was to be able to take his boots and clothes off at night and climb into a bed.

Yet in spite of all, some on both sides managed to keep their sense of humour. On 9 November, the Prince of Wales's birthday, the Navy fired a twenty-one gun salute with live ammunition. On Christmas Day, after an otherwise quiet morning, the Boers sent a shell into the town on which had been painted 'With the compliments of the Season'. Inside, the explosive charge had been removed and replaced with plum pudding.[10]

Lionel's older brother Arthur was part of the Naval Brigade attached to General Sir Redvers Buller's relieving force. On 15 December Lionel was thrilled to receive a message from him by heliograph[11] that read: 'All well at home; C [sister Cecily] is to marry 21st in London. Hope to see you soon. Remember me to all your people.' Lionel was able to get a message sent back that read: 'To Lieutenant Halsey: All well. Wire home. From Lieutenant Halsey.'

On 6 January 1900, the Boers made a determined attempt to take the town. It was touch and go at one point, but after a battle that raged for seventeen hours, they were finally driven off with heavy losses on both sides. They never tried again. By the middle of February, Captain Lambton and Lieutenants Heneage and Hodges were all down with enteric, so Lionel was the only remaining officer fit for duty. He then had a bad spell himself for a week, but was soon perfectly well again, albeit 18 pounds lighter, and now unrecognisable with a full ginger beard. Things were getting pretty desperate, and he was down to the last forty rounds for each gun – enough for one day's fighting. Then to everyone's real surprise on 28 February, exactly seventeen weeks after the siege began, Major Hubert Gough entered the town against orders at the head of the first relief column. Buller had finally managed to outflank the Boers and they retreated north in a hurry. By this time, 30 of the 276 in the Naval Brigade were dead, most of them from typhoid.

Much to Lionel's joy, Arthur rode into Ladysmith the following day. Amid all the excitement and the celebrations, there was much to do, as

---

[10] Ibid.

[11] Solar telegraph using Morse Code flashes of sunlight reflected by a mirror.

Lionel had to hand over his guns to the Royal Artillery. Then the Naval Brigade went by train to Durban, where there was a big reception. To his embarrassment as he hated such things, Lionel had to ride through the town at the head of the brigade on the way to the docks. They eventually rejoined the *Powerful* at Simons Bay, and so to England, where they were welcomed as heroes. Captain Lambton and Lieutenants Hodges and Heneage all made a complete recovery.[12] On arriving in London still bearded, Lionel is reported to have doffed his hat to his father, who did not recognise him. That evening, clean-shaven, he heard his father say at dinner, 'The young these days are not nearly so bad as people make out – a very polite young man took his hat off to me in the street this afternoon.'[13]

Early in January 1905, the central block of Gaddesden Place was completely destroyed by fire. TFH had let the house for three years to Mr John Kerr MP, who was in residence at the time. Apart from most of the library, and the contents of the wine cellar which they some how managed to save, everything was lost. Once the fire had been extinguished and the building declared safe, Mr Kerr's butler and footman set about returning the wine to the bins. Before they had the chance to complete this, a large beam fell down from the top of the house and through the vaulted ceiling of the wine cellar, killing the butler instantly. The footman died from burns the next day. A policeman, a postman and a fireman who were also in the cellar at the time had a miraculous escape. Because the damage was covered by insurance, TFH was determined that Gaddesden should be rebuilt. Walter tried to persuade his father that the days of such great houses were over and the family should cut their losses and move back to the Golden Parsonage. They ended up having a furious row about it. Walter lost, and Gaddesden was rebuilt using the very latest fire-prevention technology: the floors were made of concrete and all the wiring encased in steel cladding.

After his high-profile performance at Ladysmith, Lionel Halsey's naval career went from strength to strength. In 1912 came his appointment as captain of the new battle cruiser HMS *New Zealand*. As part of the race with the Kaiser to maintain British supremacy at sea by completely re-

[12] All three lieutenants became admirals.
[13] *A Brief History of the Halsey Family of Great Gaddesden.*

equipping the Royal Navy, the Dominions were encouraged to make a contribution, of which the first was HMS *New Zealand*, a gift from the people of New Zealand to the Royal Navy. In 1913, she called at every port in the North and South Islands. At Rotorura the captain was presented with a *piupiu*, a Maori grass war skirt, by an old Maori chief. With it came the prediction that the ship would be involved in three battles, but if the captain wore the *piupiu*, the ship would be hit only once and suffer no casualties.

The first engagement of the Great War in which the *New Zealand* was involved was Heligoland Bight. Now all sailors are superstitious, but the most superstitious of all are those in the engine room. As the ship steamed into battle, the engine room telegraphed up to the bridge to ask whether the captain was wearing his *piupiu*. As a matter of fact the captain was not, but also being superstitious, Lionel quickly put it on. The ship was completely unscathed. The second action was Dogger Bank. Again Lionel wore the *piupiu* and again the ship was completely untouched. By the time of the battle of Jutland, Lionel had been promoted to flag rank, and had handed over the ship to Captain John Green. The *New Zealand* was fifth in line of Admiral Beatty's six battle cruisers, and as they steamed to intercept Admiral Hipper's ships, Captain Green put on the *piupiu*. Twelve minutes into the action, the *Indefatigable*, immediately astern of the *New Zealand*, blew up with the loss of over a thousand men. Twenty minutes later, a similar fate was met by the *Queen Mary*, two ships ahead, with the loss of 1,266 men.[14] The *New Zealand* on the other hand, despite being in the thick of the early part of the battle took only one hit – on her aft turret and there were three minor casualties. By this time the *piupiu* was credited with near supernatural powers and the story was known throughout the entire navy. Thereafter whenever an enemy ship was even sighted on the horizon, a rating was sent up to the bridge to make sure that the captain was wearing the *piupiu*.

The *New Zealand* was eventually broken up and sold for scrap – a victim of the Washington Naval Treaty of 1922 which set a drastic limit to the capital ship strength of the Royal Navy, and Lionel was presented with the *piupiu*. It always hung halfway up the stairs in his house at Old Warden in

[14] Keith Yates, *Flawed Victory* (Naval Institute Press, New York, 2000).

Bedfordshire. After he died, Lord Mountbatten and Bernard Fergusson, then Governor-General of New Zealand, wanted it to be given to the people of New Zealand, but Lionel's younger daughter Ruth did not – she had known it all her life. After Ruth died, Lionel's grandson John Wood handed over the *piupiu* and his grandfather's sword to the head of the New Zealand Navy at New Zealand House in 2005. Together with the ship's bell, they are now in the Navy Museum in Auckland.

Back in June 1915, Lionel had become Captain of the Fleet to Admiral Sir John Jellicoe, with responsibility for ensuring that all ships in the fleet were fuelled, stored and victualled. In this capacity, he spent the battle of Jutland on the bridge of Jellicoe's flagship, the *Iron Duke*. When Jellicoe was appointed First Sea Lord the following year, he invited Lionel to join the Admiralty Board as Fourth Sea Lord, later becoming Third Sea Lord and promoted rear admiral. Lionel never knew for certain who recommended him, but in 1919 King George V offered him a temporary appointment as Chief of Staff to the Prince of Wales for his forthcoming visit to Canada and the USA. Although twenty-two years his senior (the prince was twenty-five and Lionel forty-seven) they got on extremely well and, much to the king's surprise, the prince's first visit to one of the Dominions was a huge success. An older man on the staff of his eldest son seemed to be a very positive influence, so the following year the king appointed Lionel to be Comptroller and Treasurer to the Prince of Wales, effectively his Chief of Staff. He soon had the confidence of both prince and king, which helped enormously in smoothing the flow of business between them.

Edward's charm, good looks, and genuine wish to do well by his future subjects had earned him great public esteem, and he was considered to be the very epitome of the dashing young prince. But those who knew him well knew him to be moody, egotistical and frivolous. Lionel's first-class administrative ability and experience, political knowledge, sympathy and tact, not to mention Halsey sense of humour, held him in good stead on the various royal tours around the world. The prince relied heavily on his advice, and Lionel valued the prince's respect and friendship. These tours were not without their funnier moments. When the last two coaches of the royal train were derailed in South Australia, the prince and Lionel were thrown over as their coach was dragged along on its side. It was a great relief to the ashen-faced security staff to see both the prince and the admiral appear out of one of the coach windows after a string of nautical oaths. There were plaintive cries of help appearing from a drainpipe of the ministerial car immediately ahead of them, where one of the Australian ministers accompanying the party had the misfortune to be trapped in a lavatory with the contents of that small room on top of him. 'Let's leave him there,' said Lionel. 'He always was very tiresome.' The accident would have been a lot worse if the train had not had to slow down for a cow on the line, and had not yet got up steam again. The prince later remarked that the cow deserved the MVO.[15]

In Japan, the royal party had a lot to do with the Japanese Crown Prince, the future Emperor Hirohito. Hirohito had apparently got the idea from his trip to London the previous year that golf was the British national game, so challenged the prince to a game. It was to be a foursome, Hirohito and a low-handicapped Japanese player against the prince and Lionel. Hirohito arrived at the Komazawa Golf Club resplendent in cap and plus-fours. It all seemed to be perfectly normal until it was his turn to tee off. After four complete air shots he eventually succeeded in hitting the ball down the fairway, and beamed with pleasure. Lionel and the prince exchanged glances – it was perfectly obvious that their host had never played before. Here was oriental hospitality at its best, which demanded a quick and considered response: the prince developed a disastrous hook, and Lionel was almost never on the fairway. He also kept the score. The result was extremely close, but the home team narrowly won.[16] Subsequently, Hirohito and the prince had a rickshaw race. The prince, who was extremely fit, went at great speed with Lionel as his passenger, and crashed, somewhat redesigning his rickshaw. When the ensuing photograph appeared in the British press, Queen Mary was not amused, and Lionel was severely reprimanded.[17]

By the late 1920s the traits known only to the Prince of Wales's inner circle had really come to the fore, and he was behaving perfectly disgracefully. Perhaps the most objective picture of this complex character was

[15] Member of the Royal Victorian Order, a personal gift of the sovereign.
[16] HRH The Duke of Windsor, *A King's Story* (Cassell, 1951).
[17] John Wood, personal communication.

given by Tommy Lascelles, who as his assistant private secretary saw things at first hand. His account of a crucial incident on the 1928 East African tour, which Lionel did not go on, is particularly telling. This tour was for him

the last straw on my camel's back. It was finally broken by his incredibly callous behaviour when we got the news of his father's grave illness. I remember sitting, one hot night, when our train was halted in Tanganyika,[18] deciphering the last and most urgent of several cables from Baldwin[19] begging the Prince to come home at once. The Prince came in as we finished, and I read it to him. 'I don't believe it,' he said. 'It's just some election dodge of old Baldwin's. It doesn't mean a thing.' Then, for the first and only time in our association, I lost my temper with him. 'Sir,' I said, 'The King of England is dying; if that means nothing to you, it does to me.' He looked at me, went out without a word, and spent the remainder of the evening in the successful seduction of a Mrs Barnes, wife of the local commissioner. He told me so himself, next morning.[20]

From then on, things became increasingly difficult for Lionel, but he stayed with the prince due to his loyalty to the king. He disapproved of the prince's relationship with Mrs Simpson and in no way could countenance her becoming queen. Along with everyone else who had similarly disapproved, he was dismissed the moment King George V died and Edward became king. When Lionel died in 1949 at the age of seventy-seven, he stipulated in his will that his correspondence with the king about the Prince of Wales, of which he had kept copies, should be destroyed to prevent it falling into the public domain. Much to the disappointment of subsequent historians, this was complied with.

Lionel's brother Arthur, TFH's second son, who had been part of the Ladysmith relief column, was three years his senior, and had retired from the Royal Navy as a captain before the war. With the onset of hostilities he was called up, and became naval vice-consul in Bergen. This was an

[18] Tanzania.
[19] Stanley Baldwin, the Prime Minister.
[20] Duff Hart-Davis (ed.), *The King's Counsellor: Abdication and War – The Diaries of 'Tommy' Lascelles* (Weidenfeld & Nicholson, 2006).

important job, because all communications came through Bergen, and he also had responsibility for organising all the convoys between Norway and England with the admiral based at Scapa Flow. He must have done something useful, because he was awarded the CBE at the end of the war. Arthur had a brilliant sense of humour, and a laugh that the older members of the Halsey family can hear still. 'I always enjoy family weddings and funerals,' he used to say, 'but of the two, I much prefer funerals because you don't have to talk to the other side.'

After Arthur came Freddie, who was a clergyman and had married Walter and May back in 1896. At the outbreak of war he was vicar of Rickmansworth and over-age for war service, so much to his disappointment was told by his bishop that he had to remain at home and look after his flock. His eldest son, Pat, a confirmed bachelor, was one of the most brilliant public school housemasters of the twentieth century, and the name of 'Tiger' Halsey was indelibly etched into the memory of generations of Lancing boys. His younger brother, Guy, had two sons who between them would produce the only male Halseys in the next generation. After Freddie came Lionel and then Reggie, who, breaking the mould of the law, the Church and the Navy, became a land agent.

Reggie worked for the Office of Woods and Forests, now the Crown Estates, and in 1905 was appointed Deputy Surveyor and Receiver of Crown Rents for Windsor Parks and Woods. He spent a huge amount of time shooting, and was always appearing in photographs of King Edward VII's shooting parties. In those days, a smart shooting man would have had a pair of best-quality twelve bores made by a good English gunmaker. Reggie was unusual in having a trio made by Boss – which was about as good as you could get.[21] He subsequently joined the Hertfordshire Yeomanry and went with them to Egypt when they were mobilised as dismounted troops in September 1914. By the time the regiment left for Gallipoli on 14 August 1915, Reggie was a major and second-in-command. Seven days later, the commanding officer Lieutenant Colonel S. G. Sheppard DSO was killed at the very beginning of the attack on Chocolate Hill, and Reggie took over, afterwards being mentioned in despatches by Sir Ian Hamilton. A sergeant in the regiment wrote in a letter home, 'Among the first to fall was our

[21] He left No. 3 to his nephew Guy Halsey, who shot with it for many years.

gallant leader, Lieut-Colonel S. G. Sheppard. He was bravely marching at the head of the Regiment, when he was terribly wounded by shrapnel, but as the men reached him he very gallantly sat up to urge them on. His last command: 'Go on, the Herts! Go on, the Herts!' will be remembered by all ranks for all time to come.'[22]

Reggie survived Gallipoli, but was invalided home from Mesopotamia. Twelve months later he was back in Palestine, but his health never fully recovered. He was, however, present with Bob Macalpine-Leny at the Old Etonian dinner in Jerusalem on 4 June 1918. He ended the war as a brevet Lieutenant Colonel. The next brother, Gerald, took holy orders, and became rector of Pebmarsh in Essex. During the war he spent two years as a chaplain with the Grand Fleet on HMS *Empress of India*. The youngest brother was Gavin, who became a barrister, and died unmarried at the early age of thirty.

In addition to these seven sons, old TFH also had three daughters. Florence, known as Fyffie, was the oldest of all his children, born in 1867. She lived the life of the typical Victorian spinster, doing endless good works around the parish and leaving to posterity a collection of watercolours of the Gaddesden Place gardens. She died in 1918, four months before Gavin, the youngest of the ten children. We have already mentioned Cecily, who married Walter Barnett, amidst a hail of buns. Finally there was Edith who married Lieutenant Colonel Walter Granville, DSO, in January 1903. Almost exactly two years later, Lionel married Walter's younger sister.

But back to Walter and May Halsey. After Tom and Kitty, Jean, variously known as Sally or Sarah, was born in 1901, followed by Bill in January 1903. After a gap of almost ten years, May decided that what was needed to round off the Halsey tribe was another boy, and because he was due on 30 November, he would obviously be called Andrew. When Agatha appeared she was clearly disappointed, but nothing daunted, tried for a brother to Andrew, who would naturally be called Simon. Again she was disappointed to be presented with her fourth daughter, but not nearly as disappointed as the daughter in question on discovering that she had been christened Evelyn Cecilia, two names she simply couldn't abide. So Simon she became and Simon she remained, until much later in life her husband

[22] O'Moore Creagh, *The Distinguished Service Order, 1886–1915* (J. B. Hayward, 1978).

Freddie De Butts, Manus to the family, rose to the dizzy heights of military attaché in Cairo. In those much less permissive times, it sparked off some fairly awkward questions when people were told that Freddie and Simon were coming to dinner, so it was mutually agreed that Simon would become 'Simone'.

The war put a natural stop to any further expansion of the family. Walter had started off as a captain in the 4th Bedfordshire Regiment and saw active service in Egypt. By the end of the war he was Assistant Adjutant General of Alexandria and a Lieutenant Colonel. After demobilisation he returned to his solicitor's practice. Then in December 1922 his mother died, and two months later he moved his family into Gaddesden Place. Thus began the legendary reputation for hospitality at Gaddesden that would continue for three generations. The Halseys were very family-minded and given the slightest excuse were always prepared to get together and have fun. The location of the house, in easy striking distance of London, made it a natural focal point, especially for a family so closely attached to Hertfordshire, so what better place on which to descend? And it was a very large house. In the days when many of the family played cricket, it was possible to put up both teams.

An indoor staff of twenty-two had been slimmed down to a mere fourteen by the time that Walter and May took over. There were still four taps in the butler's pantry: hot water, cold water, rain water and beer. The brewery had been closed in the 1880s when the commercial ones got going, and the beer now arrived in barrels. These ran down a ramped rack to the beer cellar under the front steps, so the next full one appeared as soon as the empty one was removed. One of the conditions of employment was going to church on Sunday, and everyone was entitled to have a glass of beer in the servants' hall on Sunday morning. Some of the old hands took advantage of this, and there were some very merry churchgoers. In those days the servants still pretty much ran their employers' houses. Walter and May were amazed to discover that the butler had the main telephone in the pantry and the extension upstairs so he could make his own calls in private and listen to everyone else's. There were two parlour maids and the old man who cleaned the shoes and knives, and always took the luggage in the back door. He also had to keep the water and the house hot, and take the meals from the kitchen, a mere 50 yards away, on a butler's tray to the food lift outside the dining room.

Walter always walked down through the park to church every Sunday morning, and naturally took the dogs. As there was nowhere to leave them at the other end, they came to church too. Before Freddie Halsey became the vicar of Great Gaddesden, there was a rather dull chap to whom preaching did not come easily, and he was rather apt to drone on. On one famous occasion, one of the dogs that had hitherto been sleeping peacefully up in the chancel (the family always sat in the chancel because they were lay rectors) suddenly got up, shook itself, let out an enormous yawn and walked out.

Meanwhile, members of the family and their friends came and went in waves, and someone likened living at Gaddesden to living at Waterloo Station. May was at the centre of it all with her finger on the pulse, a brilliant hostess and very amusing. 'I am always frightfully glad to meet Milly,' she said of her sister, 'and equally pleased to say goodbye to her.' 'They are now asking me what I am giving up for Lent: the whole of my life is one huge Lent.' May had inherited the family deafness, which she unfortunately passed on to Kitty, Bill and Agatha. In consequence the Halseys always shouted, and the noise in the house was simply terrific.

When the Prince of Wales came to lay the foundation stone for the new Hemel Hempstead hospital, his programme included lunch at Gaddesden. May laid on extra staff, the cellars were combed for the finest wines, and elaborate menus devised. Old Sir Frederick got to hear of this and was furious. 'It's Thursday he's coming, May; we always have mutton on Thursday.' After Sir Frederick died at the beginning of 1927 at the age of eighty-eight, Walter decided that the family needed to economise, so they moved from Gaddesden to the Marsh, a farmhouse about half a mile away, which he had extended. He was fond of writing little rhymes, and the following appeared in the downstairs loo there:

> Little drops of water make the ocean grand,
> Every drop of water, here is pumped by hand.
> So wash off your dirt, you must be clean and nice,
> Cleanliness is virtue, waste of water vice!

At the time that Gaddesden was empty the Prince of Wales was in the process of turning Fort Belvedere in Windsor Great Park into his new home, and wanted to furnish one of the rooms as a library. All the books were still in the Gaddesden library, so the prince said he would come over and have a look. As he was flying up to Liverpool for an official opening, elaborate plans had to be made to do a detour. Walter's daughter Agatha drove her father (who never learnt to drive) to the prearranged field, and two tiny planes came over. One dropped a paper bag that burst making a smoke bomb to act as a windsock, then they both came into land. Once at Gaddesden, the prince calculated what he needed on the floor of the marble hall with the aid of his stick: 'Yes, about five yards, and no more than eight inches high, and in English, in case I want to read them.' It was a very windy day, and the prince said he would not fly again but catch the train instead. So Agatha and her father drove him and Lionel to Boxmoor Station, which had received a telephone call asking them to stop the express to pick up a VIP. When told who it was, the assistant station master stopped selling tickets, seized his bowler hat, and came out to do the honours.

The prince must have told his brother that Walter was trying to let Gaddesden, because the future King George VI and Queen Elizabeth came out to have a look round when they were house-hunting. Simon, Agatha's younger sister, was determined that she was not going to learn to curtsey, so went and climbed the cedar tree outside the dining-room windows from where she could safely watch the proceedings. Gaddesden was evidently not what the Yorks were looking for, and the house would remain empty for about three years.

Meanwhile, both Walter and May's sons had joined the Royal Navy. Tom, the eldest, was a brilliant cricketer. He had left Eton early in 1916 to become a midshipman to get into the war, and was promoted sub-lieutenant in 1918. He went up to Cambridge as a lieutenant in 1920, and although he played for the university as twelfth man, he didn't get a blue. He played First Class cricket for the Navy until 1928 and then, in 1936, surprisingly for Egypt, captaining the side and making a century in his first innings. He was also the Navy racquets champion. Probably due to the influence of his uncle Lionel, Tom became ADC to Prince George, later Duke of Kent, and accompanied him aboard a P&O ship to join HMS *Hawkins* on the China station. All the royal princes had a decided eye for the ladies, so Tom was under strict instructions to make sure that the prince did not get into any trouble. Stealing a march on his ADC, Prince George instructed Jean Brooke, the very attractive eldest daughter of the Tuan Muda[23] of Sarawak to walk Tom round the deck while he got on with more pressing matters. Jean was heading out to Sarawak to act as hostess for her father who shared the ceremonial duties with his brother the Rajah on a six-monthly basis. The ruse worked far better than Prince George could have dared hope, because by the time the ship docked two weeks later, Tom and Jean were engaged. When she wrote to him subsequently from Sarawak she didn't even know his first name, and wrote to him as 'Dear Tim'.[24] They were married the following year.

After a spell on the Royal Yacht, Tom's first command was the destroyer HMS *Boadicea*, but it was as captain of the *Malcolm* that he assured himself a place in Royal Naval history. After Germany invaded Holland on 10 May 1940 she was hurriedly despatched to the Hook of Holland to rescue the Dutch royal family and their government. By the time *Malcolm* had docked at the only serviceable quay Tom had been on duty for more than twenty-four hours and retired tired and grimy to his cabin to attack a much-needed boiled egg. Before he could even crack the egg there was a knock on the door and a wide-eyed young seaman rushed in saying: 'The queen is here, sir, what are we to do with her?' As this might have referred to a steamer, a battleship, or many other ships, dazed with tiredness and the spoon still poised above the only thing of importance to him at the time, Tom replied, 'What queen, you fool, and where?' 'Dutch queen, sir,' came the reply, 'and her ministers, on the quay. And it doesn't seem an awfully safe place, Sir, it's a bit bomby out there. Shall I ask her to step down to your cabin?'

Wearily Tom abandoned the egg and amidst the sound of gunfire and the occasional exploding bomb, stepped off the ship to be received by Queen Wilhelmina amidst the debris on the quay. Bowing low over her

[23] The brother of the Rajah of Sarawak.
[24] Margaret Anne Farnon, Tom's daughter, personal communication.

hand as graciously and calmly as he could, as if this was an audience in one of her palaces, the following conversation then took place:[25]

T.E.H. I'm afraid the conditions are not very good, but what can we do for you, Ma'm?
H.R.H. I wish to go to Breskens.
T.E.H. I'm sorry to be so ignorant of the Dutch coast, Ma'm, but we don't know where your minefields are. We know where our mines should be, and have a vague idea where the German ones might be, so if one of these gentlemen with you could inform us of this rather important matter, we'll try and arrange it.

Calmly turning to the nearest one, she said, 'Where are our minefields?' He, poor man, turned out to be the Minister of Agriculture, and looked absolutely aghast at being asked the question. Seeing this was getting nowhere, Tom regretted that he could not escort the queen himself because he must stay to the very end, but he would endeavour to see that she was taken to wherever she wanted to go. Once the queen and her ministers were on board the destroyer *Hereward*, they received intelligence that the Germans were already in Breskens, so reluctantly she agreed to be taken to England. The voyage back was not without incident, because the *Hereward* had to swerve and alter course to avoid a magnetic mine dropped from a German bomber. It exploded only 40 yards away. The *Malcolm* did indeed stay to the bitter end.

Having done as much as possible by way of demolition to the port installations and picked up the Royal Marines who had been providing the rearguard, she prepared to return to Dover. When Tom radioed the harbour master to say they were finally leaving, he was answered in German.

On 27 May the *Malcolm*, with four other destroyers under Tom's command, was ordered to La Panne on the French coast to pick up troops. The units on the beach that day were mainly support services, and loading them aboard the *Malcolm's* two whalers and two motor boats was a rather undisciplined and painfully slow process, but eventually they set off on the return trip to Dover with 450 men on board. Subsequent trips to pick up

[25] Jean, Lady Halsey, unpublished memoir.

the regular fighting units from the mole at Dunkirk were much more efficient and disciplined affairs, but not without their nasty moments. At one point a German bomber flew straight over, and as the bombs left the aircraft, things looked serious. The stick straddled the ship, one falling just short of the bridge and one just over. Both detonated when they hit the bottom, the only result being a bridge full of muddy water. On another occasion there were ranks of Scots Guards drawn up on the mole in the darkness as if for review, and the young navigating officer, Lieutenant 'Dan' Mellis, who had nothing much to do while troops were being embarked, thought it might cheer them up if he took out his bagpipes and piped them aboard. He had learnt to play at Cargilfield, his prep school, and was a keen piper. 'Scots Guards approaching, sir,' he said to Tom. 'I've got my pipes with me. Do you mind if I pipe them aboard?' 'Do anything you damn well like that will get them aboard any quicker,' came back the reply, 'and let them know they're not on a bloody parade ground.' The Guards proceeded to come aboard in the most orderly fashion imaginable.[26]

On 1 June the *Malcolm* was returning to Dover with more than a thousand men on board, wedged so close together above and below decks that they could not fall over, let alone sit down, even if they had wanted to. As she approached the Downs a Spitfire flew low down the port side, obviously in trouble, and ditched a few cables in front of the ship. The whaler was lowered, and soon returned with the pilot. There then came the problem of hoisting the whaler, because the deck was covered in soldiers. When the moment came the soldiers were invited to man the falls and the boat came up to the davit head in style. 'Well done the Army' shouted Tom from the back of the bridge with his characteristic ear-to-ear grin, and a tremendous cheer went up.[27] By the time the *Malcolm* returned to Dover after her ninth and final trip on 4 June, she had brought back 5,851 men. Only HMS *Sabre* had made more (ten trips, but only 5,765 men). In all, Operation Dynamo had evacuated 338,226, of whom 198,315 were British troops and 139,911 Allied. The thirty-nine destroyers involved brought back 96,197 men.[28] It

[26] Ibid.
[27] Capt. D. B. N. Mellis, DSC, RN, retd, 'Mostly from the Bridge', *The Naval Review*, Vol. 64, Nos. 2, 3 and 4, 1976.
[28] Ibid.

Lieutenant Frank Quantock Shuldham, XIIIth Hussars

The wedding of Frank Quantock Shuldham and Milly Macalpine-Leny, 8 April 1890. Bob Macalpine-Leny *back row, third from left*; *front row*: Jimmy, pageboy, Harley and May Macalpine-Leny

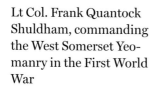

Milly Shuldham, *née* Macalpine-Leny

Lt Col. Frank Quantock Shuldham, commanding the West Somerset Yeomanry in the First World War

Captain Walter Quantock Shuldham, State Secretary to the Maharajah of Jaipur

Frank and Milly Quantock Shuldham's Golden Wedding, 1940. *left to right*: Robin, Betty Johnny, Tony, Walter and Christopher

Gaddesden Place,
Hertfordshire

May Macalpine-Leny

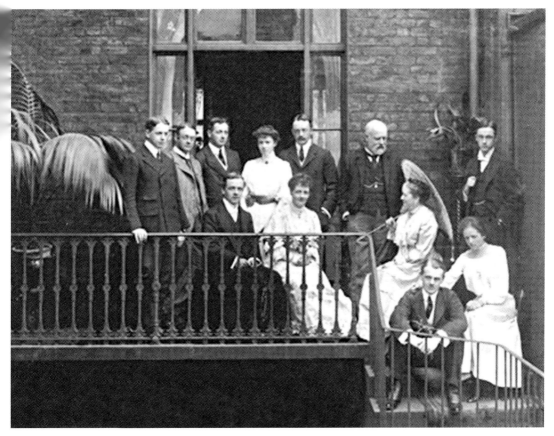

Freddy and Julia Halsey and their ten children. *Left to right*: Gavin, Arthur, Walter, Freddie, Cecily, Fyffie, Reggie, Mr and Mrs Halsey, Lionel, Edith and Gerald

Reggie Halsey (*back row, second from left*) with King Edward VII entertaining the King and Queen of Sweden

The wedding of Walter Halsey and May Macalpine-Leny, 28 July 1896

1 Edith Halsey (bridesmaid)
2 Revd Frederick Halsey
3 Florence Halsey (bridesmaid)
4 May Long (bridesmaid)
5 Reginald Halsey
6 Evelyn Shuldham (trainbearer)
7 Walter Shuldham (trainbearer)
8 Gavin Halsey
9 Mrs Macalpine-Leny
10 Arthur Halsey (best man)
11 Mrs Halsey

12 Harley Macalpine-Leny
13 Capt. William Macalpine-Leny
14 Bride
15 Bridegroom
16 Gerald Halsey
17 James Macalpine-Leny (later Macalpine-Downie)
18 Mr Frederick Halsey
19 Frank Quantock Shuldham
20 Cecily Halsey (bridesmaid)
21 Emily Long
22 Emily Quantock Shuldham (*née* Macalpine-Leny)

Revd Frederick Halsey performed the ceremony assisted by Revd A. Edwards, Rector of Norton-sub-Hamdon.

Photographed on the lawn of The Manor, Norton-sub-Hamdon, Somerset by Messers Chaffin & Sons of Yeovil

Bouquets from Messers Scott & Co's Merriott Nurseries

Golden Wedding of Freddy and Julia Halsey, 28 September 1915. *Left to right standing*: Kitty, May, Gerald, Plum, Arthur, Audrey Halsey, Freddie, Katherine, Guy; *sitting*: Sarah, Edie, TFH, Mrs Halsey, Fyffie with Judy; *front row*: Rosemary Barnett, Lettuce Halsey and Barbara Halsey

Vice-Admiral Sir Lionel Halsey with the Prince of Wales on HMS *Renown*

Lionel Halsey and the Prince of Wales after the rickshaw race in Japan

Lt Col. Walter and May Halsey, during the presentation of their eldest daughters at Court

Jean Brooke, daughter of the Tuan Muda of Sarawak, on her engagement to Tom Halsey in 1926

King George VI and Captain Tom Halsey on board the battleship HMS *King George V*

May, Lady Halsey in later life

Betsey, Addie and Mary Ann Pryor and (*front row*) Belinda Balfour as brides-maids at Simon Halsey's wedding, plus Elisabeth Balfour, who was not a bridesmaid but thought she should be in the photograph all the same (1944)

The wedding of Mary Ann Pryor
to Eric Marsden, 1948. *Left to
right*: Addie Pryor, Mr and Mrs
Marsden, Eric, Mary Ann, Kitty
Pryor, Margaret Pryor, Sir Walter
Halsey; *front row*: Andrew Bain-
bridge, Patricia Bainbridge, Sarah
Marsden and John Cawley

Kitty Pryor, eldest daughter of
Walter and May Halsey

Appin House, 1899

Jimmy Macalpine-Downie,
1902

Ethel (Effie) Blackiston-Houston on her engagement to Jimmy Macalpine-Downie, 1902

Jimmy Macalpine-Downie and the Brasier, 1907. The small boy is probably Robin Macalpine-Downie

Lt Col. Jimmy Macalpine-Downie, 1917

Borris House, County Carlow

Joane, Marchioness of Kildare, at the time she met Archie Macalpine-Downie

Lt Col. Archie Macalpine-Downie on board the *Servabo*

Crossbow, designed by Rod Macalpine-Downie, the first holder of the World Sailing Speed Record in 1972

Alison Macalpine-Downie, Mrs Effie McClintock (aged ninety-three), and Kimie and Rod Macalpine-Downie in 1972

was an achievement that exceeded all expectations, and one of which the hard-pressed nation could be justi-fiably proud. The officers and men of the *Malcolm* came away with the highest regard for their captain. Tom's tremendously warm personality and complete straightforwardness had won over every one of the ship's company. He was awarded the DSO on 7 June 1940 'for good services in the withdrawal of the Allied Armies from the beaches of Dunkirk'.

After leaving the *Malcolm*, Tom had a couple of shore postings. For someone who longed to be at sea, six months as officer in charge of the Isle of Man training establishment must have been something of a disappointment, but Tom gave it his all. His first order was to send everyone on parade off to the barber for a short back and sides. 'I can't have you known as Tom Halsey's young ladies,' he said. No one was more dumbfounded or embarrassed at the send-off he was given when he left the island. The road through Douglas to the steamer was lined with cheering boys, and the band processed slowly in front of his car laboriously playing the Eton boating song, which they had learnt especially for the occasion.

His next posting was one that any ambitious naval captain would have given his eye teeth for: flag captain of the battleship *King George V*. The KGV was the largest and newest member of the Home Fleet, and had come into service in February 1941. On 26 May she joined in the hunt for the *Bismarck*, and the following day shelled her with HMS *Rodney* for an hour and a half until the severely crippled ship stopped firing. The battered hulk was then torpedoed by HMS *Dorsetshire*. Tom took over command in February 1943, and the following January went on a top secret mission to Gibraltar to bring back Winston Churchill, who had been convalescing in Morocco. From March to July the ship underwent a substantial refit in Liverpool in readiness for joining the Pacific Fleet, and much to his pleasure, Tom was reappointed captain. Before she sailed for the Mediterranean at the end of October, the king and queen came on board at Greenock on the Clyde, bringing with them the two princesses, who had never been on a battleship before.

By the time Tom's tour as captain came to an end in April 1945 he was already showing signs of tuberculosis, which would ultimately result in his premature retirement from the Navy. There can be no better appreciation of the final stage of his naval career than that written by Rear Admiral Desmond Hoare, the first headmaster of Atlantic College:

For two years during the war I was chief engineer of the battleship *King George V.* I got the job very young, by accident, and was naturally much in awe and admiration of our captain, Tom Halsey. He was the last naval officer to have taken leave of absence as a sub-lieutenant to sail, before the mast, to Australia in a full-rigged sailing ship. He was roughly the same shape as Winston Churchill and immensely strong. When in harbour he always came up to the wardroom for a gin before dinner. If an officer happened to be standing in the way as he entered he would be picked up under the arms and thrown to the nearest sofa. One day Tom picked up the fleet constructor officer but missed the sofa. The commander-in-chief, Admiral Tovey, was not pleased.

One evening just before Christmas Tom sent for me to tell me in great secrecy that we were leaving at 0800 tomorrow to fetch Winston Churchill home from Gibraltar. We all knew that Winston had been recuperating in Morocco from a serious illness. So we left Scapa at high speed. The Germans must not know about such a precious cargo so Tom had to bring the great battleship into the small harbour at Gibraltar after dark without lights. At about 2000 a familiar bulky figure came up the gangplank and was escorted by Tom back to the captain's cabin. We had about 3000 tons of oil to take on, and I was told to report progress hourly. After the first hour I found the two of them drinking horse's necks, naval jargon for brandy and ginger ale, and Winston talking, talking, talking. After the second hour ditto, and so on to the eighth hour when I could say, 'Ready to go, sir.' Winston had to sleep in the safest place, judged to be forward just under the bridge. So the procession started, master at arms leading. All went well until the steel ladders which led up from the main deck to the bridge. Here Winston hit his forehead on a coaming and blood flowed. Never was the surgeon commander produced so fast, and Winston never stopped talking for one moment, to the fascination of the motley observers. Out of the harbour again without lights and 'full speed' was rung down to maintain thirty-one knots to Plymouth. Winston was not an early riser but spent most of the day wandering round the ship talking to the crowds that gathered everywhere. Winston had to have his war map room and this meant he had to have his WRNS to stick the pins in.

The commander organised a dance in the wardroom, and as French chalk was not a war store, the cabins of some of the more sissy officers were raided for talcum powder. The mixture of smells for the first hour cannot be described. During the dance Winston sat on a sofa and talked. We took it in turns to sit with him and listen. I have never heard anything like it, so much history, wit and wisdom stored up behind the piece of sticking plaster.

Apart from a Junkers 88 scare in the Bay, mistaken of course, in naval fashion of those days, as 'one of ours', and sliding over a wreck in Cawsand bay, the cargo was safely delivered to the Great Western Railway.

Winston went on to glory. Tom, who would have made the best First Sea Lord since the war, contracted TB and was invalided into obscurity.

Obscurity is of course a relative term. Tom had been struck down shortly after taking up his new post of commodore of the Royal Naval Air Station at Lee-on-Solent. With one lung collapsed and the other badly affected, the specialist who examined him said that he had gone through the war in a state that would have killed a lesser man, or at least rendered him unfit for active duty. After a year in a sanatorium, Tom was offered the job of Captain of Greenwich as a rest cure until he was fit to go to sea again, but faced with another shore job, he handed in his resignation.

Back at Gaddesden, Tom moved his family into the Golden Parsonage, which had been let for many years, and even been a prep school at one time. Then he set about applying his considerable talents to local affairs with his characteristic enthusiasm. He was a leading member of the Hemel Hempstead Development Corporation that planned the new town of Hemel Hempstead, a member of the County Council, chairman of the local bench, chairman of the governors of every conceivable local school, and Vice-Lieutenant of Hertfordshire. In his capacity as patron of the living of Great Gaddesden, he had the dubious duty of appointing the next vicar. While turning over in his mind which of the two on his shortlist, Mr Speed or another, should get the job, his dilemma was resolved halfway through matins the following Sunday when the priest turned to the congregation and said, 'O God make speed to save us.' So Mr Speed it was, and very good he was too. But it was the Gaddesden estate that was always closest to Tom's heart.

Family life was not without its tragedy. Tom and Jean's eldest daughter Sarah Anne died of kidney failure when she was only eight. After Eton, their son, John, did National Service in the army with the 60th Rifles. He later took holy orders and in 1965 was a founding member of the Community of the Transfiguration, a small ecumenical religious community at Roslin, near Edinburgh. Their second daughter Margaret Anne studied the cello and piano at the Royal Academy of Music, where she met her future husband, John Farnon. Tom did not think he was suitable for the daughter of one of the leading families in Hertfordshire, and even said to his daughter on their way to the church, 'It's not too late to change your mind.' But they had the happiest of marriages. One wonders what Tom would have thought of one of his granddaughters on the stage and another leading a jazz band. No doubt another case of that famous twinkle in the eye and his characteristic ear-to-ear grin.

Tom's brother Bill also went into the Navy, and passed out as a midshipman in 1921, at the same time as Prince George. His first posting was to HMS *Raleigh*, a Hawkins-class heavy cruiser that had been commissioned earlier that year. This gave him the unusual experience of being aboard a Royal Navy capital ship that became stranded. In June 1922 she headed up the coast towards Newfoundland, passing through the Strait of Belle Isle on her way to anchor in Forteau Bay on the coast of Labrador. The visibility became progressively worse, and by 1515 hours they were in thick fog and the fog siren started. At about 1530 hours Bill was walking up and down the quarterdeck talking to his divisional officer and getting the ship ready for entering harbour when he 'felt the ship slow down with a lurching motion, go on and then stop. There was hardly any jar, no more than to make one take a quick step forward. 'By God, we've run into an iceberg' was the first thought that ran through his mind. 'Collision stations' was sounded immediately.'[29] The ship had missed Forteau Bay and run aground at Point Amour, one bay further east. The engines were put full astern but it was too late: with a strong beam sea the stern swung round and then she was well and truly aground. The ship was a total loss.[30]

[29] W. E. Halsey, letter to his parents, 9 August 1922.
[30] Vice-Admiral Sir Stephen Carlill, 'The Wreck of HMS *Raleigh*', *The Naval Review*, Vol. 70, No. 3, July 1982.

At least two of the *Raleigh*'s midshipmen went on to become admirals, but Bill's naval career was cut short. By the time he had become a lieutenant he was so deaf that he could no longer continue, and he was forced to resign on medical grounds. But his short career had shown great promise, and he left with the rank of lieutenant commander. He joined Sclaters, the electrical firm, as an apprentice, and then, as recounted earlier, when his cousin Walter Shuldham took over the Norton Fruit Farm he joined him as a partner. He married Barbara Orr-Ewing[31] in 1931 and, like many of the Halseys, they spent their honeymoon with their cousins at Appin. Tragically, their son Gavin died following a motorbike accident when he was twenty-one, but his sister Bridget married and produced three very talented girls.

Jean, who became Sally and then Sarah in later life, grew up with her elder sister Kitty sharing a governess with the Cecil twins, Molly and Eve. Like her mother, she was energetic, enthusiastic and adored all games. Mixed hockey with walking sticks became a feature of Sunday life when walks had previously been the only acceptable form of exercise. With brother Tom at sea, Sarah was the only member of the family entrusted with moving his precious motorbike when the family moved to Gaddesden. Unfortunately it came to grief when she failed to negotiate the bend at the end of Gaddesden Row. She was a good sporting shot, and many a rat, magpie and even the occasional pheasant was to meet its end from either kitchen or bedroom window. In the Hertfordshire hunting field she cut a dashing figure riding side saddle, and had many admirers. One of these was considered to be unsatisfactory, and to be pursuing her a little too closely, so it was arranged that she would go out to India to stay with her cousins, Walter and Betty Shuldham. This proved to be one of the highlights of her life, and she was immensely proud of her job as one of the social secretaries to the viceroy, Lord Irwin. She was also very proud to have shot a jackal, and returned in triumph with the mask, which hangs in her daughter Elisabeth's house to this day.

While staying with Iris and Cecil Parker at Craiganour in Perthshire on her return from India, she met Gilbert Balfour, a land agent then looking after Lord Radnor's Folkestone estate. They were married at Gaddesden

[31] Her brother David had been a lieutenant on the *Raleigh*.

in 1931 – the last time both wings of the house were in full use. Life in Folkestone was very different from the one she had known, and unfortunately Gilbert became very ill, but she devotedly nursed him back to reasonable health. They were both very sociable, and enjoyed their life in Kent. Here their two daughters, Belinda and Elisabeth, were born. Gilbert and Sarah continued hunting until well into their seventies, sharing one horse. While others changed horses, this horse changed riders, Gilbert handing over the reins to Sarah – a manoeuvre that became known locally as 'doing a Balfour'.

After Gilbert died in 1975, Sarah moved back to the Gaddesden area, living happily in Studham near Whipsnade, where in her eighties she taught the author to carve a shoulder of lamb. As she had two sisters and five first cousins living within a few miles, life was never dull. She managed to continue with her bees, and was often to be found climbing a tree to take a swarm. When no longer able to drive, she sped around the neighbourhood in a bright yellow battery car, and even attempted cross-country journeys, which caused a certain amount of excitement. She had been so unselfish, always putting others first, and spared no effort in ensuring that her two daughters had as good a childhood as she had enjoyed.

Of Walter and May's four girls, Agatha always regarded herself as the original suffragette. Like her sisters she was educated at home by a succession of governesses. At the age of eighteen and decidedly extrovert, Agatha arranged to go camping in France with a cousin, Puss Sladen, driving a little Austin Seven. If either of their mothers had known they were going to camp they would never have been allowed to go. When Puss's older brother invited Agatha to a matinee when he was at Sandhurst, her mother was scandalised. 'You? A matinee? Alone in a theatre with a man? Certainly not! You can go four if you like.' So Agatha collected another girl and he collected another man and they went four.[32]

At the age of twenty-four, Agatha announced that she wanted to go nursing. Her parents threw up their hands in horror. The Halseys did not do that – aristocratic girls didn't go out to work. But eventually she got her way, and after an operation to improve her deafness, started at St George's Hospital in London. This amazed her family and all her friends, but even-

[32] Agatha Bainbridge, unpublished reminiscences.

tually her father became rather proud of her, though her mother did not really like talking about it.[33] Agatha nursed all through the Blitz in London, which was where she met her future husband, Alan Bainbridge, an Australian accountant who had served with the British Army as a volunteer. He proposed ten days later and Agatha turned him down flat, but they were married two years later in 1942 and in 1948 went out to live in Melbourne. Amusing, outspoken and unconventional, Agatha was not exactly easy to live with, especially after she had converted to the Bahá'í religion. When all the family had grown up, she and Alan agreed to split up. She ended up as a Bahá'í missionary on Flinders Island, a small island off the coast of Tasmania.

Simon was two years younger than Agatha and the baby of the family. She was always fairly small, but what she lacked in stature she made up in determination. She joined the Auxiliary Territorial Service (ATS) at the beginning of the war and drove ambulances during the Blitz in London, and even rode a motorbike as a despatch rider for a time. Later she became a land girl and worked on the farm at Gaddesden. Back in 1937 she had met a young Oxford undergraduate called Manus De Butts while on a skiing holiday to Davos in Switzerland organised by her brother Bill. Manus was destined to join the army, and shortly after being commissioned was posted to India in January 1938. He was not to return to England for six years. As soon as he did, in February 1944, he enquired if Simon Halsey of Gaddesden Place was married. She was not. They became engaged in April, and were married in July that very year.

Thus began a wonderful marriage that was to last for sixty-one years. It also saw Simon devote the rest of her life to other people, driven by a sense of duty, and fuelled by an eternal optimism. She made the perfect wife for Manus and saw to his every need, unquestioning, wherever in the world they happened to be. This was just as well as, though a brilliant soldier and highly effective at sorting out the military problems of Arabia in the 1960s, Manus was not quite so at home in the kitchen. In fact he could not even boil an egg. Simon loved entertaining for the family, but being the wife of a high-flying army officer, especially with all the official parties after Manus became military attaché in Cairo, did not come easily to her. This was not

[33] Ibid.

helped by the fact that, in the words of her uncle Gerald Halsey, she was always on time, but one hour behind. With the official guests due to arrive in forty-five minutes, Simon would start to do the flowers, completely oblivious of the fact that she still had to go up and change. She always said that the epitaph on her tombstone should read 'She got there in the end.'

Kitty, the eldest of Walter and May's four daughters, was the first to get married. Having kept him on a string for several years she finally married Tom Pryor at Gaddesden in 1925. Tom was one of ten, so the large Pryor clan was introduced to Gaddesden. Tom had won the MC during the war but had been very badly wounded. Sadly the wound led to cancer, and when he died, Kitty was left with three little daughters, the youngest of whom was only three months old. But she was very determined, and with the support of lots of Pryors, not to mention a certain amount of Pryor money, she agreed to take on Gaddesden Place, which had been empty for three years. To make it manageable she closed off both the wings and moved the kitchen into the dining room and built a larder in one corner. The saloon, between the old dining room and the drawing room, became the dining room, with French windows out to the beautiful view across the Gade Valley. Finally, she sealed off the basement and made a door at the bottom of the back stairs. Thus began a reign which was to last for thirty years.

Although the indoor staff had been reduced to six, everything seemed to go on much as before, and with three very lively Miss Pryors growing up in the house, there was never a dull moment. One day in 1938 or 1939, Guy Halsey was leading his platoon down Hemel Hempstead High Street when a car swept past carrying them, all waving and blowing kisses. To a man the platoon immediately started singing ' 'Allo, 'allo, who's your lady friend,' to which Guy respond with 'GAS!', so they all had to put their respirators on.

To the endless Halseys that came and went were added legions of Pryors, and Gaddesden continued to be very much the social centre for the entire family. When the war came, the staff were called up one by one and, with Agatha nursing and Simon in the ATS, Walter and May were left on their own at the Marsh. They weren't getting any younger, so the obvious thing was for them to move back into Gaddesden. As a young girl, May had always been incredibly athletic, but from about thirty-five onwards she suffered increasingly from numbness in one leg which heralded the onset of a rare form of multiple sclerosis. In later life, in addition to deafness, she always walked with a stick. This was incredibly frustrating to someone who had been so active, but she bore it all stoically. By this time, Walter and May were getting on increasingly badly. Walter never learnt to drive, but had a two-seater car which was driven by Perkins, the chauffeur, so he always had an excuse not to take May. There was also a four-seater car, but this was only allowed out on very special occasions. On going to the races, the car door would be held open by P.C. Dear, the village policeman, and May would always say, 'Thank you Dear,' which sent the grandchildren into absolute hysterics.

She underwent one of the very early operations to pin her hip after breaking it. Before going down to the theatre, a young nurse came to ask her if she would first remove her teeth. 'No, my child, I never remove my teeth.' 'But Lady Halsey,' persisted the nurse, 'you must remove your teeth, it can be very dangerous if you swallow them when you are under the anaesthetic. No one will see you without them.' 'Absolute nonsense, I'm never going to swallow my teeth,' came back the reply. Recognising defeat when she saw it, the nurse went off to tell the sister in charge of the ward. Sister was pretty busy, and had no time for such delaying tactics. 'Now come along, Lady Halsey, I'm afraid we must have your teeth.' With that she put her hand in May's mouth to remove her dentures, and was promptly bitten. Letting out a shriek, she beat a hasty retreat in considerable pain. The first person she met outside the ward was Dr Gregory, who was coming to check on his patient. 'That bloody old patient of yours, Lady Halsey, has just bitten me when I tried to get her to remove her teeth before going down to theatre.' 'But Sister, they are her *own* teeth,' said Dr Gregory.

Kitty's increasingly desperate search for wartime staff produced the McGraths – it transpired after they had been hired that McGrath's only butlering experience was as a baker's delivery boy and Mrs McGrath, 'Bridie', could only cook Irish stew. But they learnt fast, and thanks to the exigencies of wartime, everyone got along. One day Bridie came into the drawing room when everyone was having a cup of coffee after lunch to announce: 'Oh Lady Halsey, there's a nightingale singing outside the kitchen door.' With a certain amount of difficulty, May manoeuvred herself into position, and Bridie had thoughtfully opened the outside door off the kitchen. At this point Addie, aged about fourteen or fifteen realised that her Aunt Jean had left the pressure cooker on in their temporary basement flat, and fighting her way through the steam, rushed to turn it off. 'Oh Lady Halsey, it's gone,' said Bridie.

The man who really kept the house going was Mardle. Mardle had been with Tom Pryor in the Royal Artillery in the war, and was now the gardener. He fixed the clocks, mended the plumbing, sorted out the drains, and did everything that a large decaying house needed. He married Ethel, who had started as a kitchen maid, and risen to be parlour maid before the war. She went on into the 1970s, by then the only indoor help, and much to everyone's surprise, gave two weeks' notice after sixty-eight years. That, she said, was her notice period.

Betsey was the eldest Miss Pryor, and the brightest. As soon as she was able she joined the Foreign Office, and before the end of the war was working at Bletchley Park. Much against the family's advice she married Michael Hickling in 1949. Michael had been in the RAF and finished the war as a squadron leader flying Mosquitos. But his nerves had gone and it ended in divorce. He left her with four Miss Hicklings. Addie, the youngest Miss Pryor, was a brilliant skier, and in 1956 captained the women's Olympic ski team at Cortina in Italy. It was through skiing that she met her future husband, Digby Raeburn, who had skied for the army. After a distinguished career with the Scots Guards and gaining a DSO in the war, Digby retired as a major-general. There then followed two highly successful tours as governor of the Tower of London. It was at this time that Addie discovered that she had an amazing gift for healing – much to the discomfort of the governor.

Mary Ann was the most beautiful, and men gathered round her like bees round a honey pot. She eventually married Eric Marsden in 1949. Eric had rather an uncomfortable enforced stay with the Japanese during the war but went on to become a very successful merchant banker. He looked like a rather aloof Groucho Marx, and had a very similar gait on the cricket field. When he and Mary Ann took on Gaddesden from her mother in 1963, he tackled it in style. The kitchen wing was demolished and a tennis court laid in its place; the laundry wing was taken down to ground level and garages built in the basement; and, most conspicuous of all, a swimming pool was made in the conservatory – 'Granny's little porch'. Kitty retired to a flat on the first floor, assisted by a rather smart lift that fitted neatly into the back stairwell.

When Lizzie, Mary Ann and Eric's eldest daughter had her coming-out dance on New Year's Eve, 1969, there was no expense spared: the house was floodlit, there was an eight-piece band in the drawing room, and Juliana's, the most fashionable discotheque of the day, was downstairs in the billiard room. But in keeping with the amusing chaos that always seemed to pervade the entire establishment, the man came to service the Aga when the caterers were just getting to grips with the hors d'oeuvres. And when guests arrived from their various dinner parties to be greeted by Eric and Mary Ann at the bottom of the oak stairs, Mary Ann was overheard to say, 'I haven't the faintest idea who you are, but how frightfully nice to see you.' No party could fail after that. The following morning, May's old bath chair was full of empty champagne bottles.

The 1970s moved on with Eric and Mary Ann Marsden keeping up the Gaddesden tradition for the third generation. The numbers of people through the house, and the friendships thereby kindled, were if anything even more than in the decades before. It would have been completely impossible to have scripted any one of the conversations overheard in any part of the house, and a mock-up of the kitchen would have been a challenge even for Tracey Emin. Uncannily, the William Douglas-Home plays that were all the rage on the London stage at the time seemed to have countless members of the family amongst the cast of characters. The great event was always tea on Christmas Day, when sixty to seventy members of the family and their friends gathered round the large Christmas tree in the oak hall to wait for Father Christmas. He would land on the roof with his bell and little lantern and, clutching a large sack of presents, would slowly make his way round the various landings and down the oak stairs to the wide-eyed children below. There were endless reel parties in the drawing room, and house parties for every conceivable occasion. Thanks to Eric and Mary Ann, the next generation of cousins all grew up knowing each other well and feeling part of one huge extended family.

It was customary on those weekends for everyone staying in the house to go to the eleven o'clock service on Sunday, after which there would be drinks before lunch, outside on the saloon steps if the weather was warm enough. On one such occasion, when it turned out to be surprisingly hot, Kenny Macalpine-Leny offered to take Mary Ann's coat. 'That's one thing you can't do, Kenny,' she replied. 'I got changed for church in rather a hurry, and forgot to put my skirt on.'

Even for Eric Marsden, the task of bringing up seven children and running Gaddesden became too much, and he had to haul down the flag. When the house was finally sold on a 250-year lease in 1984, clearing it out after it had been occupied by the Halsey family for two hundred years was a nightmare. But the flag still firmly flies at the Golden Parsonage, the original Halsey house in Hertfordshire, to this day. Freddie Halsey's eldest son, Guy, took over after Tom and Jean died, in turn to be succeeded by his eldest son Nick and wife Viola. Today the estate has successfully diversified in all manner of different ways, and there are set to be Halseys in Hertfordshire for many years to come.

10 The Macalpine-Downies of Appin

Midway between Oban and Ballachulish on the west coast of Argyllshire lies the district of Appin, with scenery among the most spectacular of anywhere in Scotland. The hills seem to rise directly out of the sea, and the offshore islands provide the perfect backdrop to the endless succession of sea lochs and bays. With the clarity of the air characteristic of that part of the world, the view from Appin House, perched 200 feet above the shoreline, stretches for many miles down Loch Linnhe to Lismore and beyond. There can be no better location for a house anywhere in the British Isles.

As every schoolboy knows, Appin originally belonged to the Stewarts. It was Robert Stewart, the 8th of Appin, who built Appin House overlooking the island of Shuna sometime around 1724. In those days the Argyllshire coast was notorious for smuggling, and it is always supposed that the unusual holes in the shutters on the first floor were used as a means of signalling to ships on Loch Linnhe. According to local history, the house was forfeited because of Robert's involvement with the 1715 rebellion, but regained between 1735 and 1739. But as with so many famous historical families, fortunes waned as easily as they had been made, and Robert's son Dougal sold the property to one Hugh Seton of Touch in 1766. He in turn sold to the Marquis of Tweeddale in 1788. By 1809 the trustees of the 8th Marquis had applied to the House of Lords to sell the estate and reinvest the proceeds closer to their other landholdings. A few years later the Appin estate was again for sale.

We have seen in earlier chapters how Robert Downie had made a fortune in India and returned safely home to spend it. The ultimate sign of respectability for any returning nabob was to own a landed estate, and Robert wasted no time in buying a place in Forfarshire named Dumbarrow. But always prepared to switch horses if something better turned up, he then bought the Appin estate in March 1814 and in the late 1820s sold Dumbarrow at a profit. According to Hugh McColl, a tenant on the island of Shuna, Robert agreed to pay him between £1,000 and £1,500 for his

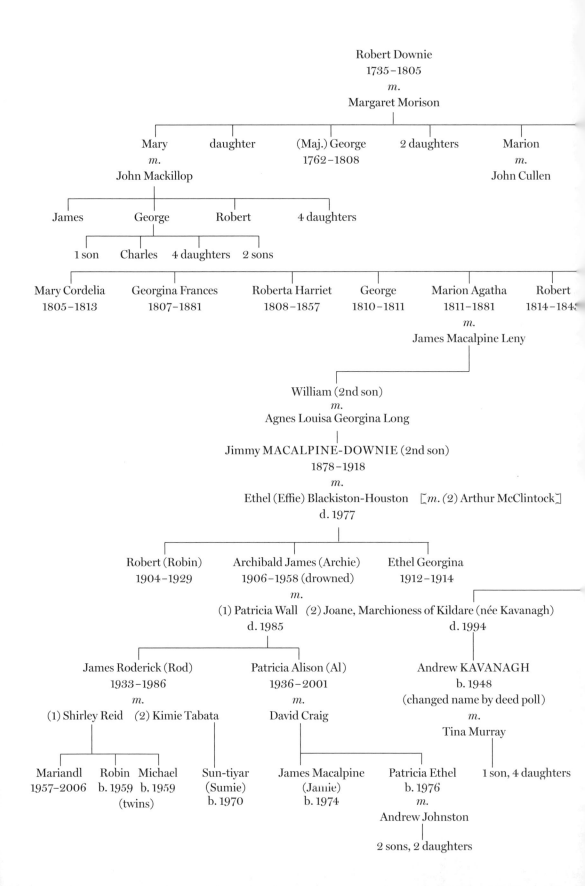

Robert Downie
1735–1805
m.
Margaret Morison

Mary	daughter	(Maj.) George	2 daughters	Marion
m.		1762–1808		*m.*
John Mackillop				John Cullen

James — George — Robert — 4 daughters

1 son — Charles — 4 daughters — 2 sons

Mary Cordelia	Georgina Frances	Roberta Harriet	George	Marion Agatha	Robert
1805–1813	1807–1881	1808–1857	1810–1811	1811–1881	1814–184:
				m.	
				James Macalpine Leny	

William (2nd son)
m.
Agnes Louisa Georgina Long

Jimmy MACALPINE-DOWNIE (2nd son)
1878–1918
m.
Ethel (Effie) Blackiston-Houston   [*m.* (2) Arthur McClintock]
d. 1977

Robert (Robin)	Archibald James (Archie)	Ethel Georgina
1904–1929	1906–1958 (drowned)	1912–1914
	m.	
	(1) Patricia Wall (2) Joane, Marchioness of Kildare (née Kavanagh)	
	d. 1985	d. 1994

James Roderick (Rod)	Patricia Alison (Al)	Andrew KAVANAGH
1933–1986	1936–2001	b. 1948
m.	*m.*	(changed name by deed poll)
(1) Shirley Reid (2) Kimie Tabata	David Craig	*m.*
		Tina Murray

Mariandl	Robin	Michael	Sun-tiyar	James Macalpine	Patricia Ethel	1 son, 4 daughters
1957–2006	b. 1959	b. 1959	(Sumie)	(Jamie)	b. 1976	
	(twins)		b. 1970	b. 1974	*m.*	
					Andrew Johnston	

2 sons, 2 daughters

THE DOWNIES

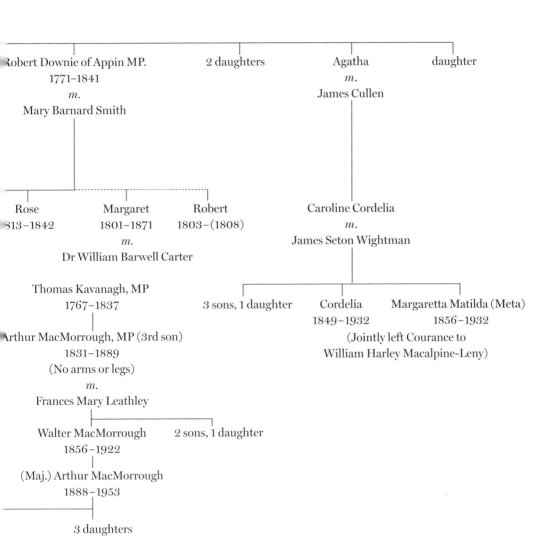

Robert Downie of Appin MP.
1771–1841
m.
Mary Barnard Smith

2 daughters

Agatha
m.
James Cullen

daughter

Rose
1813–1842

Margaret
1801–1871
m.
Dr William Barwell Carter

Robert
1803–(1808)

Caroline Cordelia
m.
James Seton Wightman

Thomas Kavanagh, MP
1767–1837

3 sons, 1 daughter

Cordelia
1849–1932

Margaretta Matilda (Meta)
1856–1932

Arthur MacMorrough, MP (3rd son)
1831–1889
(No arms or legs)
m.
Frances Mary Leathley

(Jointly left Courance to
William Harley Macalpine-Leny)

Walter MacMorrough
1856–1922

2 sons, 1 daughter

(Maj.) Arthur MacMorrough
1888–1953

3 daughters

help in securing the estate. This seemed an exceptionally large amount of money for such a task, and Robert always denied it. When he never received anything, McColl spent the next fifteen years making increasingly slanderous claims against Robert Downie to everyone from the Duke of Wellington downwards. Hardly surprisingly, the law sided with Downie and McColl was eventually evicted from his farm for not paying the rent. Robert Downie was now the owner of a substantial estate which consisted of the island of Shuna, and together with the next-door estate of Duror, some 43,000 acres on the mainland.

In addition to being chairman of the Union Canal Company, Robert had very extensive business interests. These included being governor of the Edinburgh Gas Light Company and chairman of several insurance companies. Hardly surprisingly for someone who was such an excellent networker and managed to have a finger in every conceivable pie, he was also a freemason. Then in 1820 came the ultimate pinnacle for any nabob – election as the Member of Parliament for the Stirling burghs. All this meant that he did not spend much time at Appin. He had a house in Charlotte Square in Edinburgh, and would take a house in London (interestingly, 21 Downing Street, in 1821) for use on the occasions he sat in the Commons. A contemporary account in the *Edinburgh Chronicle* gives an idea of the esteem with which Robert Downie was held in the Highlands:

I was lately travelling on the Caledonian Canal. A drizzling rain having set in, I retired to the cabin, and was amusing myself turning over the pages of a Highland guide-book, when all at once the crew got into a bustle – tables were turned up – the floor covered with a new carpet, and the cabin underwent a hurried and general change. 'What is the cause,' I enquired, 'of this unexpected movement?' A sturdy and weather-beaten Highlander with great amazement, abruptly answered, 'It's Downie o' Appin and his family, sir.' 'Who is Downie of Appin,' I asked, 'that you make such a fuss about him?' The fellow answered me with a look of wonder and surprise, turned to his neighbour and said, 'Wha can that be that disna ken Downie o' Appin?' Downie and his family shortly made their appearance, and I soon discovered they were people of some consequence in the neighbourhood.[1]

[1] The account was reprinted in the *Guardian*, 4 May 1845.

Robert Downie was re-elected in 1826 in spite of endless complaints from his opponents about illegal practices, but was outmanoeuvred in 1830, so lost his seat. He made all sorts of noises about standing again, but never did. He now devoted more time to Appin and in 1831 remodelled the house, adding a striking new wing on the east side to provide a new drawing room and dining room. Previously the drawing room had been on the first floor. His original crest of a palm tree had been replaced with a cockerel and the motto 'Courage', and this was now prominently displayed on the front of the house.

Like so many parents, Robert did not think that Robert Junior possessed either the commitment or the hunger to succeed as his father had done. He was right. Robert was packed off to India to join the 16th Lancers, the snob regiment of the day, as a cornet when he was twenty-one. He must have been bitterly disappointed, having just entered the party scene in London. He was a very good-looking, rather effeminate young man, which was probably part of his undoing. By the time he left the regiment as a lieutenant in 1839, his father saw the writing on the wall, and stipulated that his son could not inherit Appin until he was thirty, much to the benefit of subsequent generations.

Old Robert Downie died at Appin on 10 September 1841, in his seventy-first year. When he seized the opportunity to enter Parliament as the member for an unpopular and 'difficult' constituency, he became one of the minor characters of the House and was known as 'Dirty Downie'. But, a strong Episcopalian and a keen musician, he also had another side. Above all, he invested part of his fortune in a spectacular Highland estate, and provided the launching pad for the future Macalpine-Downies. He would be amused to know that the Downie family vault where he was buried at St John's Edinburgh, now forms the entrance to the crypt cafeteria.

His youngest daughter, Rose, died unmarried nine months later at the age of twenty-nine, and left her money to build the Rose Chapel at Appin. Robert Junior died intestate at his home in Ladbroke Villas in Kensington when he was twenty-nine, eighteen months after that in 1843. That left Georgina Frances, Roberta Harriet and Marion Agatha, and his half-Indian daughter Margaret, the widow of Dr William Barwell Carter, who also now lived at Appin House. Under a scheme drawn up by old Robert's trustees, the estate was divided into three, and each of his surviving legitimate daughters drew lots. Georgina being the eldest drew first, and got Kinlochbeg, Roberta Harriet drew next and got Appin House, and Marion Agatha, the only one of Robert Downie's legitimate daughters to marry, drew last and got Duror.[2] When Roberta Harriet died at Claridges Hotel in London at the beginning of 1857, she left everything she possessed to her older sister.

In bad weather, the old Pass of Glencoe road would get so washed away that the traveller could take a day or more rebuilding it before being able to cross Rannoch Moor. Marooned visitors were a regular occurrence at Appin House, and the bishop of Argyll and the Isles was a frequent visitor. It would seem that he was rather accident-prone. One morning while restoring his dentures to their rightful position he carelessly dropped them into the toilet bowl. One ill-considered flush later, and they were gone. With the house standing some 200 feet above the loch and the sewage outflow emptying straight onto the foreshore, speed was clearly of the essence. A minion was despatched with a butterfly net, and duly returned with his prize, which was restored to the bishop.[3]

Miss Georgina Downie lived on at Appin House in great state at the centre of her 37,000-acre estate, a fabulously wealthy old spinster. No wonder William Macalpine-Leny believed that as her only nephew, all his looming financial problems would be solved the moment she fell off her perch. But, as we know (p. 62), he was in for a nasty shock. When she finally died at Appin in her seventy-fifth year and her will came to be read, she had named William and Agnes's three-year-old second son, Jimmy, as her heir. Her will went on:

. . . it being my wish that the said estates of Appin and Dalswinton shall in no case devolve upon or belong to the same person or persons but that the proprietorship of Appin shall always vest in a separate individual from the proprietor of Dalswinton, and I direct that the person succeeding under these presents to my said estate of Appin shall as a condition of such succession be bound to take

[2] Patricia Pollock, letter to James Macalpine-Downie, 4 April 1899.
[3] Roderick Macalpine-Downie, unpublished final writings.

and retain as his or her final surname the name of 'Downie' and shall call or style himself or herself 'Downie of Appin'.

If Jimmy did not survive until he was due to inherit at the age of twenty-one, then William and Agnes's youngest son Harley would be the heir, and, failing him, Milly or May. Poor William – it was checkmate. The will then said she wished that 'the mansion house of Appin be not let for hire during the minority of the heir but along with the whole contents aforesaid be preserved in as far as may be possible in the state in which the said mansion house existed in my life.' Bearing in mind that it would be almost eighteen years before Jimmy became of age, this was a pretty tall order.

The bequests under the will amounted to an astonishing £46,000, equating to £3.75 million in today's purchasing power. After amounts to all her cousins and godchildren there was £500 to her lady's maid, £400 to her coachman, and £100 each to her other named servants; £500 each to the Edinburgh Royal Infirmary, Glasgow Royal Infirmary and Western Infirmary, Glasgow, on condition that they kept a bed for the relief of sick persons in the parish of Appin; £1,000 for the McCall Mission in Paris; £1,000 for the Anglo-Indian Evangelisation Society; £3,000 for a Downie scholarship; £2,000 for the Appin Mission; £1,250 for the Church of Scotland Parish Church to increase the minister's stipend by £50 per year; £1,000 to the Book and Tract Society of Scotland, and £1,000 to the Royal National Lifeboat Institute for a lifeboat to be named *The Appin*. This was a 37-foot self-righting boat that was stationed at Fishguard as the No. 2 Lifeboat from 1885 to 1907. It was launched thirty times and saved 134 lives. The old girl would have been thrilled. William was less than thrilled, but had to put a brave face on it.

James Robert Macalpine-Leny was born at Dalswinton on 21 March 1878. He followed his elder brother to Cargilfield and then Eton, where he was in the shooting VIII for two years. He had had his first lesson, with a shotgun rather than a rifle, from Tilbury at Dalswinton when he was still only nine, and proudly shot a hare on his first outing. A year later, he shot his first three partridges. He would go on to become an extremely fine shot, which would earn him an invitation to Sandringham from the king on ability alone. His introduction to his future Highland home came at the age of eleven when he went with his mother to lay the foundation stone of the new Appin Church. One cannot help wondering what became of the silver trowel with which he was presented. But his real introduction to Appin came on his twenty-first birthday, when in accordance with his great aunt's wishes, he took the name of Macalpine-Downie on becoming the laird. There was a dinner followed by dancing for all the tenants and employees of the estate, at which Jimmy was presented with a magnificent silver bowl and salver. In his reply to the toast, he said that 'it was a present that I shall value as long as life is spared to me among you'.

When he left Eton, Jimmy joined the Argyll and Sutherland High-landers, and went to Dublin with them at the end of 1899. Here he would meet Ethel Blackiston-Houston out hunting, the sixth daughter and eleventh child of John and Gertrude Blackiston-Houston of Orangefield, County Down. Anyone else appearing so far down the batting order might have found life rather intimidating, but Effie was made of strong stuff. She had attended finishing schools in both France and Germany, which gave her a thorough grounding in both French and German, and she remained able to converse in both languages all her life. Never afraid to be different, she had trained as a trapeze artist with a circus, but when offered the job, decided on marriage to Jimmy instead. They announced their engage-ment at the end of 1901, just one month before Jimmy, now a captain, sailed for Capetown and the Boer War. With their wedding announced for August 1902 after Jimmy returned from South Africa, Effie bravely trav-elled to Wennington alone to meet her future parents-in-law. Both they and Milly and May liked her enormously, and were totally entranced by her large blue eyes. Sadly Jimmy's parents were too unwell to make it over to the wedding, so the family was represented by Frank and Milly Quan-tock Shuldham, and the faithful Laing. Bob was still in South Africa and Harley (chapter 11) in Aden.

Jimmy left the regiment the following year, and in May of 1903, he and Effie sailed to New York. They travelled across the States and visited the Yellowstone National Park, and did not return home until October. This belated honeymoon did the trick and Robin was born at their home at Nevinstown, County Meath, at the beginning of January. Archie would follow two years later. In addition to field sports, Jimmy was a keen motoring enthusiast. He bought his first car in 1900, and in 1907, after a Frenchman driving a Richard-Brasier had succeeded in winning the Gordon Bennett Cup[4] in both 1904 and 1905, he invested in a 25–36 horsepower top-of-the-range Brasier. This was an extremely powerful car for its day, and Jimmy had a lot of fun doing time trials on the beach at Magillian Strand.

As Appin House was still let, the family stayed in nearby Kiel House when they went back for visits. A new front drive was put in at Appin, and shortly after they moved back in 1909, Jimmy installed hydroelectric power to the house and his sawmills. For an outpost in the Highlands, this was years ahead of its time, although hydroelectric power had been installed at Ardkinglass in Argyllshire for Sir Andrew Noble in 1906. When the young engineer sent by his company to carry out the survey work saw that his guide was none other than the laird himself, he could not believe that this slightly humpty-dumpty figure would make it up the first hill. But Jimmy was incredibly fit and tough and took it upon himself to take the man on the most circuitous route possible, with the result that the wretched chap arrived back at the house in a state of collapse. Jimmy revelled in being a thoroughly go-ahead Highland laird. He had totally embraced the Highland way of life, and had learnt to play the bagpipes when still at Eton. He even tried to learn Gaelic – a hopeless task for someone who was not very academic and had never spoken it as a child. Although an excellent shot, keen rider to hounds and expert fisherman, his knowledge and appreciation of the arts was rudimentary. He did not know the difference between Chippendale and Scottish country-style furniture and did not care, which was just as well because most of the Downie heirlooms went up in smoke – literally, thanks to a warehouse fire in Edinburgh. When Appin House needed a new carpet in the drawing room, a large and beautiful room with fantastic views down Loch Linnhe, he famously wrote to the factor in Oban telling him to go ahead and fit one, adding 'A red one would be nice'. The brown and white tiles that he had installed in the entrance hall would not have looked out of place in any public lavatory in the land.

[4] The forerunner of the Le Mans twenty-four hour race.

In the autumn of 1909, Jimmy and Sir Charles Stuart of Achara received stag dinner invitations from the reclusive Sir Duncan Campbell of Barcaldine, and their wives were far too intrigued to let them refuse. The old bachelor, who was an expert on genealogy and Scottish history, let it be known that he had something on which he would appreciate their opinion. This was the year when David Lloyd George as Chancellor of the Exchequer introduced his famous People's Budget which included a Land Tax. If this were to be passed it would have disastrous financial consequences for all landowners. Barcaldine explained to his guests that he believed that he still retained the ancient right of pit and gallows, because this had never been signed away and surrendered to the Crown. He therefore proposed that a Liberal rally be arranged in the county and Lloyd George invited to address it. He would then be enticed to Barcaldine, whereupon Sir Duncan would arrange for him to be hanged on his gate. Jimmy and Sir Charles sat dumbfounded – the old boy clearly meant what he said. As Jimmy said afterwards, it all seemed so damned reasonable. Sir Charles, being a prosperous London lawyer, immediately pointed out that by virtue of being accessories before the fact, both he and Jimmy would have no alternative but to inform the police to save their own heads. So it all came to nothing.[5]

Although a talented man in so many ways, Jimmy had no head for business, and grandiose impractical schemes followed in quick succession. He even tried to run MacBrayne's Steamers out of business for purely altruistic reasons at one point and ended up charging people so little that he was virtually paying them to go on his boat. Inevitably, he had to retreat with his financial tail between his legs.

For someone who had failed the Army Exam, which was almost impossible to do in those days, Jimmy was a natural soldier. With the outbreak of war, he volunteered to rejoin the Argyll and Sutherland Highlanders. A colourful character who had always led from the front, it was a bitter blow not to be sent to France. Instead he was asked to command a feeder battalion for the Argylls. He was indignant at first, but eventually accepted it, and poured a lot of his own money into recruiting and training the finest such battalion in the regiment. He was promoted Lieutenant Colonel in

[5] Donald Sutherland, *Butt and Ben* (Blackwood, 1963).

1915. Two years later, the battalion was based at Taverham Hall outside Norwich.[6] It was here that Jimmy received orders to go to France and take over command of 1/8th battalion of the Argyll and Sutherland Highlanders. He crossed to France on 3 October and assumed command on 19 January 1918.

When his younger brother Harley visited him at the front just before a big push, he was amazed to find every fifth man carrying a tin of petrol. 'Yes,' said Jimmy. 'Last time we overran their trenches they hid in their dugouts and popped up behind us with machine-guns. This time we'll toss down our petrol tins, chuck in a Mills bomb and fry them.'[7] By the middle of March, General Sir Hubert Gough's Fifth Army was occupying the sector around St Quentin, and all intelligence reports pointed to a big German offensive. It began with a heavy bombardment at 3am on 21 March, followed by gas and stormtroopers, and then mass infantry attacks. Never one to lead from behind, Jimmy left his reserve headquarters dugout to visit the forward positions and was mortally wounded by shell fire. It took four of the strongest stretcher-bearers to evacuate him to the casualty Clearing Station at Ham, where he died. It was his fortieth birthday.[8]

When everything had been sorted out, most of Jimmy's wealth had evaporated – lost to war, dishonesty, grandiose schemes and taxes. Poor Effie found herself being sued for breach of contract for failure to deliver railway sleepers on a contract that she never even knew existed. But she was made of strong stuff; she sold the Argyll car and bought a motorcycle and sidecar and took the boys, now aged fourteen and twelve, on an extended camping holiday round Scotland. A little daughter had been born in 1912, only to succumb to the dreaded meningitis some two years later.[9]

By now Robin had followed his uncle and first cousin to Preshute House at Marlborough where he soon stood out as a future leader of men. As a member of the Shooting VIII he represented the school at Bisley, but it was in athletics where he really excelled. He went on to Sandhurst in 1922 and

[6] Coincidentally, the author's prep school from 1956 to 1961.
[7] Kenneth Macalpine-Leny, unpublished Family History.
[8] Lt Col. J. R. Macalpine-Downie is buried in grave I.E. 17 in the Ham British Cemetery at Muille-Villette, France.
[9] She was buried at Dunoon, Argyllshire.

won the Victor Ludorum for the best athlete of his year, and gained Blues in athletics, cross country and hockey. Running against the Royal Military Academy at Woolwich, he shaved two seconds off the record for the mile, and would go on to improve this still further with a personal best of 4 minutes 18.4 seconds. In 1924 he was commissioned into the 2nd Battalion of the Argyll and Sutherland Highlanders, his father's old regiment, and joined them at Parkhurst on the Isle of Wight. Here he quickly demonstrated that the promise which he had shown at Marlborough and Sandhurst had fully borne fruit. He became battalion signal officer, and when the adjutancy fell vacant in 1928 he was selected to fill this coveted position – an appointment for which he subsequently showed he was fully qualified.[10] He still managed to compete in athletics matches and play hockey, and was selected to represent Great Britain against France and Scotland against Ireland. He was a keen horseman, and when the regiment moved to Jamaica, he took up polo. He soon outclassed all those who had started with him, and ended up playing for the regiment.

Then on 26 September 1929, the day before the regiment was to leave Jamaica for China, the news arrived that Robin had died following an operation. His family and many friends were stunned – he was only twenty-five. He was cheerful, loyal, modest and of the highest integrity. He loved Appin, and would have been an ideal laird. But it was not to be. His grave in the Military Cemetery in Kingston, Jamaica,[11] is marked by a headstone of Kentallen granite, quarried from the Appin countryside that meant so much to him.

Archie was twenty-three when his brother died. Overnight, everything changed. If Appin was going to continue, one day he would have to step up to the plate. In some ways he was very different from his brother, but had all the Macalpine charm. He had also gone to Marlborough and then Sandhurst, and was now serving with the Royal Tank Corps out in India. Here he met Pat Wall, the daughter of the retired police chief of Srinagar in Kashmir. Much against the advice of his commanding officer, who considered Archie at twenty-four much too young, they got engaged, and were married in great state at Appin the following year.

[10] *The Thin Red Line*, January 1930.
[11] Plot A21, Brigg's Park Military Cemetery, Up Park Camp, Kingston, Jamaica.

Perhaps there was some truth in the old saying – never marry a girl in India. Having been brought up in India it was hardly Pat's fault that she never took to Appin, but she tried. Roderick was born in 1933 and Alison in 1936. By the time war broke out, Archie was working in a basement at Woolwich developing a new armour-piercing shell with Dr Janeck, a Czech arms manufacturer who had fled the advancing Germans complete with his prototype. Pat left Rod and Alison in the care of Effie at Appin, and joined the ATS. Before long she had met an American sergeant, and that was the end of her marriage with Archie. She eventually married another American in Paris at the end of the war, and moved with him to Florida.

Archie worked round the clock in grim conditions developing both armour-piercing shells and tank carburettors. The pressure of the job coupled with a diet of alcohol and cigarettes eventually got the better of him and in 1944 he was rewarded with an MBE and TB. He managed to shake off the initial bout but eventually succumbed. There followed an eternity in a sanatorium at Midhurst, where he managed to keep himself amused by running a highly profitable racing book among the other inmates. Here he met Joane, a former Miss Kavanagh but now the estranged Marchioness of Kildare, who was nursing as a VAD.

The Kavanaghs are an ancient Irish family who can trace their descent back to the Kings of Leinster. Their family seat is Borris House in County Carlow, which sits in 600 acres of parkland and ancient oak woodland above the town of Borris. The house, which incorporates the remains of an old castle, was built in 1731 by Morgan Kavanagh. It was badly damaged in the 1798 uprising but restored about 1820 by Richard and William Vitruvius Morrison, who gave it a Tudor exterior and a rich and largely classical interior. When seen from the south-east, the house has a commanding position over the surrounding countryside.

The most famous member of the Kavanagh family was Arthur Mac-Morrough Kavanagh, who was born without any arms or legs. The third son of Thomas Kavanagh, MP, he was born in 1831 with only rudimentary limbs, but through incredible determination and perseverance, he managed to do almost everything that a normal man could do, and much of it a good deal better than most. His main form of locomotion was servant power, although he did have a mechanical chair that enabled him to move about the room unaided. He was totally fearless on horseback, and rode strapped into a special chair-saddle, with the reins tied to one of his stumps, and a whip to the other. Although he had a broad chest, his two stumps could meet across it, and by endless practice he had made the stumps so strong, supple and sensitive that he could control a horse as well as if he was using his fingers. He shot, and shot well using a special gun with no trigger guard, balancing the fore end on his left stump while activating the trigger with the right. He was an expert fisherman, either from a boat or a horse, moving the rod with a special jerking action. He also became a fairly good amateur draughtsman and painter, and his handwriting was more legible than most. One of his favourite exercises was chopping down trees, with a special axe attached to one of his stumps.

By the age of twenty-three he had completed two grand tours: France, Rome, Egypt and Asia Minor with his tutor the Rev. David Wood in 1846–8, and with his eldest brother Thomas and his tutor to India by way of Russia and Persia in 1849–51. In Persia he fell dangerously ill, and was nursed back to health in the harem of Prince Malichus Mirza. In addition to having the most wonderful gift with animals, he was incredibly attractive to women, and proved quite conclusively on two subcontinents that you did not need arms and legs to perform the sexual act. After he returned to Ireland and inherited the family estates in 1853 following the death of both his older brothers, people were forever turning up at Borris in later years claiming to be descendants.

In 1855 he married his cousin, Francis Mary Leathley, and they had at least three sons and a daughter. With the help of his wife he became the most philanthropic of landowners, rebuilding the villages of Borris and Ballyragget and always looking for ways to improve the lot of his tenants. He even managed and subsidised the railway line between Borris and Bagnalstown until this was taken over by the Great Southern and Western Railway. He became MP for County Wexford from 1866 to 1868 and then County Carlow from 1868 to 1880. He reached the House of Commons by sailing his yacht up the Thames and mooring her alongside the Palace of Westminster, an ancient privilege of MPs that had fallen into abeyance. He lost his seat in the general election of 1880 and became Lord

Lieutenant of County Carlow. Worn out by anxiety and overwork he succumbed to pneumonia and died at his London house on Christmas Day
1889, at the age of fifty-seven. A most remarkable man.[12]

Arthur's grandson was Major Arthur MacMorrough Kavanagh, MC,
who served in Palestine in the Great War and was present along with Bob
Macalpine-Leny and Reggie Halsey at the famous Old Etonian dinner in
Jerusalem on 4 June 1918. He only managed to produce four daughters, of
which Joane was the eldest, so for the first time in generations, there was
no male Kavanagh heir. At the age of twenty-one, Joane married Gerald
FitzGerald, the Marquess of Kildare, who was himself only twenty-two.
Gerald's father, the 7th Duke of Leinster, was a compulsive gambler and
ne'er-do-well. His mother was May Etheridge, the daughter of a commercial traveller who had graduated from her home in Brixton via the Gaiety
Chorus to a leading role in a West End show. Here she captivated the
young Lord Edward FitzGerald, who defied his family and married her in
1913. Needless to say, the marriage did not last, and Gerald ended up being
brought up by one of his father's aunts.[13] His childhood was bleak and
lonely, and at twenty-two he was naive and inexperienced. Joane was
equally unworldly, and their marriage was never going to last – they were
just too young. But they did manage to have three daughters. Pamela was a
blue baby, and died after five months; next came Rosemary (Ro), who was
born in 1939, and then Nesta (Net), born in 1942. Joane always said that it
was because she couldn't produce an heir that the marriage failed, but
most likely the wild days, stress and separations of the war were too much
for the marriage, especially after Gerald joined the fighting – he had been
commissioned into the Royal Inniskilling Dragoon Guards after Sandhurst. When he had an affair, Joane refused to take him back and they
were divorced in 1946.

Archie always had more than his fair share of the Macalpine charm,
and this was now brought to bear on a willing recipient. Rosemary and
Nesta had lived at Borris with their grandparents during the war, but the
following year Joane took a bungalow from the Wemyss family outside
Guillane so she could see Archie. The first the girls knew of her engage-

[12] Sarah Steele, *Arthur MacMorrough Kavanagh*, Macmillan, 1891.
[13] Obituary, 8th Duke of Leinster, *Daily Telegraph*, 7 December 2004.

ment was back at Borris when their grandmother called them into a room and rather hesitantly said that their mother was going to get married again. When they heard his name they thought it was hysterical, and they laughed and laughed: they had never come across anyone called Archibald before. Their grandmother was terribly put out. 'I think you should call him Uncle Archie', she said. But that was an absolute non-starter, and the girls quickly decided that they would call him Dad. Things got off on the wrong foot rather quickly because Archie took Joane to Norway for their honeymoon, where they went sailing, neither of which she enjoyed. Then it was Appin House, which Effie had finally moved out of after forty years.

Joane found Appin a real struggle from the very beginning. At Borris there were still servants, but Appin was very isolated, pretty primitive and there was no help. She could barely cook at first, and had never stoked a solid-fuel Aga in her life. There were still oil lamps, and electricity only when the turbine was running. This required water behind the dam and that the pipe wasn't choked with leaves. But the girls loved it. They were seven and four when they went to Appin, and had the run of the hill, farm and shore. Archie was the only dad they had ever known, and was always making them wooden models, bringing them back little presents and encouraging them to read. They were thrilled to be with Rod and Al, now fourteen and eleven respectively, and they soon teamed up together. The first years in particular were much harder for Joane than for the children. Archie was still only convalescent from his TB and, shortly after the Irish family's arrival, he had to be sent on a long and expensive cruise for his health, which left Joane feeling abandoned to struggle with the harshness of life at Appin.

For Joane horses were her life, and she had no interest in anyone who was not horsey. That ruled Rod out from the very beginning, who, being rather aloof, never cared for his stepmother. Al was totally different, being very good on a horse from an early age, and handsome and self-confident to boot. With the birth of Andrew the following year, Joane's long-hoped-for and precious son, the dynamic in the household changed, with him becoming the centre of attention. This led to some amusing incidents. Nesta as the youngest often had to look after Andrew, and had to push him in his pram, which was bigger than she was, up and down the Appin hills.

One day she had the bright idea of attaching the Shetland pony to the pram with binder twine. Going down the hill, the pram ran into the back of the pony which promptly kicked it and then took off at great speed in the field below the house. Nesta thought it terribly funny because as the pram bounced higher and higher, so did Andrew in his pram straps. Eventually the whole thing disintegrated and she got into severe trouble. Archie had a particularly irritable Ayrshire bull which was really cross and lived in a pen with a gap just wide enough to hook his food in. One day Nesta poked Andrew in through the gap and he crawled round in his little blue gingham rompers. Mr Chivers who looked after the cattle saw him in there, but did not dare do anything in case he attracted the bull's attention. But the bull took absolutely no notice, and eventually Andrew crawled out again.

After Andrew's arrival, the cracks in the marriage really began to show. Archie was banished to a room on the second floor, and there were tensions in the house. Archie was not a born farmer, money was always a problem and they were both unhappy. Then one day in 1953 news came that Major Kavanagh had died suddenly of a heart attack at the age of sixty-five. Joane picked up her three children and left for Borris. She never came back. Although her father had never made a will, Borris was to be left to Andrew, and Joane saw it as her job to go back and run it until he became of age.

Like so many of the family, Archie was the most wonderful company, absolutely charming, utterly honest, and he loved a party. He was a wonderful scientist and inventor, but the loss of his brother and the powerful social rules surrounding land and inheritance forced him away from his intellectual bent. All his ventures failed, whether farming lobsters or raising chickens in the drawing room. And he was absolutely hopeless with money – he had too kind a heart. If he had sold a cow in Oban he invariably met someone on the way home who had a hard-luck story, and they would end up having a few drinks together.

The alternative family holiday for Archie, Rod and Al was skiing, but it was always the sea that was Archie's great love. He eventually decided to give up farming and chartered the *Servabo*, a converted Brixham trawler which he sailed on short cruises from Oban in co-operation with the Scottish Council of Physical Recreation teaching seamanship to summer parties. His constant companion at that time became a twenty-two-year-old former debutante, Ann Chichester-Constable, who had originally answered an advertisement to join the crew of the *Servabo*. On 18 April 1958, Archie had been joined by his friend Major Richard Brooke in a hotel on the shores of Holy Loch to discuss the arrangements for the forthcoming season with the secretary of the Scottish Council of Physical Recreation. A strong wind blew up that evening and, not wishing to leave Ann alone on the *Servabo* anchored out in the loch, Archie and the Major took on some stores and set out in a dinghy. They never reached the ship. Ann raised the alarm next morning, and a search found the upturned dinghy on the shore a mile down the loch. Archie's body was not found for more than three months.

With all the disasters that had befallen the Macalpine-Downies, and more that were to follow, there was one member of the family who carried on undaunted – Effie. Faced with the loss of Jimmy at the end of the war and the reduction in circumstances that followed, she just carried on. She was made of very strong stuff, and she had no choice. Ten years later she married Arthur McClintock, an old family friend, only to be faced with Robin's death in Jamaica later that year. A year later, Arthur died; they had not been married two years. Always a lady of the outdoors, she was an excellent shot and a very keen fisherwoman, but had no interest in such things as clothes, soft furnishings or antique furniture. If she went into a shop to buy a hat she would be out again in no time with the first one she saw. She continued to run the farm on a shoestring, and endless carloads of Shuldham, Halsey and Macalpine-Leny cousins who used to go up and spend part of their summer holidays at Appin enjoyed helping Aunt Effie with whatever task needed tackling on the farm. One of her greatest achievements was to take over the tenancy of Shuna when it fell vacant in 1936, and transform the 395-acre island over a seven-year period from a bracken-covered waste to the highly productive farm it had been in days gone by. She would row across every day to supervise operations and play her part in the bracken-clearing. When farming again got under way in earnest, the highlight of an Appin holiday for young cousins was to help swim the cattle across from Shuna at low tide. Untroubled by shades of grey, Aunt Effie cut a robust path through life and ran much of the west coast of a depleted Scotland for most of the Second World War with a handful of cronies. She once received, albeit tardily, a letter addressed to Mrs E. McClintock, Scotland, and was widely loved and feared.[14]

When Archie and Pat left for London at the beginning of the war and shortly thereafter Pat left altogether, Effie brought up her grandchildren Rod and Al at Appin House. It was they that coined the name 'Gump', but she was always Aunt Effie to the wider family. She was soon joined by her niece Agatha Bainbridge and her two young children, Agatha having decided that Gaddesden was now vulnerable to bombing. When Joane arrived in 1947 as the new Mrs Macalpine-Downie, Effie moved out of Appin House and took up residence at Strathappin House, which had previously been the Manse. Here she continued to be a force to be reckoned with for miles around.

Still living alone at Strathappin when she reached ninety, Aunt Effie was only too pleased to offer a bed to a visiting young cousin. It was difficult to tell exactly where the garden ended and the house began because a trail of mud went in through the front door, through the kitchen, and out through the back door. There was a lone bulb burning unshaded at the end of its flex above the kitchen table, around which numerous flies seemed to be in perpetual motion. Having lost an eye to a splinter while chopping wood, which mercifully put an end to her driving, Aunt Effie decided at the age of ninety she was too old to have a glass one. This meant that when her remaining eye blinked the empty socket had a disconcerting habit of doing the same. She deftly skinned a chicken for dinner, and produced that great delicacy, haggis on toast. It was a bit disconcerting to go up to your bedroom and find someone else already in your bed. On closer inspection this proved to be Aunt Effie's patent bed-warming device – a 150-watt bulb inside a large wire cage that went down inside the bed. She would be up at 8am the next morning to provide porridge and her own fried eggs for her guest for breakfast.

While Andrew was growing up at Borris his mother tried to keep him, Rosemary and Nesta at home concentrating on their ponies, but at the age of fifteen he hitch-hiked over to Appin to see 'Gump'. They became

[14] Rod Macalpine-Downie, unpublished final writings.

extremely fond of each other. Years later, when Effie was well into her eighties, he went to visit her again, having hired a car at the airport. Since he said that he hoped to get to Strathappin at about 4pm, Effie set out at 3.45pm to walk to meet him. Andrew was running a bit late, and it was 5pm before he saw this exhausted figure struggling along the road towards him. She got into the car and never said a word about it.

At the age of ninety-six, Effie left Strathappin and went to live in a little cottage next to her granddaughter. When she was very ill, Dr Iain McNicholl came to see her when standing in as a locum for his father who was on holiday. Effie told him not to worry as she was not going to die on his watch because she had a deal with his father. Shortly after Dr McNicholl Senior came back from holiday, she died. She was always terrified of being buried alive so, as had been prearranged, Dr McNicholl came over and pronounced her dead, then went away and came back an hour later and re-pronounced her dead. He said it was one of the worst things he had ever had to do, but he had always promised her he would do it, so he did. She died in her ninety-ninth year, having outlived both her husbands, her three children, and to a large extent, the Appin she loved.

Archie and Pat's son Roderick Macalpine-Downie was a most unusual man in many ways. Highly intelligent and something of an outsider, he had won a scholarship to Eton where he quickly showed considerable talent for music. He played the viola, and was for two years the number-one string player in the Eton orchestra. He even considered going professional at one time. Two milestones of his musical career were in the end not playing a much-rehearsed duet with Yehudi Menuhin when he visited the school because Menuhin had caught the flu, and much later, not having supper with Herbert von Karajan because somebody else had caught the flu and von Karajan had to step in and conduct their orchestra. When he came back to Appin, Rod always played the organ in the Parish Church, but sadly, he never kept his music up.

After Eton, Rod became apprenticed to a firm of precision engineers in Motherwell, outside Glasgow, but he did not really enjoy it. Then it was a short-service commission in the XIth Hussars spent largely out in Malaya, which he loved. Here he met Shirley Reid, the daughter of an RAF pilot who had been killed during the war when he was shot down over the North

Sea. Shirley had joined the Women's Royal Army Corps as a signals officer, and went out to Singapore in 1953. She always claimed that she and Rod met in bed, and there was a certain amount of truth in that. Rod was in hospital recovering from a bout of malaria, and Shirley was visiting a girl friend who had been injured with her in a car crash. On leaving the army, he ended up at Appin helping his father with the chickens, which he loathed. Despite opposition from Archie, Rod and Shirley were married in 1956. Rod had always been a keen sailor, and they had bought a Flying 15 with their wedding money. He suddenly decided that he wanted to design boats, and went up to Glasgow to acquire books on the subject, which he read avidly and memorised.

Thus it was that someone who was not a trained naval architect or even a trained boat designer became the most outstandingly successful designer of catamarans for more than twenty-five years. With instinctive understanding of his craft, Rod had the rare quality of complete original- ity in his designs, which were always extremely elegant both in concept and appearance. He called his first design Thai (his little joke – Siamese twins), which was built in the garage of their home at Appin Lodge. He then moved south to Brightlingsea where he met up with Reg White, who offered to build for him. By the time that Thai Mark IV came along, it proved startlingly better than anything else around, and won numerous regattas. This led to Rod being invited by *Yachting World* to design a kit boat called the 'Yachting World Catamaran'.

In 1959, the American magazine *Yachting* staged a 'one of a kind' regatta, at which the fastest boat overall proved to be the catamaran *Tiger- cat*. This led *Yachting* to describe *Tigercat* as the 'fastest small boat in the world', which Rod found rather irritating. He therefore issued a challenge to the Eastern Multihull Association of the USA for a series of races to be sailed by catamarans conforming to the recently internationally estab- lished 'C' Class. The Royal Highland Yacht Club did not show much enthusiasm for this, so Rod teamed up with John Fisk, and a challenge was mounted through the Chapman Sands Sailing Club, of which Fisk was flag officer. This was accepted, and the first series of races was organised by the Seacliffe Yacht Club of Long Island in 1961, which generously donated a beautiful trophy. This became known as the Little America's Cup, because the competition was organised on similar lines to that most famous of yachting events. Rod and John put up *Hellcat II*, the second in Rod's famous series of designs of that name, and they beat the American challenger four races to one. The Americans were quite cross about this and challenged again the following year, but Rod and John defended, and swept the board. Subsequent boats in this series then held the trophy annually against all comers until 1969, when no further owner came forward to mount a challenge.[15]

Rod named many of his subsequent designs after Indian tribes. This included the *Iroquois*, the most successful cruising catamaran of the time. More than three hundred were built by Reg White's firm Sail Craft, and the basic design stayed in production for fifteen years. Compared with a typical cruising yacht of the period, the *Iroquois* was twice as fast and had four times as much room inside.[16]

Mariandl had been born in 1957, and twins, Robin and Michael in 1959, but by the beginning of the 1960s, Rod and Shirley were not getting on well. Seeing Rod looking rather depressed, his great friend Bernard Hayman, editor of *Yachting World*, sent him over to the States to report on the 1964 America's Cup. *Sovereign*, the Royal Thames Yacht Club's challenger skippered by Peter Scott, was beaten four-nil by *Constellation* off Rhode Island. The slight consolation for Rod was that Scott came up to him and said how much he had always wanted to meet him. The following month, Hayman sent Rod out to report on the Tokyo Olympics, and this would take his life on a totally different course.

In addition to *Yachting World*, Rod was also reporting for the *Times, Daily Express, Guardian* and *Irish Times*. He was billeted in a beautiful old Japanese house with Hosaka-san, its one-eyed housekeeper, and Fakuya-san, its gentle and artistic houseboy. 'Would you like to meet a nice Japanese girl?' Fakuya-san asked Rod one evening . . . Kimie Tabata was a twenty-five year-old dental hygienist who worked for a big company clinic in Tokyo. Her father was an accountant in Nagasaki and Kimie was the third of his six children. When Fakuya-san called her to ask her to have dinner that evening, she was very hesitant – it was rare for her to have dinner with someone she did not know, but she finally accepted. There were

[15] David Pelly, *Faster! Faster!* (Macmillan, 1984).   [16] Ibid.

ten people for dinner, six or seven journalists from all over the world plus Rod, and she was the only Japanese lady. She could not enter into the conversation because although she understood English, she could not speak it. Rod was very busy, but they did meet a second time for tea, and then he left for New York.

A postcard arrived from him asking what she was going to do in the future. Kimie wanted to see the world and, since she had an aunt who had married an American, was thinking of going to the USA. Rod suggested that she should come to the UK first, and if she did, he would fix her up as an au pair with friends. The following year she sailed to Marseilles and then flew to London, where Rod met her. By this time Rod was living on his own. They were married the following year. 'What's he asking?' said Kimie when questioned by the registrar at the registry office. 'Just say 'Yes',' said Rod, under his breath.

They were very hard up at the beginning with two families to maintain, and Kimie went out to work, first in a restaurant in Hampstead to improve her English, and then for Nomura, where she would end up as personal assistant to the president. The marriage was an instant success. Rod was the perfect gentleman; he was friendly, but with an intensely analytical brain. He could not be superficial about anything and always wanted to get to the bottom of things. He could have excelled at endless different things. Needless to say, he did not suffer fools gladly. Being Japanese, Kimie was very correct and reserved, but also highly intelligent. It worked, and a daughter Sun-tiyan (Sumie) was born at the end of 1970.

When the world sailing speed record was introduced in 1972, millionaire Tim Coleman asked Rod to design his challenger. The resulting catamaran, *Crossbow*, was revolutionary, and set the first record over a timed course at 26.3 knots. This was progressively raised in successive years to 31.1 knots. In 1976, *Crossbow II* was launched, and the record pushed to 31.8 knots. In 1980, *Crossbow II* achieved 36.0 knots, a record that would remain unbroken for six years. So Macalpine-Downie designs held the world sailing speed record from 1972 to 1986. At the time of his death, Rod was working on the design of *Crossbow III* with which he hoped to take the record to 50 knots.[17]

[17] Ibid.

The increase in taxation on luxury goods at the beginning of the 1980s killed the boatbuilding business in the UK, and the US company, although having done extremely well initially, was forced into bankruptcy by the cost of successfully defending two product liability claims. Ever resourceful, Rod resorted to driving a minicab. And then cancer caught up with him. He never thought it would get him and he was incredibly brave about it, but it did in the end. Sumie was only just sixteen.

Rod's sister Alison, always known as Al to the family, was seriously good with the horse. Almost grown up by the time Joane returned to Ireland, she wanted to stay in Scotland, so went and lived with her grandmother at Strathappin. Good-looking, self-confident, with plenty of Macalpine charm, she was not going to be hindered by a somewhat unconventional upbringing. She broke in horses very successfully for the Duchess of Portland, and made a good business of supplying horses and riders for films made in Scotland. She even appeared as a mounted redcoat extra in *Kidnapped*, but by the time *Highlander* was made, the definition had improved to such an extent that it was impossible to have ladies masquerading as mounted soldiers without the audience smelling a rat. Every winter she would go down to Exmoor to hunt for three months with the Exmoor Fox Hounds, and was completely fearless over the drystone walls. She was equally fearless on the ski slopes, and would have made an even better skier if she had not spent quite so much time chatting up the ski instructors in the coffee shop.

History does not relate how many would-be suitors her grandmother turned away, but David Craig refused to be deflected. His connection with Appin began when his father, who was chairman of Scottish Steel, bought the island of Shuna from Archie in 1955. Archie was short of money as usual and had agreed a deal with Tom Craig, only to be reminded that Shuna actually belonged to his mother, and he hadn't told her. Eventually the deal went through, and the Craigs became the new owners of Shuna. David had done his National Service in the army and then converted to a regular commission in the Cameronians (Scottish Rifles). It had always been understood that he would follow his father into Scottish Steel, but after nationalisation, this proved no longer possible. Thus it was that David arrived at Appin in 1969 to take over the farm on Shuna. The Craigs had been sold a piece of land at Lettershuna to act as a supply point for Shuna, and promptly proceeded to erect a house for David on it.

His first real contact with his future wife was when Al hired him and his lorry to collect a farm-cart from Skye that she needed for the next film. One thing led to another, and they were married in 1973. They were granted the tenancy of Shuna, bringing the island once again back into the family, and set up the Lettershuna Riding Centre. Jamie was born in 1974 and Ethel followed in 1976.

Back at Borris, the future of the estate looked bleak. The house was vast and totally impractical, and Joane had tried to rationalise it by pulling down the kitchen wing which connected the main house to the chapel. To inherit the estate, Andrew had changed his name from Macalpine-Downie to Kavanagh, so once again there was a Kavanagh heir. Having married the high-spirited and immensely capable Tina Murray in 1970, Andrew rode as a National Hunt jockey for Clifford Nicholson in Lincolnshire before returning to Borris to pick up the pieces after his mother moved to a smaller house on the estate.

By dint of sheer hard work and an immense stroke of luck when the house was hired by an American film producer for six years, Andrew and Tina were able to turn the tide and start to restore Borris. Today it is one of the leading wedding and event locations in Ireland, but the house still retains its charm complete with a wonderful mix of Macalpine and Kavanagh hospitality. The kitchen is always full of children and dogs, the laird has been seen wearing gumboots in the drawing room, and dinner cannot begin until he has finished watching a horse race on television. Before the new heating system was installed, the day began with Andrew chucking huge logs into a Heath-Robinson-type furnace at the back of the nursery wing, and it was always rather disconcerting to go up to your bedroom and find it full of smoke. 'It always does that when the wind's in the east,' was the response.

Poor old Appin has not fared so well. After his father died in 1958, Rod found that the estate was largely owned by the banks and there was no alternative but to sell. He never really cared for Appin anyway. The Forestry Commission bought a lot of the land, and Appin House was sold. It was in a pretty dreadful state by then, with Archie's chickens in the drawing room ('Mansion Chickens'), and as Effie had never locked the house in her day, quite a lot of things had been stolen over the years. The most distressing thing to subsequent researchers was that in the hurry to empty the house, all the old papers, books and records were put on one huge bonfire and set alight. It burnt for two days.

The new owner pulled down most of the house, and only Robert Downie's 1830s extension remains today. The main part of the house has been replaced by a smaller modern building, surrounded by numerous chalets and cottages. This is barely visible from the road thanks to a large number of conifers that have grown up over the last forty years. But turn your back on the house and all the change that it has seen, and there is that same incredible view down Loch Linnhe that first attracted Robert Downie all those years ago.

Appin always will be a very special place.

11 Harley – 'The Smallest of the Litter'

At 2.20am on Sunday 28 November 1880, Agnes Macalpine-Leny's fifth and final baby was born at Dalswinton. It was a boy. He would be christened William after his father and Harley after his godfather General Harley Maxwell, a close family friend who lived at Portrack on the other side of the River Nith. Always known as Harley, he was initially rather a sickly child, but a late developer who would grow up to be incredibly strong.

At the age of eight Harley was packed off to Cargilfield to follow in his brothers' footsteps, but by the time it came to move on to his public school, the family were already drawing in their horns and had moved to Guernsey. William thought that Eton was not at all the right thing given his reduced circumstances, so Harley was the first member of the family to be sent to Marlborough. To cheer him up as he set off for his first term, his father gave him two new half-sovereigns. He never spent them, but passed them on to his son Kenny when he took him to Marlborough for the first time. Harley did not particularly enjoy the school, in fact he was rather bewildered by it. No one ever told you anything – you were supposed to have read it on a notice board. The whole school seemed to be run by notice boards – there was one for everything. There was a Set Notice Board outside your classroom, a House Notice Board, an Upper Passage Notice Board and a Lower Passage Notice Board. There was also a terrifying erection in the 'Quad' known as The Notice Board. The porter even had one all to himself in his lodge. All prefects had canes which were used freely, but they could only give two strokes for any one offence – leaving shoes about or forgetting to hang up a towel, etc. In addition, all form masters were provided with the handles of old racquet bats, which they were not frightened of using. Harley arrived in a strange classroom one day and was seized by a choleric assistant master and given the pasting of his life. 'I'll teach you to come in late' he thundered. Harley meekly explained that he had been sent over with a note from his own form master.[1]

[1] Kenneth Macalpine-Leny, unpublished Family History.

Harley spent his holidays in Guernsey and was a martyr to seasickness during his frequent crossings. Once, he was supposed to be staying the night at Gaddesden and going on to Marlborough the next day. He was so seasick during the crossing that he was beyond all rational thought when he reached London, and boarded the Marlborough train instead. This meant he arrived back at school a day early. His housemaster, the fierce old bearded Joe Mullins, must have had a soft streak in his formidable make-up, for he was sorry for the boy. He hired a pony so Harley could enjoy a day's riding on the Downs and fed him at his own table.[2]

One day Harley happened to glance at The Notice Board and found a list saying. 'The following boys will be confirmed next Sunday.' His name was on it. Mindful of the terrible fate that befell any boy rash enough to disobey The Notice Board, he decided he had better show up. He had had no instruction, and with his Presbyterian upbringing the whole thing meant absolutely nothing to him, but confirmed he was.[3]

By now William had decided that he would send Harley to Woolwich so he could go into the Royal Artillery – a poor man's regiment with certain pay advantages. This meant that he had to switch from the classical to the modern side, but fortunately he turned out to be a brilliant mathematician. About this time he suddenly started to develop both mentally and physically, so by the time he enrolled as a cadet at Woolwich in February 1898, the 'Little White Mouse' had disappeared. But he always resented not going to Eton.

Passing out from Woolwich in June 1899, Harley was posted to Aden and sailed on the *Britannia* in September. Aden was not a popular posting. As his column marched into the fort the sentry presented arms, tilted the muzzle of his rifle into his mouth, and shot himself. Harley soon discovered that there had been a wave of suicides among the other ranks about the time he joined. The commanding officer was a wise old major who lived in the Aden Club. Leaving the comfort of the club, he pointed to some derelict guns out in the desert and gave the instruction that they should be brought in. Upwards of two hundred men were then employed salvaging these useless weapons in the most appalling conditions of heat and discomfort. There were no more suicides.

[2] Ibid.   [3] Ibid.

The following May it was India for Harley and promotion to lieutenant. Here, in addition to his regular soldiering, he succeeded in attending the Delhi Durbar on New Year's Day, 1903, and of all things, an Old Marlburian dinner later in the month. The Durbar was mounted to celebrate the coronation of Edward VII. There was also polo and mixing with a number of well-heeled young cavalry officers. Unfortunately, he was inveigled into playing poker for very high stakes. After the first session, Harley left the table with £500 in his pocket. Thinking this was a source of easy money and that he had finally arrived, he played again and lost the lot – and a good bit more besides. What was to become of him? Was it disgrace and the native moneylenders? As a last resort, he cabled his father: 'Please send £500 urgent stop writing.' William wired back: 'I will do nothing of the sort.'

Fortuitously, about this time, the Aden Political Resident decided to launch the Aden Hinterland Expedition. In 1873, after an interval of 240 years, the Turks had reoccupied the Yemen. This threatened the security of the nine Arab tribes in the Aden Hinterland who many years previously had been granted protection by HM Government. The solution was to delineate Turkish-occupied Yemen from the nine tribes' cantons, not to interfere with the people, but to protect the Arabs from the encroachment of the Turks. A joint boundary commission was set up, amidst much haggling by the Turks who were reluctant to accept the proposed boundary; they had sent troops to occupy some of the villages in the cantons, and generally stirred up the Arabs against the British.

The commissioner in charge of the British team was a Colonel Waller who reported through the Aden Political Resident, Brigadier-General P. F. Maitland, to both London and India. When things went wrong, the Turkish Ambassador in London, Musurus Pasha, complained (in French) to the British Foreign and Colonial Secretary, Lord Lansdowne, who got the British Ambassador in Constantinople, Sir Nicholas O'Conor, to deal (ultimately) with the Sultan. Following advice from the Russian Ambassador and, at the eleventh hour, from the German Ambassador, the Sultan agreed to HM Government's demands, and part of the dispute was resolved on 18 March 1903 with Turkish troops subsequently being withdrawn.[4]

[4] National Archives Ref. FO78 5319.

The problems of the Boundary Commission were not resolved because the Arabs were forever stealing each other's camels, and had a nasty habit of taking it out on its surveyors. In response, the Political Resident reinforced their escort and mounted a punitive expedition to restore British authority in the area, as well as protect the surveyors. This was unlikely to be a particularly popular expedition, so they called, rather half-heartedly, for volunteers. It is no good being a brave subaltern in the middle of the Arabian Desert – you have to arrange for a few very senior officers to be there to see you. But day-to-day expenses in the desert would be nil, so Harley volunteered to restore his finances after the poker losses. The force initially consisted of two hundred infantry and two 7lb guns of No. 6 Mounted Battery.

Part of the purpose of any such expedition was diplomacy, and Harley had the foresight to have a gramophone sent out from England. The first time he played it to his Arab guests he was disappointed that they took not the slightest notice. They assumed it was just a musical box, and they had their own musical boxes. But he had one record of farmyard noises, and when the cows mooed, the sheep baaed and the hens clucked, his guests went wild with excitement and insisted on seeing what was inside the box. Harley sent for a screwdriver and removed the top of the machine, only to reveal a simple coil spring and governor. When diplomacy and the gramophone failed, blowing up the occasional village usually had the desired effect.

Things started to go wrong when they were deep in the hinterland many miles from Aden and their much-needed supplies had failed to get through. They still had plenty of water, but had been reduced to quarter rations and were running dangerously short of ammunition. It was then that they learnt from scouts that Saleh, the disaffected brother of one of the sheikhs, was massing a force of eight hundred Arabs and was planning to attack their camp at dawn. As the only remaining officer, Harley reviewed the camp defences and then called a conference of all his NCOs to agree a course of action. There were two alternatives: to take up defensive positions and hope that they could survive long enough for the Arabs to give up their attack, or to attack giving the impression that they had been resupplied, in which case the Arabs would never press home an attack. The conference settled on the former course, and they started to strengthen their defences.

Sitting alone in his tent and turning the two options over in his mind, Harley realised that their decision was wrong. Hurriedly reconvening the conference, he told his NCOs that having thought it through carefully, he was convinced that they would be overrun if they just waited to be attacked by a numerically larger force when they had a limited supply of ammunition. They must attack, firing off all their remaining shells, and so give the Arabs the impression they had been resupplied. Eventually the NCOs agreed.

The whole force was stood-to an hour before dawn, and first light revealed a tightly packed mass of Arab cavalry providing a perfect target for the two seven-pounders. When Harley gave the order to fire, the first two shells landed right in the middle of the cavalry with devastating effect. There followed a half-hearted charge which was quickly beaten off, and with that the Arab force scattered and melted into the desert. When it came to recovering the dead and wounded, Saleh was found among them. It was unanimously agreed that his magnificent silver *khanjar*, powder horn, necklace and Lee-Enfield rifle covered with silver plates should be presented to Harley, whose decisive course of action had won the day.[5]

After it was all over, Harley's Battery sergeant major, a hardened veteran of several campaigns, came up to him.

'Do you mind if I ask you a personal question, sir?'

'Of course, sergeant major, go ahead.'

'How old are you, sir?'

'Twenty-two.'

With that the old soldier sat down on a nearby rock, pushed his helmet back on his head, and mopped his brow. 'My Gawd.'

By the time the survivors of this sadly depleted force finally struggled back to Aden, Harley had spent the last 80 miles unconscious on the back of camel with a severe attack of malaria. There was no alternative but to be invalided home, and he arrived back at Tilbury at the end of April 1904. There followed a long period of recuperation, endless quinine injections

[5] The *khanjar* (traditional curved dagger), powder horn and necklace are at Doddington to this day. The Lee-Enfield was stolen during the move from Courance to Doddington in 1952.

and finally six weeks in the convalescent hospital at Osborne. But his promotion to captain came through in July, so that raised morale. His next
posting was to 20th Company, Royal Garrison Artillery, based at the
Nothe Fort in Weymouth.

Once Harley had the opportunity to play games he quickly showed that
he had an exceptional eye for a ball. He would go on to play cricket for
Dorset and hockey for Dorset County and the West of England. He also
played a very good game of tennis, as well as being pretty useful on the
rugby pitch. His untiring strength seemed to be only rivalled by his zest for
games. After a hockey match his soldier servant had instructions to have
his bicycle ready for him. He would then change and cycle the 30 miles or
so to Norton sub Hamdon to spend the weekend with his sister Milly.
There are stories of him playing more than one game at once. He would
stroll across the road from the cricket match when he was not batting and
play off the semi-finals in the tennis tournament. He was also a brilliant
game shot in later life as well as a very effective marksman with a rifle, particularly at long range, and a frequent competitor at Bisley before the First
World War. He had had his first shooting lesson from Tilbury at Dalswinton when he was ten, and that had held him in good stead. When asked by
his son Kenny why he always fired his choke barrel first, he said that when
he was first being taught to shoot at Dalswinton, he had used a double-
barrel muzzle loader and it was always much easier to reload the left-hand
barrel. You would have thought by 1891 Dalswinton might have been able
to find a hammer gun for him . . .

By this time Harley's strength had become legendary. One of his particular parlour tricks was to carry his major round the anteroom in his
teeth on guest nights. He liked to walk out of Weymouth on fine Sundays
and stop for lunch at a pub some 5 miles outside. Here he would have a
pint of beer and as much bread and cheese as he could eat. The bill was
six pence ($2\frac{1}{2}$p). He was a noted trencherman and would have certainly
got his money's worth. On another occasion one of his brother-officers
expressed surprise at finding him alone in the mess sitting down to a plate
of chops and mashed potatoes. Harley explained that he was going out to
dinner and never got enough to eat.

The halcyon existence of a popular officer with Harley's physical gifts could only have one end. The fashionable clergyman of the day was a certain Canon Weldon, a great Irish gentleman, who filled Holy Trinity Weymouth with his eloquence. Canon Lewen Burton Weldon was the youngest of the seven sons of Sir Anthony Weldon. He had apparently got into trouble with the Church hierarchy in Dublin over some religious matter when he was a canon of Christchurch Cathedral there, and had to move to England. Here he became a canon of Salisbury Cathedral and the very popular vicar of Holy Trinity Weymouth from 1894 until his death in 1914. He married Olivia Barrington, and the Weldons had two sons and three daughters, the youngest of whom, Felicia, caught Harley's eye.

All the Weldon family were great fun. Lewen, the eldest, was wonderful company and the most amusing raconteur. He worked for the Egyptian Government in the Survey Department. At the outbreak of war he became an intelligence officer, and had a fascinating time landing agents behind enemy lines on the Syrian coast, and directing two French sea planes on reconnaissance work from his floating base – a requisitioned German cargo ship. Sadly his gift for being amusing did not extend to the written word, and his account of his wartime experiences is rather disappointing.[6] Still, he won a Military Cross for his efforts, and would become Surveyor-General of Egypt after the war. His younger brother Kenneth was in the Royal Dublin Fusiliers, seeing action in both the Boer War and the First World War, winning a DSO in 1917. When the regiment was disbanded in 1922 he transferred to the Sherwood Foresters as Lieutenant Colonel. Of the three girls, Mary married Bryan Gwynn and their son-in-law, George Simms, would become successively Archbishop of Dublin and then Archbishop of Armagh. Hilda, who was Commandant of VAD for Dorset during the First World War, married the Rev. Cyril Pugh after the war, but they had no children.

Felicia was not only the youngest but also the prettiest, and always had a string of young men in tow. She was also very musical and wrote most beautifully – talents that she would pass on to her son. Not surprisingly, she was the first of the three sisters to become engaged, having accepted Harley's diamond-and-sapphire ring in March 1908. They were married in great state at St Jude's, South Kensington, with a reception afterwards

[6] Capt. L. B. Weldon, MC, *Hard Lying* (Herbert Jenkins, 1925).

at 15 Bolton Gardens, the home of Felicia's aunt and godmother. Her father married them, and her brother Kenneth gave her away. There were no fewer than five Miss Weldons as bridesmaids,[7] and Master Robin Macalpine-Downie as the page. After that, Harley carried his young bride off to a fishing honeymoon in Killarney.

From adjutant to the Royal Garrison Artillery in Weymouth and Portsmouth for three years, Harley's next posting was as adjutant of the 4th Highland Mountain Brigade (TA) based at Tarbert Loch Fyne, a lonely fishing village in Argyllshire. This was quite a change for Felicia, who had been brought up on the south coast amid a string of friends and relations with frequent trips up to London, but she took it all in her stride. A son was born on 20 October 1909, christened Kenneth after his godfather Kenneth Weldon and Harley after his father, but always known as Kenny to the family. Harley's mother was insistent that the baby, initially rather a sickly child, should be christened immediately, so he was. Shortly thereafter the minister called in the true Scots manner to christen the new baby, so he was rechristened. Canon Weldon then wrote from Weymouth with plans for the christening in Holy Trinity with Felicia's aunt supplying the christening robe. Harley was long past all argument by this time, so Kenny was christened a third time. He always claimed subsequently that it never seemed to do him much good. We shall hear more of him in the next chapter.

Harley's next posting was to Malta and he sailed from Southampton at the beginning of 1914 leaving Felicia and Kenny in lodgings on the south coast. But it was short-lived. War was declared on 3 August and by the end of September he was back at Southampton. A week later he was at the front, having not been able to get leave to come and say goodbye to Felicia and little Kenny, now almost five. The horrors of the next four years on the Western Front in France and Belgium are all too well known, and will not be repeated here. Suffice to say that Harley, now a major commanding the 29th Brigade Royal Garrison Artillery, lived to tell the tale. On 23 February 1915 he was awarded an immediate DSO on the orders of General Sir John French. The citation read: 'For conspicuous ability and courage at Wulverghem on 24th and 27th January, when he succeeded in destroying

[7] There were plenty to chose from: Felicia had seventy first cousins.

houses occupied by the enemy by the fire of his battery, during which period he had to observe the firing of his guns from a very exposed position.'[8] This was three years before the DSO awarded to his elder brother Bob, which must have given rise to quite a lot of leg-pulling at the time.

A very clear impression of what life was like is given in letters Harley wrote to his sister May from the Somme the following year:

2.5.16

Many thanks for your Punches that you have sent me. We move off to another place tomorrow & I shall not be sorry to say goodbye to this spot. When not actually on our guns or observing, I have lived underground in cellars – always half full of water and a perfect rain of shell all day and night going over – & still worse the Hun shell come from 3 sides of one. And we have had to stick this for 5 weeks on end. However, I had a jolly day in my front observation post today and got some Huns and blew some of his day out. I think I told you that in 5 days last month we had 3,700 heavy shells in my battery – makes one think a bit & here we are alive and very fit and into another month. I must say I never thought I would live to see May but now I think I shall probably live through anything. Cheer oh old girl and give my love to the family. The Thames still flows under London Bridge.

Ever your affectionate brother, Harley

1.7.16

I was so shocked to hear of dearest mum being dead and buried by the time I got the wire today. It seems as if the centrepiece of our home has gone.

I am on the Somme next the French & we have had today the biggest battle I suppose the British Army has ever been in. The dead Germans in front of me now are in places 6 high – I suppose on average along our front 1 dead per 3 yds. & we took about 2000 prisoners but you will see this much more interestingly told in the papers. Today has been some fight & as an interested spectator in my forward observing station I have learnt some yarns . . .

11.7.16

I was so sorry not to see dear mother again or to be able to get leave for the funeral, I am now at Montaban & of course you will probably have seen all the news about this show. I left my last choice spot in the middle of June & they

[8] *London Gazette*, 10 March 1915.

brought us here. I have a lot of yarns to tell you when we meet & have really seen quite a new side of life. Do you remember laughing at me when I spoke about the chance of getting Hun infantry massed in the open? Well I have had the chance and did my best to impress on them it is a dangerous thing to do. One of my subs, a sargt & myself got buried last night but I am quite fit again this morning . . .

9.10.16

Everything goes cheer oh here with a bit of melodrama and a hell of a lot of farce. Let's hear from you soon old girl. I still survive after nearly $3\frac{1}{2}$ months of the Somme and over 2 years of the War so can't expect my luck to go on for ever . . . I am now at Morral. Had a great time at the capture of Comblas . . .

Sometime later Harley was lucky enough to bump into his brother Jimmy in London when they were both on leave, and Jimmy suggested he should give him dinner at the Army and Navy Club. Their father had been in the habit of entertaining his sons at the club and lecturing them on the evils of drink. By way of illustrating his point, he would take them into the smoking room and point out one of his fellow-members who sat in a chair all day and read the newspaper. He never spoke, but would press the bell at regular intervals, holding up one or two fingers to indicate the size of his whisky. This was not just for an hour or two – he did it all day long and had never been known to speak, even to the waiter. After dinner they strolled into the smoking room and Jimmy said, 'I wonder, Harley, whatever happened to that funny old character who Dad used to warn us about?' They looked over to the accustomed chair and there the old villain was – ringing his bell and holding up fingers to the waiter. Their father had been dead for years.

Sooner or later Harley's luck had to give out. He had received splinters in a leg at Wulverghem, a shell wound at Montauban in July 1916, then finally a nasty gash in his head together with concussion at Favrins Court on 21 December 1917. This last resulted in him being invalided home. He would make a full recovery, but from then on was missing a piece of his skull, so had to be very careful about putting his head down, otherwise his brains would fall out – literally. Nowadays a plate would have been put in, but he just had a fold of skin. All his hats had to be specially made with a piece taken out of rim so there was no pressure on that particular spot. But he had done well – not only had he survived against all the odds but he had come away with a DSO and five mentions in despatches. His faithful charger Felice almost went all the way through with him. She was wounded at the first battle of Ypres and killed at Cambrai in 1917.[9]

During these four years, Felicia and Kenny, who were joined at one time by her sister-in-law Constance Weldon and her son Tony, lived in thirteen different lodgings in Brighton, Weymouth and Bournemouth. Kenny never thought he would see his father again. Towards the end of this time, an event occurred that would change the fortunes of Harley and his family. Kenny was alone in their lodging house one afternoon when an enormous Daimler drew up in the street and out stepped two charming old ladies who rang the bell. Kenny, who was only eight at the time, answered the door, and they introduced themselves. These were the two Miss Seton Wightmans of Courance who had come to inspect Harley's family. Kenny had not the faintest idea who they were but thought they must be relations, so invited them in and called for tea. Kenny learnt from them long afterwards that he had made himself thoroughly agreeable and gave all the right answers to their rather startling questions: did he go to church? Was he a card-playing boy, etc., etc.? Anyway, wee Kenny seemed to have completely captivated them and they went away and changed their wills. Not a bad afternoon's work for an eight-year-old boy. Harley, when he was informed, was sworn to secrecy. It later transpired that Harley's brother Bob and son Roy had been invited to stay at Courance sometime earlier. It can only be assumed that Bob spent too long in the smoking room ringing for more port because the two Miss Seton Wightmans decided that this was not the branch of the family that they wished to inherit Courance.

Courance is a small lowland estate outside Locherbie on the road between Dumfries and Moffat. It was originally a Wightman place, but after John Wightman married Margaret Seton in 1799, their son James changed his name to Seton Wightman. He in turn married Caroline Cordelia Cullen, a niece of old Robert Downie. James was a good friend of James Macalpine-Leny of Dalswinton, and would succeed him for a time

[9] One of her silver-mounted hooves sits on the drawing room mantelpiece at Doddington.

as chairman of the Commissioners of Supply. His children knew the Macalpine-Leny children well and they would spend a lot of time in each other's houses as they grew up. James was a keen shooting man, and in his day the 2,750 acres of the Courance estate included a grouse moor. The estate was much reduced when this was requisitioned by the Forestry Commission. The mansion house was not large by Dumfriesshire standards and was built about 1840 in the local pink stone typical of the period. It is not a particularly attractive house, but has a nice setting. In addition, the family had a house in Edinburgh at 6 Darnaway Street.

The Seton Wightmans were consumptive, so none of the three boys married and all died relatively young. The estate was then left jointly to the two surviving unmarried daughters, Cordelia and Margaretta Matilda, always known as Meta. After their mother died in 1903, they continued to live at Courance in great state and something of a time warp, and were known in the family as the two 'girls'. Harley could remember Courance as a child, and was thrilled to think that one day this would become his home and he could move back to Dumfriesshire.

Once he had recovered, by now a brevet lieutenant colonel, Harley saw out the remainder of the war in various home postings. Then, after a spell back in Weymouth, he returned to Tarbert in 1920 to command the 26th Highland Mountain Brigade (later 13th Highland Pack Brigade). With a distinguished war record and having inherited the Duror estate from his mother, he was the perfect choice to unveil the Oban War Memorial on Armistice Day, 1923. This imposing memorial in Doddington stone by one of Scotland's leading monumental masons, Alexander Carrick, rests on a high cairn of granite boulders on a promontory overlooking Oban Bay.

After four years in Tarbert, Harley did a short spell in Ireland as officer commanding troops at Loch Swilly. Then it was India and the plum job of officer commanding the 24th Indian Pack Brigade based at Kohat,[10] and later Commander, Royal Artillery, Peshawar. So Harley and Felicia sailed from Southampton the week before Christmas, 1924, leaving Kenny, who was now at Marlborough, to be shuttled round the aunts.

[10] Then a key base on the north-west frontier of India but now a district in the north-western frontier province of Parkistan.

Judging by the confidential reports from his superiors, Harley was extremely well thought of and destined for great things:

Possesses energy, force of character & the qualities to command & lead men – a popular officer, who has the confidence of his subordinates – a fine sportsman.

(sd) H. Cecil Potter, Col. Comdt. Comdg 3rd Indian Inf. Bde.
    Peshawar, 19.12.25

Lt. Col. Macalpine-Leny has commanded his Brigade during the past year to my entire satisfaction. His military knowledge is up to date & sound & he is in himself most reliable & gets down to whatever he is asked to do without any fuss or worry. He performed the duties of C.R.A. to the Blue force during the recent manoeuvres most efficiently & I should always be content to have him under my command in this capacity either in peace or war.

(sd) R. A. Cassels, Major-General, Commanding Peshawar District
    21.12.25

A thoroughly sound & capable Brigade Commander with a good knowledge of his profession – recommended for promotion to Colonel.

(sd) H. W. Newcome, Colonel Comandant Royal Artillery, Northern Command
    9.1.26

I was very struck with the efficient way in which Lt. Col. Macalpine-Leny carried out the duties of C.R.A. at the recent manoeuvres & recommend him for promotion.

(sd) W. H. Kay, Major-General R. A. India
    15.1.26

I entirely agree.

(sd) Alan W. Jacob, General, G.O.C. in Chief, Northern Command, India
    22.1.26

But it wasn't to be. Six months later Felicia became desperately ill with bowel cancer and Harley requested leave to take her back to England. As things continued to deteriorate, she was put ashore at Port Said and operated on in Egypt. Kenny was very excited to learn from his father that his parents were coming home on leave – he had not seen them for eighteen months. But he was shortly informed that his mother was really very ill, and his Uncle Lewen would take him out to see her. The journey was very exciting for a sixteen-year-old, but Kenny found his poor mother trying to recover from a terrible cancer operation, while his father wasted his leave in visits to the hospital knowing there was little hope. Lewen took Kenny to see the sights, including a trip to Cairo and the Pyramids. Here there was at least one amusing incident that he would remember for the rest of his life. They both went to a very formal lunch and Kenny was absolutely hypnotised when at the end of the meal their Egyptian host took out his false teeth, washed them in his finger bowl, and put them back in his mouth again. At the end of the day, there was nothing for it but to take Felicia back to England. When the ship docked at Southampton the General Strike was raging and Harley and Kenny had to carry the stretcher themselves while the dockers looked on. They took Felicia to the Quantock Shuldhams at Norton and she died there on 6 October 1926.

Despite all his undoubted talents, Harley was hopeless on his own. He simply did not have the stomach to go back to India alone, and wrote to the War Office accordingly. This effectively put an end to his military career, and he was made commandant of the Clarence Barracks at Portsmouth. He needed a home-maker, someone to come back to in the evening who could help him bring up his son. He didn't have to look very far. Georgiana Henley had set up house with her older unmarried sister in Norton sub Hamdon and they had settled down to the comfortable life of two middle-aged spinsters. Tall, striking and highly intelligent, Georgiana (pronounced Georgina) had been brought up in Ireland and spent part of the war nursing in Paris. As friends of Frank and Milly Quantock Shuldham at the manor, the sisters would have met Harley when he came back from India and known all about Felicia's sad end. Five months later Harley and Georgiana had started to correspond. Seven months after that they were married at Norton.

Georgiana was very good for Harley. Strong and determined, she helped him to escape the family alcohol problem once and for all.

Although always the most generous of hosts, Harley would remain teetotal for the rest of his life. She also, as we will see, was a huge help to Kenny when he was growing up. Phlebitis as a result of being hit on the leg by a cricket ball finally put paid to Harley's army career, and he retired in 1929 as a lieutenant colonel. They then moved to Long Sutton House, about 7 miles north of Norton. Harley still owned Duror, but he never liked it. He liked it even less when he was forced to put in a bathroom and inside loo into two of the cottages – something he could ill afford. The next time he was at Appin, he went along with Georgiana to inspect the work. When they got to the first cottage Georgiana was sat down in the front room, while Harley went to have a look at the new bathroom. Driving away, he was absolutely furious. 'The bath was full of coal, and the loo seat was missing,' he told Georgiana. 'But didn't you see it?' she said. 'Of course I didn't see it – it wasn't there.' 'Oh, yes it was,' she said. 'It was framing their wedding photograph in the front room.'

Then one day in March 1932, the news reached them that Meta, the younger of the two Miss Seton Wightmans, had died at Courance. Harley hurried north for the funeral, which took place in the Kirkmichael Church at Parkgate, followed by the burial in the Seton Wightman plot in the old Garrel Kirk yard just above Courance. Walking back to Courance afterwards, Harley was startled to find Meta walking beside him. 'Look after Cordelia,' she said, taking his arm. He turned to speak to her, but she was gone. Three months later in June, Cordelia died, and Harley again went north for the funeral. Walking in the grounds before the service, there was Cordelia beckoning him, as if drawing him towards the house. Now whatever else you might say about Harley, he was certainly not the sort of man to believe in ghosts, but he always did after that. Kenny fully expected to see him after he died, but he never did.

Harley lost no time in selling both Long Sutton House and Duror and moving to his beloved Courance, which he had known since a child. Every drawer in the house was stuffed full, but slowly, with Georgiana's help, everything was eventually gone through. Harley became a much-loved and caring laird who was hugely popular with everyone on the place. He was always ready to stop and pass the time of day with any of the men. For all her many strengths, Georgiana didn't exactly have the common touch, and if any of the men saw her they would earnestly concentrate on whatever they were doing, absolutely terrified that she might stop and speak to them. As the only member of an old Dumfriesshire family to return, Harley was readily accepted into local society and enthusiastically set about doing things in the county. But a tough war had taken its toll, and he died at Courance in his seventy-first year in 1951. Georgiana immediately announced that she could not live there without him, packed her bags and moved back to Somerset. In later life she became a much-revered, much-respected remnant of a Victorian world. When her grandson drove her into the local town to go shopping, people on the street would stand aside to let her pass. Back at her home, Manor End in Misterton, she had a rudimentary lift installed after arthritic hips meant that climbing the stairs became an increasing problem. Like something out of *Doctor Who*, a high-pitched whirring noise then a crash was followed by this Victorian apparition appearing out of one of the kitchen cupboards. She continued to hold court until her ninety-sixth year, reading *The Times* every day, but had to admit she could no longer finish the crossword. She was rather apt to hold forth shrewdly at lunch on some item of foreign affairs. You only discovered afterwards that she had read it in the *Times* leader that morning. Her final journey north was to join her beloved Harley in the Garrel Kirk yard.

It is tempting to wonder what would have become of the family fortunes if Harley had been born the eldest rather than the youngest son. To everyone from the people on the Courance estate to his daughter-in-law, he was the most charming man. But the final verdict belongs to Jim Weir, the last tenant of the Garrel Farm at Courance: 'He was a real gentleman.'

12 Officer Leny and the Bergne-Couplands of Skellingthorpe

Kenneth Harley Macalpine-Leny, Kenny to the family, was born at Tarbert Loch Fyne, Argyllshire, on 20 October 1909. He was a sickly child, and by the age of five had somehow managed to survive scarlet fever and diphtheria, as well as an operation to try and correct a double mastoid. The resulting deafness was to hold him back all his life. As he himself was to remark many years later, he had ten per cent hearing in one ear but the other ear was just something else to wash. His hearing improved with modern technology, and in the last two years of his life he could finally hear the birds sing.

Having been brought up in the Highlands, he always wore a kilt, which looked a bit incongruous playing on the beach at Weymouth with his cousin Tony Weldon. In fact he did not wear a pair of trousers on a regular basis until he went away to prep school at Cothill. After that it was Marlborough, and his father presented him with those same two half sovereigns that his father had given him on his first day at the school. To Kenny's eternal shame he spent one in a tea shop in Taunton in the late 1920s, long after they had been withdrawn from circulation, but he was hungry and needed petrol for his motorbike. The other he kept and gave to his own son on his first day at Uppingham.[1] Harley explained to Mr Sandford, the new housemaster of Preshute, that his son was deaf, so needed to sit in the front of the class. But this never happened, and Kenny spent most of the next four years at the back of every class sending ink pellets up to the ceiling out of sheer boredom.

One day there was a knock on the door of the study that Kenny shared with Richard Waddington, and there was the housemaster with his father. Richard could still remember that day almost seventy years later as if it

---

[1] I never spent the remaining 1893 half-sovereign, but gave it to my eldest son William on his first day at Harrow on 2 September 2003, together with a 2000 issue to make up the pair. Jamie likewise was given two new half-sovereigns when his turn came two years later.

THE BERGNE-COUPLANDS

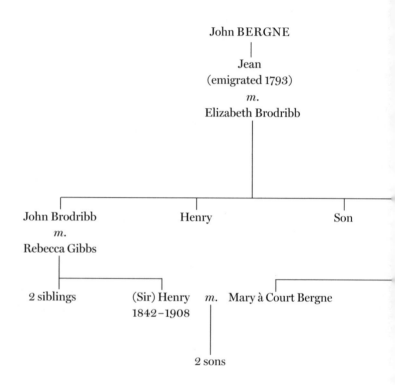

John BERGNE
|
Jean
(emigrated 1793)
m.
Elizabeth Brodribb

John Brodribb   Henry   Son
m.
Rebecca Gibbs

2 siblings   (Sir) Henry   *m.*   Mary à Court Bergne
                 1842–1908

2 sons

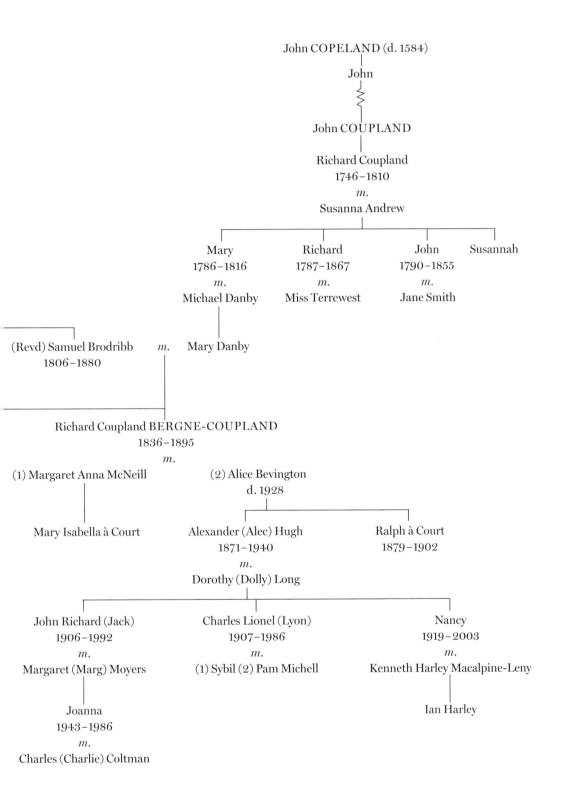

John COPELAND (d. 1584)

John

John COUPLAND

Richard Coupland
1746–1810
m.
Susanna Andrew

Mary
1786–1816
m.
Michael Danby

Richard
1787–1867
m.
Miss Terrewest

John
1790–1855
m.
Jane Smith

Susannah

(Revd) Samuel Brodribb   *m.*   Mary Danby
1806–1880

Richard Coupland BERGNE-COUPLAND
1836–1895
m.

(1) Margaret Anna McNeill

(2) Alice Bevington
d. 1928

Mary Isabella à Court

Alexander (Alec) Hugh
1871–1940
m.
Dorothy (Dolly) Long

Ralph à Court
1879–1902

John Richard (Jack)
1906–1992
m.
Margaret (Marg) Moyers

Charles Lionel (Lyon)
1907–1986
m.
(1) Sybil (2) Pam Michell

Nancy
1919–2003
m.
Kenneth Harley Macalpine-Leny

Joanna
1943–1986
m.
Charles (Charlie) Coltman

Ian Harley

was yesterday.[2] Mr Sandford left, leaving Kenny's father alone with the two boys. 'I've got very bad news for you,' Harley began. 'Your mother has died.' Kenny just looked completely blank, as if he simply couldn't take it in. Kenny hated Marlborough, and in those days, particularly for a boy who had any sort of handicap, it was simply barbaric. Much to his relief, his father took him away at the end of the summer term of 1927.

A stepmother was never going to be an easy thing for either of them, but Georgiana was determined to take Kenny under her wing. She was horrified to find he was virtually illiterate and way behind in every single subject. Shrewdly realising that his one passion in life was motorbikes, she proceeded to buy him motorbike magazines at least to get him reading something. It paid off. Although a late starter, he was highly intelligent and, with the help of a crammer, passed the exams necessary to get into Trinity College Dublin, which was where all his Weldon cousins had been. He loved it, and took a BA degree in Politics, Philosophy and Ethics in 1932. After graduating, he somehow managed to do a spell at Grenoble University, which helped to improve his French. Despite his deafness, he had shown a real talent for acting, and developed a life-long love of Oscar Wilde. The Weldon influence also showed through in some musical ability and it wasn't long before Kenny was playing the ukulele – all the rage at the time, as well as the mouth organ and the bones. But it was a natural ability to write where he really excelled – something else that he got from his mother. He had an infuriating ability to compose verse straight onto the typewriter.

Being an excellent mixer, a great raconteur and a very good dancer, particularly of reels was all very well, but no help in getting a job. He had always wanted to join the army, but a regular commission was out of the question because of his deafness. He then thought of journalism, but this would have meant starting off as a reporter on a provincial newspaper, which was again a non-starter because of being so deaf. A couple of non-jobs materialised before his father realised that he was just beginning to

[2] Richard Waddington was to take a thirty-year lease on the Glenlivet estate from the Crown Estates in 1947 and start the successful transformation of the grouse moor which made his name. He also wrote books on salmon fishing, and invented the Waddington fly. We met for lunch in 1995 after he had spotted my name at the Flyfishers' Annual Dinner, and looked me up in the London telephone book.

drift and go to too many parties, so arranged for him to go out and work on a sheep station in Western Australia. He also thought that the dry air might help his deafness. Kenny was dismayed to find on arrival that it was impossible to buy made-up cigarettes, so another chap on the station had to roll them for him until he had learnt to do it himself. Having once learnt the trick, he rolled his own with St Julian tobacco for the rest of his life.

Kenny returned from Australia towards the end of 1936 to a commission in the 5th Battalion, the King's Own Scottish Borderers, a territorial battalion. So at last began the army career that he had always hoped for, and he became known among his friends in Dumfriesshire as 'Officer Leny'. He proved a natural soldier, and by 1940 had been promoted to captain. Unfortunately the army discovered his deafness in the process and sent him before a medical board. There was no hiding this from them, so Kenny realised that his chances of being sent to France were slim.

On 10 May, Germany invaded France. Two weeks later, the news from France was grim, and the evacuation of the majority of the British Expeditionary Force was completed from Dunkirk on 4 June. It was intended that the 51st Highland Division, who had been fighting alongside the French to hold up the German advance long enough to allow the majority of the BEF to be evacuated, should fall back to Le Havre, but Rommel cut off their line of retreat. Instead they fell back on the coastal town of St Valéry, which they prepared to defend until the Royal Navy could take them off. But despite heroic resistance, a shortage of ammunition and supplies and the German army being in position to shell the town from the surrounding high cliffs meant that rescue was impossible. Major General Victor Fortune had no alternative but to take the difficult decision to surrender on 12 June. The general and more than eight thousand officers and men were taken prisoner. Meanwhile, in a desperate attempt to keep the French in the war, Churchill ordered the 52nd Division to Cherbourg. This included the 4th and 5th Battalion King's Own Scottish Borderers (KOSB).

The commanding officer of the 5th Battalion, Lieutenant Colonel K. A. T. McLennan, sent for Kenny on 8 June and asked if he had heard any more from the doctors. He hadn't. The CO then asked him what he wanted to do. Kenny answered that he would like to go to France with the battalion. McLennan replied that if he was in such an almighty hurry he could go there at 7am the next day as battalion advance party. Kenny was given a packet of sealed orders, and went off happily to look for a truck, driver and batman. He also went to rather a good dance that night on the strength of it.

The little convoy set off for Southampton the following morning and, although they were not expected, the staff captain, John Sheene, made a great deal of noise and succeeded in getting everyone on to one ship and their vehicles on to another. Their ship was packed with troops – Glasgow Highlanders, all singing 'I belong to Glasgow'. Whenever you hear a disgusting noise like that you can be pretty certain that the morale of the troops is high. They passed another ship coming in and their entire ship's company scrambled to the rail to cheer. Knowing what those incoming did, the sight of fresh troops outward bound must have seemed rather gallant.

They disembarked at Cherbourg the following morning, 10 June, but then had to wait for a day for their vehicles to arrive. As the battalion liaison officer, Kenny was responsible for organising all the local billeting and logistics for the battalion. Although he spoke pretty respectable French, he was assisted in this by a charming interpreter, Matthieu de Durford, who would end up going back to England with the battalion and being one of the first to join General de Gaulle in London. There was slight consternation when Divisional headquarters discovered that all their maps were of the wrong part of France. The problem was solved by Kenny buying a whole load of oranges and exchanging them for Michelin maps with the refugees who were starting to flood into Cherbourg.

Having sorted out the logistics as far as he could, Kenny was ordered to meet the 157th Field Ambulance who were arriving the day before the battalion, and had lost their transport and had no guides. The first person off the train was the former battalion medical officer, Captain Hutcheon, who had spend months trying to get Kenny boarded out on account of his deafness. His face when he saw Kenny on the platform with a map and instructions on where he had to go had to be seen to be believed. Kenny took pity on him and ended up giving him a ride in his truck. All the battalion's transport arrived later that night and with great difficulty, because all the drivers were dead on their feet, Kenny led them to the forest outside Le Mans where the battalion was going to be billeted. He and Mat then returned to the station and spent the night on the platform as the battalion was arriving early the next morning, 14 June. They duly did, and rather grumpily marched the 12 miles to their forest in appalling heat on empty stomachs, arriving safely at midday.

That afternoon Kenny had to take the quartermaster to Divisional HQ. By now the roads were choked with refugees, so they did not get back until midnight that night. By then things had started to unravel in a major way. Paris had surrendered, the Germans were breaking through all over the place, and the battalion was ordered back to the coast immediately. All surplus stores were to be destroyed. No one got any sleep that night, and in consequence, the drivers were completely exhausted. Kenny travelled in the last vehicle with the second-in-command, Major Tom Murray, and they took it in turns to drive. Whenever they found a broken-down vehicle they destroyed it and picked up the crew. It was a long haul, but they arrived outside Cherbourg the following night and slept well at a farm.

The following day, instructions were received for the 5th Battalion to hold the Cherbourg peninsula with the help of the French in a rearguard action to enable the rest of the 52nd Division to withdraw. Kenny was to be divisional liaison officer reporting to General Marshall-Cornwall. He found himself a motorcycle and spent the next day, 17 June, running errands. That evening he was instructed to report to Divisional headquarters on the outskirts of Cherbourg, taking 2nd-Lieutenant John Maxwell and four KOSB policemen who had turned up with him. Needing to find billets for his little party that night, Kenny broke into the roulette room of the Casino. Everything was just as it had been left: chandelier hanging from the ceiling and bogus Louis XV furniture covered in dust sheets. He established his party on various satin couches and put his Li-Lo on the roulette table. The general had said that it was his intention to hold on for three days and evacuate all stores, and Kenny was to report to him at 9.30am.

Kenny met the brigade transport officer in the town the next morning, 18 June, and they went and had breakfast at the club. Everything was as usual, and they had omelettes and croissants with their coffee. They even debated as to whether it would be correct to tip the waitress as it was a 'club'. All of a sudden the war seemed a long way away. The general had a different story to tell. The Germans had spent the night in Carantine. All stores were to be destroyed owing to lack of shipping and everyone evacuated by 3pm. Officers were to be sent out on motorcycles to obtain up-to-date information.

Before Kenny's turn came, he bumped into the Padre and Major Johnstone, who told him that the French had blown the middle of the three roads running into Cherbourg, which was very important information. He set off on his allotted scouting mission, but had only reached the first village before orders caught up with him for a total withdrawal. When he got back to Cherbourg, A company was streaming in at great speed, but two platoons took a wrong turning in Valogues and never showed up. The road was kept open for an extra half-hour, but they never arrived.

John Maxwell and Kenny then set to destroying documents at Divisional HQ. When they had done all they could, they jumped onto the only remaining motorcycle and headed for the quay. The whole town was by now a mass of burning vehicles, as there was no chance of evacuating any of the transport, so everything had to be destroyed. What could not be set on fire was simply driven into the sea. When they reached the quay, the *Manxman* was just casting off, but HMS *Fernie*, the destroyer escort, was still alongside as the demolition crews completed their final preparations to blow the legs off the dockyard cranes so they tipped into the sea. With the motorbike destroyed, Kenny and John hopped onto the *Fernie* as the captain gave the order for the charges to be lit and to cast off. As the third leg of the furthest crane exploded and it toppled into the harbour and the ship started to move off, three men were seen running along the quay. It was Lieutenant Greenhalgh, the medical officer, and two of his NCOs who had gone ashore to recover some medical supplies. Quickly checking his watch to see when the nearest crane would go up and block their escape, the captain gave the order for full astern and they managed to get them on board, and, of all things, a dog. They were not popular. With Dornier bombers flying overhead the ship's guns were swiftly into action, and the escape from Cherbourg harbour was quite exciting. But they made it safely home, with the rescued infantrymen being royally entertained by their hosts in the wardroom. Although a number of stragglers subsequently made it home by various heroic means, Kenny had the melancholy distinction of being one of the very last British infantry to be evacuated from France.

The dog, actually a bitch, was quickly adopted by the ship's company and christened Cherbourg. Having been a miserable specimen on arrival, she soon became quite fat and lived off the best that the galley could provide. Not being able to be officially landed because of the quarantine laws, she lived on the ship, but would always go ashore with the liberty boat. But the day came when she missed the return trip and started to swim after the boat, and was sadly drowned.

The Navy landed their human cargo at Portsmouth from where they repaired to Victoria Barracks, who helpfully organised hotel rooms. Kenny's parents were considerably relieved to receive the following telegram the next day: 'Hopped last destroyer last night Victoria Barracks looks charming very fit and well writing.' The rest of the battalion had been landed at Southampton, so it was a couple of days before Kenny and the other stragglers caught up with them. Thus began a long period of regrouping and retraining for the 5th Battalion KOSB, first in Norfolk and then in Scotland. They would not see active service again until 1944. Unable to circumvent the dreaded Medical Board a second time, Kenny was not among them. He had a long spell based on the island of Benbecula in the Outer Hebrides which built up a large army presence for the remainder of the war, and boasted, among other things, some excellent wild fowling. Then when the battalion was engaged in the invasion of the Low Countries after D-Day, Kenny found himself in Lincoln, of all places, as the adjutant to the Ruston & Hornsby Home Guard. This must have seemed a pretty depressing alternative at the time, but it opened the door to the next phase of his life.

Ruston & Hornsby was founded in Lincoln by Joseph Ruston in 1857 as Ruston & Proctor & Co., a company employing twenty-five people making a small range of agricultural implements. By 1889 it had become one of the largest engineering companies in the country, employing 1,600 men producing traction engines, steamrollers, locomotives, portable and stationary steam engines, as well as a range of agricultural equipment.

Thanks to the sales ability of Joe Ruston, the firm had an extensive network of overseas agents from the beginning which would hold it in good stead. During the First World War, Ruston made all manner of war materials including guns and ammunition, and became the third-largest producer of fighter aircraft, building 2,750 planes and more than four thousand aero engines. At the end of the war came the acquisition of Richard Hornsby & Sons of Grantham, who had developed the world's first oil-engined tractors and locomotives as well as the first fully tracked vehicle in 1905. Sadly, world markets were not ready for this new means of locomotion, and Hornsby sold its ideas very cheaply to the American Holt Tractor Co. – now Caterpillar – and the rest is history.[3] As part of expansion into a number of new markets after the war, Ruston & Hornsby made cars from 1920 to 1925, but could not compete with the mass production of dedicated motor manufacturers. Petrol and oil engines of all sizes were very successful, as was its joint company with Bucyrus Erie, Ruston Bucyrus, making excavators. Then the Second World War brought new demands on the company. Ruston engines powered minesweepers, landing craft, patrol boats and midget submarines; stationary engines were used in every field of operation, and one factory produced tanks. As a result, the workforce reached a peak of ten thousand, and Rustons was the major employer in Lincoln.

For Kenny, life in Lincoln came as a bit of a shock. He was somewhat taken aback to be told in his first week that someone he needed to talk to had gone out to buy some maggots. Until then he had no idea that he had been posted to the coarse-fishing capital of the country. But he had that wonderful gift of being equally at ease with a duke or a dustman, was extremely popular, and so was soon very much at home. The Home Guard Major turned out to be Jack Bergne-Coupland, the works manager, who had been prevented from joining the Royal Naval Reserve at the beginning of the war because he was needed to run the works. They soon became good friends, and Jack arranged for Kenny to be billeted with his mother, who had moved out of Skellingthorpe Hall, and was living at the Wooden House a quarter of a mile away across a 60-acre field. It was not long before he met Jack's sister, Nancy, who drove for the American Ambulance

[3] Ray Hooley, web-based Ruston & Hornsby Company History.

Harley Macalpine-Leny aged eighteen

Captain Harley
Macalpine-Leny, Royal
Artillery, 1904

Saleh's silver *khanjar*, presented to Lieutenant Harley Macalpine-Leny during the Aden Hinterland Expedition, 1903

Felicia Macalpine-Leny, *née* Weldon

Major Harley Macalpine-Leny, DSO, 1915

The Courance, by Lockerbie, Dumfriesshire

Lt Col. Harley Macalpine-Leny, *c.*1946

Kenneth Macalpine-Leny as a young man

Officer Leny

Alec Bergne-Coupland,
Esq., with his beagles in
front of Skellingthorpe
Hall, *c.*1900

Alec Bergne-Coupland, Nancy and Jack

Jack Bergne-Coupland

Lionel Bergne-Coupland

Nancy Bergne-Coupland,
while serving in the
American Ambulance
of Great Britain

Dorothy (Dolly) Bergne-Coupland with *papier mâché* animals in the drawing room of the Wooden House

Dolly Bergne-Coupland and her deterrent to hitch-hikers

The wedding of Nancy Bergne-Coupland and Kenneth Macalpine-Leny, 1945. *Left to right*: Lt Col. Harley Macalpine-Leny and Georgiana, Kenny, Nancy, Pru Johnston, Major Arthur Jardine-Paterson (Best Man) and Dolly Bergne-Coupland

Kenneth Macalpine-Leny with baby Ian

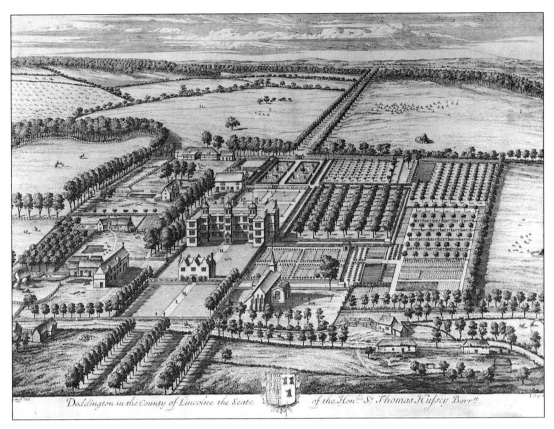

Doddington Hall engraved by J. Kip, 1707; *below*, as it is today

The Old Rectory, Doddington – the south front

The Doddington shoot, 5 October 1957. Colonel Ralph Jarvis, Jack Bergne-Coupland, Charlie Dickinson, 'Nim' Nelson, Newham Cade (guest) and Kenneth Macalpine-Leny

Kenneth and Nancy Macalpine-Leny and Linda shooting at Doddington, 1963

Col. Ralph Jarvis and Kenneth Macalpine-Leny

Kenneth and Nancy
Macalpine-Leny at Addie
Pryor's wedding, 23 April
1960

Nancy Macalpine-
Leny 'picking-up'
with Busy, January
1999

Anne Ailes and Ian
Macalpine-Leny on
their wedding day, 21
March 1986

Peg Adams, Christmas
1997

22lb cock Atlantic salmon, just before being returned to the River Rynda in Russia (photo Araminta Lowes)

Pheasants appearing over the pine trees at Edwinsford, near Talley, Wales (photo John Perry)

Another high Edwins-
ford pheasant lives to
fly another day (photo
John Perry)

William and Jamie
Macalpine-Leny

of Great Britain, when she was home on leave from the Military Hospital. It is time we took a look at the Bergne-Couplands.

The Couplands, originally spelt Copeland, were farming at Skellingthorpe outside Lincoln in the middle of the sixteenth century. Interestingly, John Copeland of Skellingthorpe had, among other things, a registered swan mark.[4] By the end of the fourteenth century, the practice of keeping semi-domesticated mute swans had become widespread in certain parts of England, particularly the Fens, East Anglia and on the Thames. Where a number of owners kept their birds on the same stretch of water it was obviously important to be able to distinguish one from another. This led to the practice of marking the birds, usually on the upper mandible, with a pattern unique to their owner, analogous to the branding of horses and cattle. Swans were valuable both as food and gifts, so theft was not at all unusual. When John Copeland died in 1584, his swans were inherited by his son, another John, and the original swan mark 'differenced' by the addition of a cross near the base of the bill. There were certainly Couplands in Skellingthorpe at the beginning of the seventeenth century, but because the church records were badly damaged when the church caught fire on 2 April 1916,[5] there were no more Couplands recorded in Skellingthorpe until the end of the eighteenth century. By then the family farmed at Heighington, Waddington and Washingborough as well as Skellingthorpe, all villages near Lincoln. They clearly prospered because Skellingthorpe Hall was built on the site of a much earlier farmhouse as an imposing gentleman's residence in 1812, complete with lodge and front and back drives, by John Coupland, a Lincoln maltster. He left Skellingthorpe to his older brother, who in turn would leave it to his great-nephew, Richard Coupland Bergne.

The Bergnes were French Huguenots who came to England in 1793 to escape the Reign of Terror in France. Jean Bergne was naturalised in 1794 by Private Bill in the House of Lords and went on to marry a Lincolnshire girl, Elizabeth Brodribb. They had four sons. The eldest, John Brodribb Bergne, became head of the Treaties Department at the Foreign Office; the

---

[4] N. F. Ticehurst, *The Mute Swan in England* (Cleaver-Hume Press, 1957).

[5] The fire was always supposed to be caused by enemy incendiaries, but was actually caused by what the vicar called the 'heating apparatus'. He had complained to the boy who stoked the boiler that the church was cold, and the boy in question vowed that the vicar would never complain again (Cyril Taylor, personal communication, 1967).

youngest, Samuel Brodribb Bergne, was a Congregational minister in Lincoln. Samuel married Mary Danby, whose mother, another Mary, was a sister of John Coupland who built Skellingthorpe Hall. To complicate matters further, one of John Brodribb's sons, Henry, later Sir Henry Bergne, head of the Commercial Department at the Foreign Office, married his first cousin Mary à Court, daughter of the Rev. Samuel Bodribb Bergne. Insanity, never far below the surface with the Bergnes, was given yet further encouragement.

Samuel's eldest son, Richard Coupland Bergne, was an intelligent young man. He had a good knowledge of the Scriptures and ancient history, and had studied both Latin and Greek. He had always known that he would inherit the Coupland farms, so had a keen interest in farming from an early age. He was also blessed with a good sense of humour. When he was twenty-two, his father, who had many friends and contacts in Europe through his ministry, took him on the Grand Tour to the Holy Land. They left London on 17 August 1859 and travelled by train and steamer to Paris. Then it was on to Mâcon, then Turin, Milan and Venice. In parts of Italy the railway had been destroyed during the war with Austria, so the party had to resort to stagecoaches. Everywhere they stopped, Richard was eager to look at the great buildings, particularly the cathedrals and churches, and works of art, especially pictures. After Venice they took a steamer to Trieste and made the mistake of going to the Hotel de Ville for dinner: 'a most execrable hotel and ruinous charges'.

The first of September found the party in Vienna, but being a keen shooting man, Richard's 'thoughts today are more of partridges than anything else. I rather sigh after my gun and old Rake.'[6] At Budapest they boarded a steamer and sailed down the Danube, transferring to a smaller steamer at one point to negotiate some rapids. Two days later they arrived at the port of Galaez where they were to change for a sea-going steamer to take them down the Black Sea to Istanbul. Richard found Galaez to be 'a most filthy place. Even after this long dry time there a pools of liquid filth in the streets a foot and a half deep. In one of the streets there was a very large heap of manure of the filthiest description; at one end of the heap was a cow, a pig and some fowls; at the other end the owner (I suppose) of

[6] Richard C. Bergne, *Rough Notes of a Pleasant Tour from West to East, 1859*, unpublished.

the manure, the cow, pig and fowls was lying taking his morning nap. He was stretched full length on the heap with his face on it.'[7]

Much to Richard's disappointment the Bosphorus was covered by a thick blanket of fog when they arrived, but by the time they reached their hotel in Pera (now Beyoğlu) they had the most magnificent view of Stamboul and the Bosphorus. Over the next eleven days he would see many of the major buildings of Constantinople, and spend hours haggling in the bazaars to buy various bits and pieces. On one morning their party turned out to see the Sultan[8] go to Mosque. 'He rode a quiet bay horse and was surrounded by a body guard on foot. The Sultan is a small pale man. He looks excessively sulky, worn out and all used up. No wonder he looks so ill leading the debauched life he does. He was very plainly dressed – white trousers, black frock coat and red fez, a large black cloak with a very large clasp of gold set with jewels.' Richard didn't think much of the Turks. He goes on:

The Turks set no value on time and I should think there is no word in the language for punctuality. They are a slow, stolid, immoral race. Statistics tell you that they are dying off fast; infanticide is very common. I am told that few Turks have more than two or three children – the rest are strangled when young. It is a great pity that so fine a country should be so wretchedly mismanaged; the land is fertile and naturally there is everything that a nation could desire. The Government is rotten and the people lazy. Fancy a government imposing a duty of 5% on imports and 10% on exports – taxing every tree that is planted too. This is what the Turkish Government does and the wonder is that with this sort of ruling it has stood so long. As for the Courts of Justice I can learn but little of them. It is with great difficulty that a man can be brought to trial; he is put in prison for some real or imagined offence and there he is left to languish without his case being heard. If he is brought to trial for a serious offence he is persuaded by ever means to confess. He is cajoled by promises of all sorts, patted on the back, threatened, bullied and in the end often gets so confused that he promises to confess on condition of receiving his pardon as promised. His pardon is made out in due form, signed, sealed and delivered to him. The poor wretch on the

[7] Ibid.
[8] Abdülmecid I, who reigned from 1839 until his death in 1861.

strength of this confesses and is immediately led off to be strangled or drowned in the Bosporus!

Then on Sunday, 18 September 1859:

We were rather startled this morning at breakfast to learn that a plot of a most serious nature had just been discovered and quashed. A large number of conspirators had determined to murder the Sultan and all his ministers and pitch into the Christians in Pera afterwards. The priests and the military seem to have been the originators of the plot. The priests are disgusted to see the Sultan's liberality to Christians and the soldiers have not been paid for a long time. Thirteen of the chiefs have been taken and no doubt ere this made acquaintance with the Bosporus. There will be no public executions as the Sultan cannot be induced to sign a death warrant – but the Pachas have no scruples and will drown and strangle without mercy. Not long ago an English ship in the Bosporus brought up two priests with the anchor.

The next day they heard that three hundred conspirators had been drowned the previous night.

In Athens they took horses and climbed Mount Pentelicus about 10 miles out of the city, where the marble was quarried to build the ancient city. On the return journey, they met the king and queen,

. . . riding attended by six or eight ladies and gentlemen and a few grooms. The Queen is rather stout and red faced, certainly not good looking. She was very plainly dressed in a grey habit and felt hat. The King who is by no means a beauty was dressed in regular Albanian costume. My bow was returned in the most gracious manner by both their majesties . . . The king seems to be an indolent shilly shallying sort of man. I am told that he can scarcely be got to sign the necessary documents. The saying here is 'The King reads everything and signs nothing, the Queen reads nothing and signs everything.' Rather difficult to say which extreme is the worst; they seem to be almost as well matched as the immortal Jack Sprat and his wife.

After eight days in Athens they set sail for Smyrna (now Izmir) on the west coast of Turkey. Their stay in this city was somewhat blighted by their accommodation: 'The only place for unfortunate travellers in Smyrna is the boarding house of a Madame Girot or Giraud. A more wretched place could not be; dirty and filthy and comfortless. Our hostess is a fat, dirty, noisy old woman; walking weight I should say 17 stones, wearing a huge chestnut-coloured wig and occupying her time in abusing the servants in the shrillest of voices.'

On leaving Smyrna the party called briefly at Larnaca in Cyprus before disembarking at Beirut. This was to be the start of their overland journey to Jerusalem which would take them through Baalbek, Damascus, Nazareth and Samaria. Richard's father had the foresight to have saddles sent on ahead – very important as the ladies in the party would be riding side saddle. Their first task was to hire a dragoman to be in charge of their expedition, and they selected one Abdullah Joseph, who proved to be an excellent choice. In addition to Abdullah their party would be swelled by the addition of two servants and four muleteers and consist of a total complement of twenty-one horses and mules.

After an eventful fifteen days they arrived in Jerusalem. At one point three Bedouin Arabs with guns at the ready came out of a hiding place and walked swiftly towards them. Abdullah who was leading the party immediately drew his gun and cocked it, and Richard who was riding last cocked both his pistols. The moment they saw that the party was armed and not afraid to fire on them the Arabs halted for a moment, and then swiftly walked away. Abdullah said afterwards if they had not been armed and prepared to shoot they would have been robbed and beaten at the very least.

Jerusalem was rather a disappointment. It was ruinous and the fleas were worse than anything yet encountered. The city had not benefited from being under Turkish rule; the general way things worked was for the Turkish soldiers to collect the taxes. If an unfortunate citizen could not pay, the soldiers quartered themselves in his house and ate his victuals until he could. Having paid the appropriate bribes to obtain a safe passage up to the Jordan, the party set off, and of course, Richard swam in the famous river. They then returned to Jerusalem. As his subsequent diaries have not survived we know nothing more of the return journey to

England, other than the fact that they all lived to tell the tale.

Richard's travel diaries contain many references to the physical attributes of the various women they encountered on their travels, so it was hardly surprising that two years after returning home, he married Margaret Anna McNeill of County Antrim. A daughter, Mary Isabella à Court, was born two years later, and then two years after that, Margaret died, probably in childbirth. She was only twenty-eight. The following year, Richard's great-uncle died, leaving him Skellingthorpe with the stipulation in his will that he take the additional name of Coupland. Thus in 1868 Richard became Richard Coupland Bergne-Coupland. Two years later he married Alice Bevington from Streatham. When she moved to Skellingthorpe she celebrated the fact by taking all the family furniture out to the shrubbery and burning it. That partially explains why the Bergne-Couplands never had any particularly good furniture. Richard and Alice went on to have two sons, Alexander Hugh, born in 1871, and Ralph à Court, born in 1879. Ralph died after a mountaineering accident in Switzerland when he was twenty-three; Alec inherited Skellingthorpe when his father died in 1895.

Alec was an extremely keen sporting man who had a great gift with both horses and dogs. He never did learn to drive a car. When he was a young man he had his own pack of beagles, but these were among the first things to go in the economy necessary for married life. He almost certainly met Dorothy (Dolly) Long out hunting, the highly talented and extremely independent fourth daughter of the Rev. Hamilton Long, long-time vicar of Swinderby, some 9 miles from Skellingthorpe.

Charles Hamilton Kellet Long was the second son of an old Norfolk family whose family home was at Dunston, outside Norwich. A new Dunston Hall had been built in 1845 by Hamilton's father to replace a much older building on the estate. But like so many families, the Longs did not prosper, not helped by a strong line of insanity running through the family. Despite more than twenty grandchildren, after two generations the Longs of Dunston had ceased to exist. The eldest son, Fortescue, was declared insane in 1877 and spent the remainder of his life in various mental institutions. Both Hamilton and his younger brother Ernest followed family tradition and went first to Harrow and then into the Church after university – Hamilton following his father to Trinity College, Cambridge, while his brother went to Christ Church, Oxford. It was said at the time that the Longs were either vicars or mad or both, and there was a certain amount of truth in that.

While at Cambridge, Hamilton showed a considerable gift for all forms of games, and represented Cambridge at the Inter-University Sports in 1866 and 1867. In 1866, he ran a dead heat in the 2 Miles with the celebrated Oxford runner, Lang, which caused immense confusion among the wildly cheering supporters at the finish line.[9] He would go on to be the highly respected and much-loved vicar of Swinderby for thirty-five years. During this time he carried out a complete restoration of Swinderby Church. Very much the parson-squire, he rode to hounds and was captain of the local cricket team. He always had a keen interest in woodcarving and employed people in his workshop to produce furniture for both the vicarage and the village. One of the highlights of the church year was the summer fête, an all-day affair culminating in a pageant involving members of the village and the vicar's eight children, and usually the vicar himself. One year it was Cowboys and Indians in the very best tradition, with 'An attack on a Settler's hut'. When the rescuing cowboys galloped across the field to avenge the scalped settler's family they were led by the familiar figure of the vicar on a black pony, who, on being killed by one of the Indians, proceeded to throw himself off his horse most convincingly. His parishioners loved it.

Hamilton and his wife produced three boys and five girls; Dolly was the only one of the girls to marry. The eldest son, Ernie, went out to Canada to seek his fortune in the Klondike Gold Rush. He did not find it, and would show up at Skellingthorpe several years later with only the clothes that he stood up in and no shoes. Edward, who came next, rather rashly married a first cousin. They had a mentally disabled son Hugh, and then Marie died giving birth to Malcolm, their second son. She was eighteen. Malcolm contracted measles during an epidemic at his prep school[10] and died when he was twelve. After their Uncle Fortescue finally died in 1933, Edward and

[9] The silver tankard he was presented with to commemorate the event is at Doddington to this day.

[10] Taverham Hall, the author's own prep school.

Hugh moved into the hall and ended up living in four rooms in considerably reduced circumstances. Edward had been chief electrical engineer to Vickers at Barrow-in-Furness and, following in his father's footsteps, a very keen cricketer. 'Daddy' Long, as he was always known in cricketing circles, was one of the last survivors of the underarm bowlers. He appeared several times for Lincolnshire in the Minor Counties competition, represented Leicestershire Seconds, and in 1923 played six matches for Norfolk. His final appearance in a senior match was for Norwich Wanderers against one of the Cambridge colleges just after the Second World War. Meanwhile, Hamilton's third son, Walter, had followed family tradition by going into the Church. After Edward died, Dunston Hall and the estate, with the exception of the Manor and 4 acres, were sold. Hugh, who could not look after himself, was cared for by a family on the estate who moved with him into the manor until he died. And that was the end of the Longs. Today, Dunston Hall is a very smart five-star De Vere hotel.

Dolly married Alec Bergne-Coupland on 26 September 1905. He was thirty-four and she was twenty-five. A quiet man with a very dry sense of humour, he was rather overshadowed by his new wife. She had studied art under the up-and-coming animal painter Lucy Kemp-Welch, and was already a very talented woodcarver. Setting out in life with the philosophy that you must be able to do everything, she proceeded to do just that. She was a good shot, an extremely elegant side-saddle rider and knew a lot about dogs. But it did not stop there; she was extremely good with her hands, and could make anything, and mend anything, whether it was a spot of mechanics or changing tap washers. And she became one of the first lady bell-ringers. In consequence she could not have been that easy to live with, but they managed. She did have time to have children: John Richard, always known as Jack, was born in 1906, and Charles Lionel (Lyon) in 1907. Then after a gap of twelve years, very much as an afterthought, came Nancy.

When Nancy was born in 1919, the family were living at Nettleham Field, a farm a couple of miles to the east of Lincoln. But they needed to be nearer Skellingthorpe, so shortly thereafter they purchased a wooden house complete with stabling. This had to be dismantled before being taken to Skellingthorpe and re-erected half a mile from the hall across a field. The Wooden House was soon the home of numerous horses, goats, dogs and animals of every description that the boys had captured on their various excursions into the Lincolnshire countryside. Dolly bred greyhounds, and even ran boarding kennels for a time, while Alec looked after the family farms at Skellingthorpe, Washingborough, Branston and Heighington. One night a car that had been garaged in one of the stables caught fire, taking a substantial amount of the stabling with it. Dolly would remain in fear of fire for the rest of her life.

After Alec's mother finally died in February 1928 the family moved up to the hall and the Wooden House was let. For all her energy and capabilities, Dolly was essentially an outdoor person and had no interest in indoor comforts. She was also heavily involved with village life, and above all, the church. She started the Women's Institute and the Nursing Association, and raised the money for the building of the village hall. She was always one of the first to visit anyone in the village who was ill or in trouble, usually on a horse. But in consequence, living at the hall was fairly basic. It had also become somewhat run-down, and the roof leaked in various places. Nancy always remembered the buckets in strategic places, each giving a different sound as it caught the drips. In addition, Dolly economised on staff by taking on inexperienced young girls and training them up. But despite all this, life at Skellingthorpe Hall was always fun – Jack and Lyon made sure of that, as we will see.

Alec suffered from angina, which could not be treated in those days, so progressively gave up farming in the 1930s by either giving up the tenancies or selling his own farms to his tenants. As he never drove, Nancy would drive him round his farms after passing her driving test on her seventeenth birthday. Then one day in the summer of 1940 he had a heart attack while feeding the hens, and that was that. Dolly had been up all night with a sick horse and Mr Hamilton, the vicar, was in tears. Alec's new daughter-in-law would never forget it, and was left wondering what sort of family she had married into.

Dolly moved back to the Wooden House and, at the age of sixty, threw herself into the war effort. The Saucepans for Spitfires campaign had just been launched, and soon there wasn't an aluminium saucepan left at the hall or the Wooden House. Old wrought-iron gates and railings soon

disappeared, and it was even rumoured that Dolly had sold all her jewellery to donate to the war effort. She became a salvage officer and tackled
her new responsibilities with characteristic gusto. Appalled by how much
people threw away, even in wartime, she had an idea, which bore fruit after
the war when she started to experiment with making life-sized dogs out of
papier-mâché. By incorporating old flat irons to give them weight, these
made excellent doorstops, and she soon discovered there was a ready market out there. These she started to sell to raise money for her favourite
charity, the RSPCA. Her concern for sick or maltreated animals was even
greater than for humans, and she was only too prepared to shoot a badly
injured dog that had been run over, or dispense with unwanted cats in her
'lethal chamber' with aid of the appropriate amount of cyanide. She had
started the Mid Lincolnshire branch of the RSPCA in the mid-1920s and
remained its chairman until she died. She would be horrified to think that
the charity which had originally been started by three Masters of Fox
Hounds would eventually join the anti-hunting lobby.

Not content with turning out doorstops, she tried her hand at bigger
and bigger animals. Soon the drawing room of the Wooden House boasted
a tiger, a donkey complete with trappings, a kangaroo with her baby in her
pouch, a polar bear and even a giraffe. Rigidity was given to these larger
models with clever use of bits of old television aerials, and the horses were
even strong enough for the children to ride. The larger animals really came
into their own on RSPCA flag days when they were strategically placed
throughout the city. These drew surprised crowds of shoppers and inquisi-
tive children, and the RSPCA collection boxes benefited accordingly.

The larger animals had other uses. The family decided when Dolly
reached eighty that she was becoming something of a liability driving
around in her large old Wolseley – even perched on a large pile of cushions
she could only just see over the dashboard. So she was given one of the new
Minis. Hitch-hikers were a problem when she drove to Norfolk to stay
with her brother, Walter, so she solved it by putting a chimpanzee in the
front passenger seat. The back of her Mini boasted a large dent. She hadn't
backed into anything, but always forced it shut with her knee trying to
cram too much into the undersized boot. Driving with her was always an
experience, even in the Mini. Once going into Lincoln with her grandson

she decided she needed to return to Skellingthorpe and started to do just that. 'But Granny,' he protested, 'you can't do a U-turn in the middle of the High Street.' 'Don't worry,' she said, performing the manoeuvre in one, 'they all know me here.'

With her artist's eye, Dolly became a collector long before it was fashionable and when things could still be bought for a few shillings. She built up a large collection of Staffordshire greyhounds and horses, and a collection of Staffordshire cow cream jugs which, much to the family's horror, she gave to the Usher Art Gallery in Lincoln. She was extremely generous both to Lincoln Cathedral, where she had been confirmed by one of its most famous bishops, Edward King,[11] and Skellingthorpe Church. It was all the family could do to prevent her propping up the Cathedral singlehanded. Her lasting gift to Skellingthorpe Church was a new stained-glass East Window to replace the one lost in the 1916 fire.

She always kept her sixteen-bore shotgun handy in her bedroom to pot the occasional rabbit which dared to venture onto the lawn. One foggy November night, some unfortunate motorist became completely lost and eventually stumbling on the Wooden House, knocked on the front door. Always frightened of burglars, Dolly opened her bedroom window and fired both barrels into the night. The unfortunate motorist was never seen again. She continued to ride until well into her eighties, and shot a brace of partridges in the field next to the Wooden House not many months before she died at eighty-eight.

Jack and Lyon grew up doing all the things that country boys do. With their great friend Denzil Wright from nearby Brattleby, they fished in Lord Liverpool's lake at Hartsholme; they drove starlings over hedges and shot them with a .410 (they behave exactly like driven partridges); they made a collection of birds' eggs; they collected caterpillars and hatched them into butterflies and moths, and they kept ferrets. What they did not do, except under extreme duress, was to go anywhere near a horse. After prep school at Bramcote they were both sent on to Uppingham, together with the occasional ferret.

Jack left Uppingham in the summer of 1924, and was accepted as an apprentice at Ruston & Hornsby in Lincoln. He would leave forty-three

[11] Bishop of Lincoln 1885 to 1910.

years later as deputy managing director. He started off by bicycling into Lincoln from Skellingthorpe every morning. When he graduated to his first car – a very small Austin Seven, his 6 feet 7 inches presented a problem, quickly solved by removing the front seat and driving from the back. Once he got to grips with engineering, there was no stopping him. He built one of the first motorboats ever seen in Lincoln out of an old flying-boat hull, and the maiden voyage was on the Fossdyke Canal.[12] This, hardly surprisingly, attracted a huge amount of attention from everyone on the canal bank. The two brothers had the foresight to put together a picnic lunch worthy of the occasion, but a problem arose when faced with cocking their legs afterwards under the gaze of so many excited onlookers. This was solved by reusing the pint beer bottles from the picnic, which in those days came with a screw-top stopper. Imagine their horror when at Sunday lunch at the hall with their grandmother the following day, the same beer bottles were produced and put on the table. Life was tremendous fun, and the two boys lived it to the full.

After a five-year apprenticeship in Lincoln which typically included playing cricket for the Oil Engine Shop Eleven, Jack did a spell in Ruston's Manchester office. Then it was out to the Far East, where he spent a fascinating time, initially in Shanghai, setting up new Ruston agencies in China. By 1933 he had moved to Hong Kong, and was appointed Ruston's resident representative in the Far East in 1936. Good-looking, immensely popular, and with a huge capacity for fun and hard work, Jack would stand out in any crowd, quite literally. His detailed account of setting up and installing two Lister diesel generating plants 200 miles inland at Luichow in the centre of Kwangasi Province in early 1934 gives a very good idea of what life in mainland China was like away from the cities.[13]

The main means of travelling in the interior over the appalling roads was by bus, which presented special problems: 'Apart from the excessive overcrowding, the fact that all women passengers are continually sick makes the journey rather unpleasant, especially when you are in the bus for sometimes 12 hours at a stretch, getting out only when crossing a river

[12] Thought to have been dug by the Romans about AD 120 to connect the River Witham with the River Trent.
[13] Lincolnshire Archives, Misc. Dep. 229/2/7.

or bad bridge with the planking missing in a number of places.'[14] When it came to stopping anywhere for the night, finding accommodation was a particular challenge: 'The Chinese inns in the interior districts are extremely primitive and probably like inns in England some hundreds of years ago. We discovered the kitchen across the yard at the back, in which we found a couple of pigs helping themselves to the food on the cooking benches. There were also sundry pigeons and ducks feeding on the food that was lying on the ground. It is amazing that such good food can be produced from such foul kitchens.' Hardly surprisingly, Jack became an expert on Chinese food. He always maintained that what made the difference between a good Chinese restaurant and a really good Chinese restaurant was that in the latter the waiters always spat into the soup.

Halfway to their destination, they were fortunate enough to meet up with a Ford representative who was driving two Ford cars another 450 miles beyond Luichow, so offered to give Jack and his two colleagues a lift. This produced excitements of a different kind:

After breakfast of oranges and stale bread we started off, having first got our pass to travel on the road. The day was cold and a light rain was falling which gradually got worse until it was a downpour. The road was sand and very bad in parts. As we went further from the river the country got wilder and we rattled and skidded along the track which ran between very fine mountains. The second car which was following us about half a mile behind was fired on by bandits, but the shots went wide and they got away quite safely. We had to be very careful driving as the coolies, particularly the women, would suddenly cross the road right in front of the car. We enquired the reason and it appears that if they have been having bad luck they think there is a devil after them and by crossing the road just in front of the car the devil which is following close behind them gets killed! A driver who knocks down anyone on the road is liable to be shot, and this happens frequently unless the driver manages to run away before the arrival of the soldiers or the local magistrates. Most of the buses go along with the door next to the driver open in order that he can make a hasty exit if anything happens!'[15]

[14] Ibid.   [15] Ibid.

The following year, Jack had a narrow escape when he was ship-wrecked off the Ninepin group of islands east of Hong Kong. Three of them were travelling back from a cruise in US Vice-Consul Merritt Cootes's yacht *Wasp II* when the engine seized and they fell behind the other seven boats in the party. A sudden squall sprang up, and having left their reefing tool behind, they hacked the mainsail down and tried to get the boat into the wind. Every time they did so she was forced over and took water in the cockpit until she filled and sank. They managed to jump clear, and clung to an inflatable mattress which they had blown up. When they realised that the tide was taking them away from the islands they decided they had better swim to Green Island about half an hour away. After two hours in the water they eventually made it, and spent the night huddled together on the uninhabited island. In the morning they managed to hail a passing sampan, and got a ride home.[16]

While home on leave the following year to be best man at his brother's wedding, Jack met Margaret Moyers at a party in London organised by his cousin Graham Martin. Marg was extremely pretty and soon found herself invited back to Skellingthorpe. But then Jack returned to Hong Kong and she would not see him again for three years. Meanwhile, Jack had got himself engaged and was due to be married in Hong Kong Cathedral. Ever one with an eye for the ladies, he always maintained that sex was a very poor spectator sport. At the beginning of 1939, Jack came home on leave and lost no time in picking up with Marg. Things moved quickly: he broke off his engagement and an elaborate wedding was planned for 4 September. But this turned out to be the day after war was declared, so they had to be married by special licence. The invitations were never sent out, and poor Marg never even wore a wedding dress. By then his return to Hong Kong had been cancelled. With his love of the sea, Jack always wanted to enlist with the RNVR, but Rustons needed him to run the ironworks, so he would spend the war in Lincoln. There was a danger that the army would requisition Skellingthorpe Hall, but fortunately they selected nearby Stone's Place instead, so Jack and Marg moved back from Lincoln. Being very close to Skellingthorpe aerodrome, they had an RAF family billeted on them who had a young son. Even in wartime, some things went on regard-

16 *The Hong Kong Telegraph*, 6 August 1935.

less, including the daily measurement of rainfall in a gauge sunk into the lawn. At one point this started to produce the most highly erratic readings without any obvious connection with the weather. It was then discovered that the little boy was peeing into the rain gauge every morning.

Jack and Marg produced an only daughter, Joanna, a wonderful girl who was everything any parent could have hoped for. Tall, attractive and with a marvellously sunny personality, she made everyone feel better the moment they met her. She married Charlie Coltman the day after her twenty-first birthday and they in turn produced two daughters. Sadly, she succumbed to breast cancer at the tragically early age of forty-two.

Faced with what must be every parent's nightmare, Jack and Marg somehow managed to carry on. Jack had joined the Rustons board back in 1950. He had a real gift for industrial relations and was respected from the top to the bottom of the firm. By the time he retired as deputy managing director, he had left his mark on the entire business. Shortly afterwards he was afflicted by osteoarthritis, the curse of the Bergne-Couplands, and would end up on two crutches for the rest of his life. But that did not prevent him from continuing to fish for trout in nearby Teal's gravel pit with the help of his amphibious car, and keeping up his ongoing battle with the vicar. This eventually ended by bringing the vicar before an ecclesiastical court in his own church. The result was declared a draw; the vicar was not allowed to dig up any of his former parishioners to install a total immersion font in the church, but did not have to reinstate all the pews and the choir stalls, most of which had been given by the Bergne-Couplands.[17] Jack continued to work for the good of the community in retirement and was chairman of the local bench, High Sheriff and a deputy lieutenant for Lincolnshire. He had a huge sense of fun, a cruel wit which was never malicious, and was extremely good company.

His younger brother Lyon was also tremendous fun, but in other ways very different. He was in the running VIII at Uppingham and would go on playing cricket and rugby after he joined the Eastern Telegraph Company, later Cable & Wireless. He had a great gift for writing verse. When Arthur Claire, who clearly had a gift for one or two other things, was a tenant at the Wooden House, Lyon wrote:

[17] Judgements of Consistory Court 29 March 1988, 15 April 1991 and 12 January 1993.

What! Never heard of Arthur Claire,
Who stripped the Bishop's daughter bare?
The Bishop, who was on the rears,[18]
Hearing sounds like fighting steers,
Or Morris Oxfords changing gears,
Forgetting paper in his fears,
Rushed out!

After attending the Eastern Telegraph training school at Hendon, Lyon was sent to Carcavelos outside Lisbon for five years. Here the junior staff lived like fighting cocks on a minimal salary with shooting, fishing, cricket, rugby and tennis and all the pleasures of a well-stocked mess. Carcavelos was where important transatlantic and African cables came ashore and was a major centre for the company. Returning to England in 1931, his next posting was to Alexandria in Egypt in 1933. Here he met and fell in love with Sybil Michell, the eldest daughter of Eastern Telegraph's manager there. Sybil was very athletic and an extremely good hockey player, which made her subsequent crippling with arthritis all the more cruel. After Lyon returned to England in 1936 at the end of his posting, he and Sybil were married on 30 September, with Jack as best man. After a spell in Hendon, Lyon became the first manger of the new Cable & Wireless office in Belfast in 1939 and apart from a spell in North Africa and Italy in the second half of 1944, spent the rest of the war there. Sybil became the Belfast county borough organiser for the WVS, and was awarded an MBE for her efforts. After the war, Lyon decided that a change of direction was called for, so he resigned and bought a 10-acre smallholding outside Heathfield in Sussex. From then on it was a new life of growing loganberries, blackcurrants and daffodils commercially with the occasional pig thrown in for good measure.

Sadly, Lyon and Sybil had no children, because if anyone would have made good parents, it was them. Running a smallholding was a pretty precarious existence, but they always got by with plenty of enthusiasm. Lyon threw himself into local affairs, being chairman of the Rural District Council for three years and a churchwarden for over thirty. He always

[18] Uppingham School slang for lavatory.

maintained his keen interest in shooting and fishing and all aspects of natural history, and was horrified when his nephew gave up a career in zoology to go into the City.

Sybil became increasingly crippled with the most terrible arthritis which she bore uncomplainingly for many years, before finally dying in 1974. After a decent interval, Lyon married Pam, her younger sister. Lyon finally came into a bit of money when his uncle Walter Long died in 1964. For the first time he was able to take his foot off the pedal and relax a bit. A trip to the Galapagos Islands followed in 1968 when he met Lloyd Swift, of whom more later. He turned the top 4 acres of his smallholding into a large pen for ornamental pheasants. A particular Bergne-Coupland touch was to have large numbers of guinea pigs running wild, that mowed the grass paths most beautifully. While Jack was very much the captain of industry, Lyon was more the smaller-picture man, but they were both great fun to be with.

Their sister Nancy was thirteen years younger than Jack. Her mother's idea of a decent education was being good on a horse, something Nancy achieved with ease, and she rode in her first show at the age of two. But she was never allowed to go away to school. In consequence she was educated at home by a series of governesses whose principal concern was to avoid the amorous intentions of her two older brothers. Her elder brother Jack had many talents, but teaching anyone to do anything was not one of them. He gave his sister her first driving lesson and telling her she had done very well, left her to put the car away. Nancy drove it straight into a wall in the stable yard. At the outbreak of war she drove Dr Wells-Cole for a time before joining the American Ambulance of Great Britain as a driver.

The war gave Nancy the education she had never had. She was young, high-spirited and an extremely good dancer, and even learnt to tap dance, which was considered rather *risqué* at the time. This probably attracted the young Philip Mountbatten to her, and she well remembered that she only came up to his tunic buttons when he danced with her. She served in Nottingham, Liverpool and London during the Blitz, which cost her her hearing when her ambulance was blown across Oxford Street by a bomb. Earlier she was supposed to have gone to a party in the Café de Paris the night it was bombed, but was in bed with flu, so survived.

One day in August 1943 she was driving her ambulance between Grantham and Nottingham and came upon an overturned blazing car with two airmen trapped inside. Unable to open the doors, she broke the windscreen with a spanner, and dragged them both out. She applied a splint to a broken arm, gave them both first aid, then delivered them to hospital in her ambulance. Other missions were not so successful. She managed to lose two prisoners in Lincoln when her escort got out to buy a paper and they both hopped out of the back of her ambulance. On another occasion, she succeeded in getting stuck in the middle of the level-crossing gates on Lincoln High Street, which was rather embarrassing. All ambulance crews were instructed to salute the Princess Royal when delivering patients to Harewood House, her home in Yorkshire. Needless to say, the only one who ever met her was Nancy. Stepping smartly backwards to salute, she promptly fell over her stretcher. But the job had its grisly side: she once had to put someone into a sack after he had the misfortune to walk into a rotating propeller blade on Skellingthorpe aerodrome. Never one to miss an opportunity, she whipped in for the Burton Hunt on her day off from the military hospital when they were short of hunt servants.

Kenny suddenly developed a keen interest in horses, and by all accounts was a very good rider. This clearly helped with the ensuing courtship, but from the moment they were married on 2 June 1945, he was never seen on a horse again. The best man was Major Arthur Jardine-Paterson, who had served with Kenny in the KOSB, and would go on to command the regiment. Arthur had had the misfortune to lose the bottom half of his left arm while crossing the Rhine at the beginning of the year. Ronnie Selby Wright,[19] the padre, inevitably known in the regiment as 'Seldom Tight', was standing with him at the time, and had the presence of mind to recover his signet ring. Incredibly, Arthur managed to do virtually everything from tying his shoelaces and his bow tie to opening a bottle of wine. He became an absolutely deadly one-armed game shot, using a pair of sixteen bores presented to him by his wife Fearne for his birthday. After

[19] The Very Reverend Dr Ronald Selby Wright (1908–95) was minister of the Canongate, Edinburgh from 1936–77 (Emeritus), chaplain to the 51st Division but managed to escape from St Valéry, senior chaplain to the 52nd Division, one of the BBC's most successful radio padres, and Moderator of the General Assembly of the Church of Scotland 1972–3.

retiring from the army, he became Lord Lieutenant of Dumfries & Galloway.

Kenny and Nancy's honeymoon started by taking the train to London with many of the returning wedding guests, and spending their wedding night at the Dorchester Hotel. They then went down to Weymouth for a week, which Kenny knew well from his youth. They started married life in the upstairs of the two flats that Jack had created in the servants' wing of Skellingthorpe Hall, which was ideal because they certainly did not have the money to buy a house. Kenny was now the Rustons Transport Manager, having got on extremely well with everyone at Rustons, and demonstrated that he could get things done with remarkably little fuss. On the desk in his office sat a large clock that he had been given by his stepmother's brother, Cecil Henley, the main feature of which was the most remarkable set of Westminster chimes. One day the managing director, Viv Prehn, was on the phone at twelve noon, and the clock burst into life. 'Good God, Leny, where are you, in the belfry of the Cathedral?'

About this time there was a vacancy for a churchwarden at Skellingthorpe Church; Kenny put his hand up and was duly elected. He then thought he had better get in touch with one of his ordained uncles, Gerald Halsey, to find out what his duties would be and see if he had any advice for him. Gerald kindly wrote back at great length, finishing off, 'and be sure you keep the dogs out of the church'. Kenny didn't like to tell him that he was the only person who took a dog to church – his yellow labrador Zena.

The vicar, Mr Pond, had been behaving increasingly strangely, and one Friday night, finally crossed the line. He claimed he had invented the atomic bomb. This consisted of a wing nut on the end of a piece of string, and was activated by turning the lights on and off. Mrs Pond brought him round to the hall as Jack Bergne-Coupland was a magistrate. While Marg kept Mr Pond distracted by feeding him slices of Christmas cake, Jack rang up the Lawn, the asylum in Lincoln, and arranged for him to be admitted. He was clearly going to need some assistance with this, so rang up Kenny in the flat next door and asked him to come and help. Kenny and Nancy were going to Scotland the next day so were already in bed, but Kenny got up and put on a mackintosh over his pyjamas. When they arrived at the Lawn and the member of staff at the desk was confronted by

the smartly dressed vicar wearing his dog collar and the rather dishev-
elled-looking apparition wearing a mackintosh over his pyjamas, he
naturally thought that it was Kenny who was going to be admitted.

A son, Ian Harley, had been born at the end of December 1947, and
Mary Partridge was engaged straight out of the Norland Nursery Training
College to look after him. As Nancy rather feared, she turned out to be not
terribly maternal, and had a dislike of babies for the rest of her life. Arthur
and Fearne Jardine-Paterson nobly cut short their honeymoon, in the
Grand Hotel at Brighton of all unlikely places, so that Arthur could be
Ian's godfather. He was joined by Jack Bergne-Coupland and Kyra Long,
Viv Prehn's daughter. A brother or sister for Ian was planned, but never
materialised.

The end of Kenny's career at Rustons came about in unfortunate circumstances. He had planned to celebrate St Andrew's Day over lunch at
the Station Hotel, which being a Friday and market day, was open all day.
Unfortunately that was the day that an officious Ministry of Transport
vehicle inspector chose to make an unannounced visit to Rustons. Spotting
a couple of things he was not happy with, he demanded to see the transport manager. Knowing what was probably going on in the Station Hotel,
the faithful Mrs Price did her level best to make various excuses, but in the
end, had to send for Kenny. When he returned to the office considerably
the worse for wear, the vehicle inspector was not best pleased and, as his
parting shot, tipped off the police, who stopped and arrested Kenny as his
car weaved its way home. The following morning, Kenny's good friend at
Rustons, Richard Gimson, who had joined the firm from Cambridge after
the war and was a rising star, received a call from Kenny at home. 'Will you
still speak to me?' 'Of course I will, my dear chap,' said Richard, and set off
for the magistrates' court.

There were only two prisoners up before the rather po-faced spinster
magistrate that Saturday morning. The first had been arrested for being
drunk and disorderly outside the Stone Bow in Lincoln. 'Did the accused
having anything to say, Sergeant?' said the magistrate. He certainly did,
and the police sergeant read out a whole string of expletives from his note-
book. She was not impressed, and dealt with him accordingly. Next came
Kenny. 'Did the accused have anything to say?' she asked again. 'No, your

worship,' said the sergeant, 'he blew a raspberry.' 'He blew a what, Sergeant? What on earth is that?' The sergeant made the appropriate noise, and Kenny promptly lost his driving licence for three months. Richard Gimson, who was in the back of the court, drove Kenny back to Skellingthorpe where his brother-in-law, now on the board of Rustons, was not best pleased. A major engineering firm cannot have a transport manager who loses his driving licence, so Kenny resigned.

Such things are soon forgotten. After his father died, Kenny and Nancy wisely decided that living at Courance was beyond their means and had already started to look for a house in Lincolnshire. They did not have to look far.

13 An Island in the Jarvis Sea[1]

In his capacity as a Skellingthorpe churchwarden, Kenneth Macalpine-Leny would drive over to nearby Doddington once a month to collect Mr Crathorne, a retired parson living in the rectory at Doddington, to take the early communion service in the interregnum created by the absence of Mr Pond. He then took him back to their flat at Skellingthorpe Hall for breakfast and drove him home again. One day the poor old boy fell into the drawing-room grate at the rectory and cremated himself, and Kenneth thought the least he could do was to go to the funeral. In an attempt to make polite conversation with Mr Crathorne's two old sisters who lived with him, he asked what was going to become of the house. 'Oh, we think it's going to be sold,' they said. For some reason best known to itself, the Diocese of Lincoln had decided to put every large rectory on the market at the same time. Kenneth bought the Doddington rectory in 1952 for £3,000, a large sum of money at the time. The Doddington estate was the under-bidder.

Doddington, or Doddington-Pigot as it appeared in the Domesday Book, is a small village 6 miles west of Lincoln and $2\frac{1}{2}$ miles from Skellingthorpe. It is dominated by a stunning Elizabethan mansion house, and the history of Doddington is really the history of the families that owned the house and the Doddington estate. This has been documented up to the end of the nineteenth century in meticulous detail.[2] The house was built by Tommy Tailor, a very wealthy man who was registrar to the Bishop of Lincoln and had bought the estate from John Savile, later Lord Savile of Pontefract. Tailor employed Robert Smythson as his architect, who had already designed Longleat, Hardwick Hall and Wollaton Hall in Nottingham. Work commenced in 1595 and, at a time when most people lived in mud-and-stud cottages, the sight of such an enormous building rising up must have been nothing short of astounding. Completed in 1600, the

---

[1] In 2005, the Doddington estate passed through the female line for the fifth time, and is now owned by James and Claire Birch.
[2] Canon R. E. G. Cole, *History of the Manor and Township of Doddington* (James Williamson, 1897).

house is built in the shape of a letter E facing east–west, with three storeys surmounted by three turrets topped by leaded cupolas. The main entrance on the east front is reached through a triple-gabled gatehouse connected to the house by brick walls to form a quadrangle.

Tommy Tailor died in 1606 so did not have much time to enjoy his magnificent house. The estate passed first to his son, and then his grand-daughter, who was married to the Royalist Sir Edward Hussey. Their second son was killed nearby at the battle of Gainsborough in 1643, fighting for the Royalist cause, and his armour, complete with hole made by the fatal musket ball, is on display in the hall to this day. Fortunately, Lady Hussey had not inherited Doddington when her husband suffered heavy fines for supporting the king. Fortunately, too, Doddington did not share the fate suffered by so many local houses – being sacked and burnt during the Civil War. This may in part have been due to the Husseys' eldest son's widow, who had gone on to marry Ferdinando, 2nd Baron Fairfax, General of the Parliamentary forces in the north and father of the famous Thomas 3rd Lord Fairfax, commander of the New Model Army, thus giving Doddington supporters in both camps.

The next great family to inherit Doddington was the Delavals. Sir Thomas Hussey, who inherited from his grandmother to become the fourth owner of Doddington, outlived seven of his ten children, and Doddington passed to his last surviving daughter, Sarah. Then it went to her daughter Rhoda who had married Captain Francis Blake Delaval, RN, heir to the family estates of Seaton Delaval in Northumberland. Francis's uncle, Admiral George Delaval, had bought back the ancestral estate from a cousin in 1717, and immediately hired the leading architect of the day, Sir John Vanbrugh, to build a suitable mansion. The resulting great Baroque palace, built on rising ground above the mouth of the Tyne looking north-ward over Blyth and the Northumbrian coast, was certainly that. A writer who saw it in its splendour described it as follows: 'This magnificent seat has an air of dignity and grandeur which surpasses every other mansion of the north of England; it appears like a vast quarry lifted out of the earth, and fashioned after the most exact symmetry.'[3] Admiral Delaval was a

[3] Hutchinson's *View of Northumberland*, 1776, vol. ii, p. 330, quoted in Cole's *History of Doddington*.

bachelor, and when he died following a fall from his horse out riding after dinner at Seaton Delaval, the estate passed to his nephew. When Captain Francis in turn died, following a fall down the long flight of stone steps that led up to the south façade of Seaton Delaval, Doddington passed under his mother-in-law's will to his second son, John, on condition that he took the additional name of Hussey. This proved a wise decision on her part because the eldest son, Sir Francis Delaval, although kind and loyal to his friends, was an extravagant socialite who lived a life of fun, excess and frivolity. When he died penniless at the relatively early age of forty-four, his younger brother also inherited Seaton Delaval and its related estates.

Sir John Delaval, later Lord Delaval, was very different from his elder brother. From the moment he married in 1750 he used Doddington as his country home. When he inherited on his mother's death in 1759 he set about restoring the hall, which by then was in a ruinous state. He gave the house an elegant Georgian interior, but apart from enlarging some of the windows, had the wit not to touch the outside. In 1761 he put in the grand staircase, and a new floor in the long gallery. Not content with improving the hall, he set about enclosing and improving the land, and then turned his attention to the church, having obtained permission from the bishop to do so at his own expense. A south aisle was constructed, copying the surviving north aisle, and a tower added. This all took a considerable time, and it was not until 18 June 1775 that the church was reopened. But the Delaval family were not among the eight hundred reportedly at the opening service: Sir John's only son was dying at Bristol. When he died at the age of twenty he was buried in a specially constructed family vault underneath the south aisle, and the whole of the inside of the church was painted black.[4] This remained for twenty years, and patches of it are visible to this day. Despite Sir John having seven brothers and four sisters, his only son John was the sole male Delaval heir.

When Sir John inherited Seaton Delaval on his brother's death, he should, under the terms of his mother's will, have passed Doddington on to his next brother, Edward. Instead he agreed to pay Edward £400 a year so he could retain Doddington. He now set about trying to repair the financial damage that his elder brother's profligate lifestyle had inflicted

4 Canon R. E. G. Cole, ibid.

on the main family estates. He rebuilt Ford Castle in Northumberland, purchased the Hartley Glass Works at Seaton and at great expense carried out the plans of his brother Edward to cut a channel through solid rock to make a new entrance to the harbour at Seaton Sluice. He then employed a fleet of vessels to transport coal, glass and other products of the estate to their appropriate markets. Being a man of many parts, he also rented the rectory at Doddington from 1787 to 1804 from the rector, who lived at one of his other livings, so that he could conveniently house his mistress close by. There was always supposed to be a secret passage linking the cellar of the hall with the cellar of the rectory, but when the trench for the mains sewage pipe was dug between the two houses in 1970, nothing was found.

When Lord Delaval died during breakfast on 17 May 1808 at the age of eighty, his titles died with him and his sole surviving brother, Edward, inherited Doddington. Edward Delaval was already in his eightieth year, a Fellow of the Royal Society and a distinguished scientist who is best remembered for designing the lightning conductor that protected St Paul's Cathedral. When he died six years later, Doddington passed to his only daughter, Sarah, who was married to James Gunman. The Gunmans were a distinguished naval family, and James was collector of taxes and Mayor of Dover. He was twenty-five years older than Sarah, and by the time he died in 1824, she had become romantically linked with a dashing widowed soldier, Colonel George Ralph Payne Jarvis, who was governor of Dover Castle. They had clearly planned to get married, but six months later she died of consumption, leaving Doddington to George Jarvis in her will. When Sarah's mother died in 1829, he became the sole owner of Doddington.

The Jarvises trace their family back to the beginning of the eighteenth century in Antigua, an island in the Leeward group in the Caribbean. George's father was Thomas Jarvis, Chief Justice of Antigua and President of the Council, who had bought the sugar-cane plantation of Mount Joshua. This was reputed to be one of the most fertile plantations on the island, and had five hundred slaves on it at the time of emancipation. Old Thomas must have had something about him, because he fathered no fewer than twenty-one children with his wife Rachel Thibou. Of these, George Ralph Payne, who owed his last two Christian names to Sir Ralph

Payne who was governor at the time of his birth, was the youngest.[5]

George came back to England with his mother after his father died in 1785 and, at the age of seventeen, received a commission in the 36th Regiment. He served in the West Indies and Ceylon, and then in the Peninsular War, and was present at the battles of Rolica and Vimeiro under Sir Arthur Wellesley, later Duke of Wellington, and then at Corunna under Sir John Moore in 1808–9. He was promoted lieutenant colonel in 1819. On succeeding to Doddington he made it his principal residence and settled down to the life of a country squire. In later life he taught himself woodcarving, and some of his beautiful oak carvings hang as pictures in the hall and the church. All the Jarvis family were great sportsmen, happy to kill anything. The early family game books, which date from 1830, record bags of fieldfares, moorhens, corncrakes, water rails and even on one occasion a crossbill, in addition to the more conventional partridges, pheasants, woodcock and snipe. On three occasions between 1831 and 1837 a blackcock was shot, which shows how the habitat has changed over the last 180 years. These game books also record the first cuckoo and the first swallow, the number of puppies the various dogs had, and on another occasion, after recording the bag for the day, that 'Edwin [Colonel Jarvis's fifth son and youngest child] was married today.'

When Colonel Jarvis died he was succeeded at Doddington by his eldest son, George Knollis. His second son, Charles Macquarie George, became rector there from 1837 to 1861, and was responsible for extending the drawing room and adding the bay windows to the rectory.[6] Next came Mary Eden, who married Lieutenant Colonel Robert Cole. Their eldest son, Canon R. E. G. Cole, succeeded his uncle as rector in 1861 and is best remembered for his incredibly detailed *History of the Manor and Township of Doddington*. He also went on to transcribe all the parish registers for both Doddington and Skellingthorpe, so obviously had plenty of time

[5] Ibid.

[6] According to Canon Cole (p. 235), Lord Delaval added a new north-facing front (now the back of the house) when he rented it in 1787, and the whole of the new front was added by Col. G. R. P. Jarvis and the Rev. C. M. G. Jarvis in 1840. However, Anne Coltman believes that the north-facing back of the house is much earlier than that, and that the Georgian south-facing front was added around 1780. It is constructed of completely different bricks from the 1840 bays and drawing-room extension.

on his hands. Colonel Jarvis's third son was Henry George, who died serving with the 70th Regiment in Grenada. Next came another daughter, Anne Fector, who as Mrs John Bromhead founded the Bromhead Nursing Home in Lincoln. Finally there were two boys – John George, who only produced daughters, and Edwin George, who had three sons. When George Knollis died in 1873, he was succeeded by his only son, George Eden Jarvis, always known as 'Tuppenny' in the family because of his small size.

Tuppenny Jarvis lost no time in resigning from the XVIII Hussars and taking up the life of a country squire at Doddington. The estate was then a thriving agricultural enterprise of more than 7,000 acres. His life revolved around sport. First there were the race meetings: Lincoln, Doncaster, Chester, Newmarket. Then in July and August the family went to Norway for the salmon fishing. The first of September found them back at Doddington for the partridge shooting, with Tuppenny travelling widely to shoot, and taking Fieldsend the butler to load. Shooting away generally meant staying away because of the travelling time, and Fieldsend was expected to help wait at dinner in their hosts' houses. In addition, Tuppenny had his own pack of hounds, 'Mr Jarvis's Hounds', and hunted the country around Doddington as Master of Fox Hounds (MFH) with the help of two whippers-in. In 1891 he sold half the pack, fifteen couple, to the Burton and half to the Blankney. This could hardly have been for reasons of economy because he went out and bought a steam yacht, the *Elspeth*. In addition to Mr and Mrs Jarvis and three guests, the ship's complement consisted of Fieldsend acting as steward, a footman and lady's maid from Doddington, the captain, chief engineer, second engineer, mate, cook and second cook, and seven deck hands. The first year they went to Norway in the *Elspeth* they left at the end of May and returned to Doddington at the beginning of September. Another year they went up to Orkney, back to Inverness and through the Caledonian Canal to Oban, over to Mull and back down to Southampton via Dublin. On another trip the Jarvises went over to the Scilly Isles and stayed with their friends the Dorrien-Smiths at Tresco Abbey.[7]

Tuppenny and his wife Alice never liked having guests on Sundays

[7] John Fieldsend, unpublished memoirs.

because it prevented the servants from going to church. This was not always an uplifting experience at Doddington because Canon Cole's sermons, which he always read, lasted for half an hour. To make matters worse, Mrs Cole played the harmonium, but so badly that one day old Tuppenny replaced it with a barrel organ. She was furious, and they never spoke again.[8]

Tuppenny died in 1919 with Fieldsend, his faithful butler for twenty years, by his side. He had no children, so the estate passed to his cousin Canon Cole. Cole was by this time long retired and almost ninety, and had no wish to move back to Doddington, so it was agreed that, to avoid further death duties, the estate should be advanced to Edwin Jarvis's only grandson, Charles Francis Cracroft Jarvis. Captain Bobby, as he was always known when he came to stay at Doddington after he returned from the Boer War, had married the former Helen Constance Hunter Blair, widow of Captain Stair Johnston Johnston Stewart. She was fifteen years his senior, but to her second husband's great delight she produced a son at the age of forty-three. Ralph would turn out to be extremely good-looking, highly intelligent and very musical. By the First World War, Bobby was a brigade major in the Lincolnshire Regiment. When it was all over he returned to join the insurance brokers DeFalbe Halsey & Co. in London.

The 1920s were a low point for the Doddington estate. Saddled with double death duties after the deaths of Tuppenny and then Canon Cole in 1921 and with farm rents at absolutely rock bottom, there was no alternative but to sell land, and the estate shrank from some 7,000 acres to around 2,500. After the Second World War it would shrink again to its present 1,900 acres.

The year 1940 saw the arrival of Thérèse de Holtorp. Thérèse's extraordinary story began in Paris at the end of the 1920s. She then moved to Warsaw to leave her past behind and start a new life. Here she married, but the marriage did not last and she was left a house in Warsaw as part of her settlement. However, she needed to earn money to live, so became governess to the Tyszkiewicz family. The Count had been killed in a civilian air crash before the Second World War and the Countess lived on in Warsaw. When the Germans invaded in 1939 she hurriedly moved with Thérèse

[8] Ibid.

and her three young children to their estate in the east of Poland, hoping to escape the German advance. But here the threat was from the advancing Russians, so it was decided to make for the Baltic. It was a fairly simple matter to cross into Lithuania because the Tyszkiewicz estates extended over the border. Thérèse did not have a passport, so she had to be smuggled across at night by their gamekeepers. Eventually they made it to the coast and were able to escape to Sweden and from there to England.

Anyone who had any spare accommodation that they could make available for refugees did so, and so one day in 1940 the Countess and her three children, Isa, Zigmunt and Anita, plus Thérèse, arrived at the Littlehouse in Doddington. After nine months they moved to a bungalow on the Well Vale estate, an hour away but still in Lincolnshire; Thérèse stayed behind as a companion for Bobby's wife, now seventy-six. Eleven months after Constance Jarvis died in 1948, Bobby and Thérèse were married in Lincoln Cathedral. All the indoor staff promptly handed in their notice. Thérèse was still glamorous and an extremely good cook, and she and Bobby had eight very happy years together visiting friends and spas all over Europe.

On the night of 31 January 1953, the combination of a high spring tide and a severe wind caused a storm tide in the North Sea. The tidal surge caused the water level to rise 18 feet above mean sea level, and overwhelmed sea defences, causing extensive flooding along the east coast. At 10.30pm, the telephone rang in the hall.

'*Allô*,' answered Thérèse.

'Madam, this is the police. May we speak to the colonel?'

'But he is asleep. What is it?'

'There is a national emergency. We need to borrow your Land Rover.'

'But Rover he is asleep too. Why do you need him?'

'Madam, we need your Land Rover. There has been extensive flooding and we need all four-wheel-drive vehicles to get through the water.'

'*Non, non*, he is very old – and he cannot swim,' said Thérèse, getting increasingly agitated. At this point Bobby woke up and taking the receiver, discovered that the police did not want to borrow Rover, their red setter, but the estate Land Rover. He agreed immediately and a driver was sent round to collect it.

Bobby continued to shoot until he was eighty. When he finally died in 1957 at the age of eighty-one, Thérèse could not bear to be in the hall by herself, so Nancy had to go and sit with her while they waited for the doctor to come. Every now and then they heard a thump, thump, thump on the ceiling above their head and Thérèse said in the heavily accented English that she had all her life, 'It is Bobbee, he is still alive. It is his stick banging on the floor.' Very nervously, Nancy had to go and check, only to find that it was Rover, scratching.

Bobby was succeeded by Ralph, who had joined the leading merchant bank M. Samuel & Co. when he came down from Cambridge. He had married Antonia Meade, always known as Coney, in 1933, and Caroline had been born in 1935 followed by Antony in 1938. Ralph ended the war as a full colonel in intelligence, and would retire in 1968 as the senior director of Hill Samuel. In retirement he was the UK chairman of the Banque de Paris et des Pays-Bas and one of the founders of the City University.

When Kenny and Nancy bought the rectory in June 1952 it was in a pretty poor state. The roof leaked so badly that Mr Crathorne's two old sisters had umbrellas over their beds. There was only one bath, but perhaps that was just as well because there was no mains water. Mr Lillyman, the under-gardener at the hall, would come and pump water from the well up to the tank in the roof every morning on his way to work. There was much to do, and with building materials still difficult to obtain after the war, it all took time. One of the innovations was to dismantle the rather *shenzi* enclosed passage linking the house with the Victorian kitchen, and turn the latter into a garage. For a house on a relatively small plot of land ($1\frac{1}{4}$ acres), the rectory had an amazing array of outbuildings; substantial stables and coach house, former hothouse, two privies – one a two-seater – pig sty, wash house, game larder and yet further additional outhouses. When the garden and orchard were finally cleared it transpired that it was enclosed on two sides by a brick wall. In the 1930s there had also been a grass tennis court and a beautiful flower garden. Inside, the house boasted an elegant drawing room and dining room and the rector's study. Beneath the house was an extensive wine cellar complete with stone bins. But the most interesting thing was that the main ('new') part of the house was designed as a miniature country house with all rooms leading off a central hall. This was fine until it was realised that the dimensions did not allow enough room for the stairs, which are in consequence incredibly steep. Like many houses of the period, every room, however small, has a fireplace. The indoor staff in days gone by lived in rooms in the attics at the back of the house reached by the back stairs. This part of the house had a very steeply pitched pantiled roof that had originally been thatched. Not large by country-house standards, what then became known as the Old Rectory, Doddington, was definitely a gentleman's residence.

Kenneth decided that one of the things he was going to do in retirement was to make a vegetable garden. With the help of Kemp, the gardener at Skellingthorpe Hall, he set about doing just that. Kemp went home and had his tea at five o'clock and then bicycled the $2\frac{1}{2}$ miles over to Doddington to teach Kenneth how to set the garden. Within a couple of years he was giving vegetables to all and sundry. He always said that he had no interest in growing anything he couldn't eat. The truth was that, being red-green colour blind, all the flowers had to be yellow, otherwise to him they looked the same colour as the leaves.

The Old Colonel, as Bobby Jarvis was known in the village – he had been colonel of the Home Guard during the war – soon realised that Kenneth could be an asset to the village and set about cultivating him. He could read and write, had time on his hands, and above all, held his knife and fork properly. In no time at all Kenneth was playing for the village cricket team, was secretary to the Parochial Church Council, and was parish clerk. There was soon a long succession of coffee mornings and wine and cheese evenings at the Old Rectory to raise money either for the church or the Conservative Association. When it came to replacing the church heating, Kenneth and Nancy spent a lot of time helping to raise the money. Once installed, it always infuriated Kenneth in the days when churches did not have to be kept locked that people would leave the door open, so he sat down and wrote the following and pinned it on the church door:

> The Faithfull comes from far and near,
> To stand and kneel and shiver here,
> Lest he should find his chilly soul,
> In temperatures beyond control.

> But lo, he now can take his seat,
>
> In auto thermostatic heat.
>
> So join him stranger, and what's more
>
> Be kind enough to SHUT THE DOOR!

There was an occasion when Sir Benjamin and Lady Bromhead drove over to Skellingthorpe from Thurlby to have lunch with Jack and Marg Bergne-Coupland. This necessitated crossing the Lincoln to Gainsborough B1190 road at the Skellingthorpe crossroads. All went well on the way there, but on the way back, Sir Benjamin somehow managed to collide with the crossing traffic, and ended upside down in the ditch. Fortunately no one was hurt. Kenneth reached for his typewriter and promptly sent his brother-in-law, a past chairman of the local magistrates' bench, the following:

> At the cross roads it's a sin,
>
> To go and do a Benjamin.
>
> The liquefaction of a lunch,
>
> Can lead to quite a nasty crunch.
>
> And magistrates are apt to frown
>
> On those who motor upside down.

As with large country houses up and down the country, the critical moment for Doddington Hall came after the end of the second World War. They were beyond the means of their owners to maintain, and many were pulled down. Others were given to the National Trust. Ralph Jarvis, now an astute banker, had a preliminary discussion with the Trust, but they were only prepared to accept the house if they were given the land as well. If they reckon they can get the land to support the house, why can't we? Ralph thought to himself. But what really turned the tide was receiving a grant from the government in 1951, under the Bill introduced by Sir David Gowers, to replace the lead roof with copper. The *quid pro quo* for this was that the house had to be open to the public. Initially visitors were shown round by the keeper's wife, but this was not entirely satisfactory, and Kenneth, with his interest in social history and rapidly increasing knowledge of fine arts, was an obvious choice; he was somehow talked into taking the job. In those days all visitors were given a guided tour, even in one case in Kenneth's rather rusty French.

Although he never fished, Kenneth had the keen family interest in shooting and had been given a gun for his twenty-first birthday. In the Courance days his father had one small shoot a year for friends which always finished with a drive in front of the house. One year Kenneth thought he was frightfully clever to drop a high pheasant through the roof of the conservatory. His father was furious. In Lincolnshire he never had much regular shooting until Ralph Jarvis started up the Doddington syndicate. In the old days, Ralph's father used to invite only two guests, invariably Lord Liverpool and Lord Glasgow, and just the three of them shot. But the economics of shooting in the 1950s meant that more and more estates were resorting to syndicates, and Doddington was no exception. This was run in the 1950s and 1960s by 'Nim' Nelson, the 23-stone son of the former Doddington agent.

The tales of the Doddington syndicate are legion. Ralph Jarvis took two guns; then in addition to Kenneth there was Jack Bergne-Coupland and his brother-in-law Gerald Moyers, Richard Gimson, who by then was a director of Ruston, and two local farmers – Wilf Wells and Charlie Dickinson. In those days much of the shooting was done in the large Doddington woods, and on one occasion, as he walked along the line of guns on the first drive after lunch Nim found the guns round a right-angle bend all pointing in the opposite direction.

Jack Bergne-Coupland had a large and very strong labrador called 'Sweep' who was not particularly well behaved, especially if a hare ran through the line of guns. In consequence he was always anchored to Jack's shooting stick. On one occasion a hare appeared which Jack promptly missed with both barrels. This proved too much for Sweep who set off after it, shooting stick and all. As this was across a deeply ploughed field, every so often the shooting stick was catapulted upwards and gave Sweep a crack across his back. Thinking that his irate master had caught up with him, he stopped and sat for a moment before setting off again, when the whole performance would be repeated.

When Kenneth and Nancy first moved to Doddington they brought with them their old yellow labrador, Zena. Dinner was always punctually at 7.30pm and began with freshly made soup. Kenneth didn't like puddings, so after the main course there was always a savoury. When Nancy went into the kitchen to spread the savoury of the evening onto newly made toast, Zena woke up from her position in front of the fire and arrived in the dining room at the same time as the savoury. Here she would patiently sit by Kenneth's chair until he cut off a finger of toast and gave it to her. Then she returned to her position in front of the fire.

Kenneth had continued to roll his own cigarettes with pipe tobacco ever since he came back from Western Australia in 1936, and inevitably this caught up with him. In 1960 he was diagnosed with lung cancer, and had his left lung removed. No keyhole surgery existed in those days, and he ended up with 150 stitches and a very impressive stitch line. As he said at the time, 'Half a crown to see round the hall, five bob to see the hall and my stitch line.' Thanks to taking plenty of exercise walking his labradors, he made a complete recovery, but did not give up smoking.

On 11 December 1969, Kenneth and Nancy had been to Lincoln in the afternoon to have their photographs taken. At about twenty past four in the afternoon, when Nancy was getting the tea ready, there was a loud report from the boiler room where the guns were kept. Rushing in she could see at once what had happened. Kenneth was dead. In the days and weeks that followed there was endless speculation as to why he should have taken his own life, but you can never know what goes on in someone else's head. He had even bought all his Christmas presents. A kind, talented and most amusing man, his life had been unfulfilled. But he had been a good husband and father. If he had been born fifty years later, medical science would have been able to help him to a far greater extent, and the outcome might have been very different. Always irritated by his father's habit of earmarking possible burial spots up and down the country, Kenneth said that he wanted to be buried in the asparagus bed, but when the time came . . .

At times of great tragedy, inner reserves of strength somehow allow people to carry on. Nancy, who never dreamt for a moment she would ever be left on her own, set about making a life at Doddington with the help of a few very good friends. It came to revolve around training gun dogs and picking up on shooting days. She was hard-working, popular and always had good dogs, so she was never short of invitations. She was also one of those people that things just happened to – Kenneth always said that if there was one drunk on the London train he would come and sit next to her. On one occasion after driving a guest gun round in her four-wheel-drive all day she drove home the 40 miles back to Doddington. When she came to unload her two labradors, three jumped out. The guest gun had left his in her car, and was not at all impressed having to drive 40 miles in the wrong direction to retrieve it. On another occasion she was accompanying a gun who had been detailed to walk level with the beaters until he came on to his peg towards the end of the drive. Halfway through the drive he turned to Nancy and held out his gun as if to hand it to her, so she took it, and with that he died. There she was with a dead man whose name she did not even know, and his gun. What on earth was she to do? She couldn't even stop the drive.

Through determination, good luck and an extremely good first labrador called Spider, Nancy became a very useful part of the Lincolnshire shooting scene for thirty years, not giving up until she was eighty. This gave her a wide circle of friends that included a great naval friend of Prince Philip's, who lived on the Sandringham estate. The first time she went there to 'pick up' on what was to become an annual event, she was told that they would be going to have Sunday lunch at Sandringham House. Assuming that it would be a party of forty or fifty and that she could blend in with the wallpaper, Nancy never gave it another thought. Imagine her horror when she discovered they were just a party of ten. Her hand shook so much that she could hardly hold her glass of sherry, and all Prince Philip said, rather unhelpfully, was 'What's the matter, we don't bite.' The queen, on the other hand, was simply delightful and had the wonderful gift of making even Nancy feel at ease. She motioned her to sit down, but there was not anywhere to sit – there was a corgi on every chair. Not that there was ever any doubt about it, but Nancy was confirmed as a life-long monarchist because Prince Charles remembered the name of her labrador from one shooting season to the next. It was no good trying to tell her that he would have received a list at breakfast time of everyone attending the shooting day, complete with the names of their dogs – she simply would not hear of it.

When a new district nurse arrived who knew that everyone over seventy-five should receive a visit, she called one day at the Old Rectory. 'Mrs Macalpine-Leny is very busy, she's plucking pheasants,' she was told by Nancy's housekeeper. Undaunted, the district nurse set off down the garden to where Nancy was just visible in a cloud of feathers. After introducing herself, she set off on her list of prepared questions. 'Can you get out of the bath?' 'Get out of the bath?' replied Nancy, still plucking, 'Of course I can get out of the bath.' Thinking that she would try another tack, the district nurse struggled bravely on. 'Is there anything you can't do?' At this Nancy stopped plucking, and thought for a moment. 'Yes, doing the hoovering.' With that the wretched district nurse turned on her heels and fled.

Very much a Bergne-Coupland, Nancy demonstrated the family traits of being frightened of illness, disliking being on her own, and making an instant decision, never changed, on whether she liked or disliked someone. Needing someone to cut the grass, she happened to see an energetic man mowing the churchyard. Engaging him in conversation, she said: 'Do you know the parson? He's mad.' Now, as the newly arrived incumbent meeting one of his Doddington parishioners for the first time, Richard Billinghurst proceeded cautiously. 'I don't think he is, I'm the parson.' 'No you're not,' said Nancy, in full cry by this time. 'He's mad. And what's more, he's got a club foot.'

As *anno domini* began to leave its inevitable mark, Nancy could not face up to the fact she had become old and could no longer do the things that she had always done. Now over eighty, she came dragging back up the farm track one day with her ageing labrador and said: 'I've got this dreadful thing the matter with my foot, it's absolute agony, never had anything like this before. What do you think it can be?' 'Oh, I don't know, Mummy,' I replied, 'I should think it's old age.' 'Don't you dare say that to me,' came back her reply. On another occasion she said, 'I've been to the doctors at Saxilby and they are completely baffled as to what's the matter with me, what do you think I should do?' 'Oh,' I replied, 'I think perhaps I should take you to the vet and have you put down.' This did not go down well. But when the end came, she showed no fear, and it all happened peacefully and fairly quickly.

Although it was Bobby Jarvis's son Ralph who really turned the ship round and saved the hall for the future, and with his wife Coney worked tirelessly when they were at Doddington, their home was in London and they used the hall as their weekend cottage. It was their son Antony and his wife Vicky who really left their mark on the hall. For thirty years they painstakingly restored the inside of the house and Antony laid out and extended the wild garden. In 2005 their eldest daughter, Claire, and husband James Birch took over, and have taken things on to the next level. With flair, foresight and sheer hard work, not to mention the benefits of James being a retired managing director of Goldman Sachs, a number of additional ventures have been started that both support the house and feed off the visitors to it: a stunning farm shop and café supplied with produce from the restored 2-acre kitchen garden, a thriving Christmas shop complementing the well-established Christmas tree business, and a wedding reception business. All go forward together to ensure that Doddington Hall and the Doddington estate will be around for many generations.

In the middle of it all, calm and peaceful with the flag firmly flying, sits the Old Rectory, which will continue to be the home of the Macalpine-Leny family for many years to come.

14 Go West, Young Man

Most people have an opportunity at some stage of their life to change fundamentally how their future unfolds. This may not necessarily be a blinding flash on the road to Damascus, and often can only be detected in retrospect. Whether or not it is taken depends on the ability to recognise some part of the potential there in the first place, and the initiative to grasp it. Mine came one day at the office photocopier.

I have always been envious of people who knew from the age of two that they wanted to be a missionary or an undertaker. I never knew what I wanted to do. I was good at biology at school, and got an A grade in zoology A-Level in the days when such things were unheard of. So my future career seemed to tend towards becoming either a doctor or a vet. Since I did not like the idea of being a vet – all those horses and cows and things – it had better be a doctor. My father invited the local GP round for a glass of sherry before lunch, and he waxed lyrical about the whole idea, and was kind enough to suggest some medical schools. I duly applied and then went out to stay with school friends in western Turkey for a month and forgot all about it. When I came back I found that I had been offered a place to read medicine at the Queen Elizabeth Medical School in Birmingham.

If I found living in Birmingham a bit of a shock when I went there a month later, it was nothing compared with being a medical student. Dissecting dead bodies was no problem – they were, after all, well and truly dead, and the physiology was fascinating. But it being a go-ahead medical school, the medical students went round hospitals and saw real patients on two afternoons a week. I will never forget going to the accident hospital. Some poor chap was brought in on a trolley writhing in agony, and everyone else gathered round to see what was the matter with him. I just wanted to go out and be sick. After three weeks I began to realise I had made the most dreadful mistake. My nice tutor, Dr Valerie Hind, persuaded me to stay until the end of the term. By then I had negotiated a place in the Biology School for the following year, and so I fled.

The problem of what to do in what now would be called a Gap Year was solved by going back out to Turkey again, this time for four months. My friends' father, Victor Whittall, was the Lloyd's agent in Izmir, so I took him up on his offer to get me a passage out on one of his cargo ships. As the Moss Hutchinson Line was not allowed to carry passengers, I signed on as a member of the crew for three weeks, but waived my shilling a day (this was back in 1967). My time on the MV *Karnack* comprised three of the more interesting weeks I have ever spent, and I will never forget being in the bath during a gale in the Bay of Biscay.

I thoroughly enjoyed my three years at Birmingham, but was then faced with the same old problem of what to do next. My parents always wanted me to be a land agent – 'It's such a nice life' – and I spent three weeks going round with the senior partner of a Lincoln firm. But I was left with the strong conviction that I did not want to spend the next forty years looking over *someone else's* gate, so that was the end of that. Faced with no better suggestion, the offer of a place to do a PhD suddenly seemed rather a good idea, especially when Denis Bellamy, Professor of Zoology at the then University College, Cardiff, offered me a radio telemetry[1] project in conjunction with the Department of Medical Electronics at St Bartholomew's Hospital, in London.

Here I worked with the brightest people I have ever worked with, either before or since, and learnt to build very small radio transmitters. These I put on the backs of redshanks that had been reared from eggs in the laboratory, and on free-swimming tufted ducks at the Wildfowl Trust at Slimbridge, having collected as an additional supervisor its Director of Research, Dr Geoffrey Matthews. As Watergate was going on at the time, when I grew bored I made bugging devices. But the life of a research student, especially one who is not allowed to do any demonstrating to students, is a lonely one and is not for everyone. I well remember sitting in my basement laboratory eating a cold Chinese take-away one Saturday night and thinking there must be more to life than this. What did I have to look forward to? Spending the next forty years in some fourth-rate university teaching a lot of long-haired socialists zoology? And I would probably starve. It was then that I resolved to go and work in the City, and set about looking for an opening.

[1] Literally, remote measurement.

I discounted stockbroking because I had never had any feel for it, and accountancy (wrongly) as being too boring. I could not find any merchant banker who could actually tell me what he did, and I did not have any contacts in ship broking or metal broking. That left insurance, which did not sound particularly exciting. But my uncle Jack Bergne-Coupland had always enjoyed working with Willis Faber & Dumas, Ruston's insurance brokers, so offered to get me an interview. Willis made it sound interesting and offered me a job. The bad news was that, when I was hoping to return to London, I was going to have to train in the Cardiff branch office for eighteen months. But the good news was that I could defer my start date to allow me to complete the second year of my research. When I told my three supervisors that I had accepted a job with a firm of international insurance brokers and would be resigning at the end of September, you would have thought I had said I was going to live on Mars. As so often happens my luck on the research front then changed dramatically and I was able to produce some really interesting work in my last six months. Looking back on it now, this was way ahead of its time. It was all written up for an MSc five years later when I was trying to save money for a trip to India – sadly I had not done enough work for a PhD – and it was even published.[2] The other great thing about having a delayed start date was that it enabled me to go and stay for a month in Kenya with my ancient honorary aunt (see pp. 97–99).

Willis Faber really suited me and I got on well. In those days a graduate trainee was something of a rarity, particular on the retail side,[3] and I was well trained in the Cardiff office. Returning to London in 1974, I was given plenty of scope to learn the business by reviewing a large number of small Japanese-owned accounts that had been rather neglected on account of their size. The first great opportunity came when I was sent out to visit our American correspondent, Johnson & Higgins, universally known as J&H, in April 1979. I was asked to spend a week in their New York head office, and a week in a branch office – would I please tell my managing director,

[2] P. N. Ferns, I. H. Macalpine-Leny and J. D. Goss-Custard, 'Telemetry of Heart Rate as a Possible Method of Estimating Energy Expenditure in the Redshank, *Tringa Totanus*' in *A Handbook on Biotelemetry and Radio Tracking*, ed. C. J. Amlaner Jr and D. W. Macdonald (Pergamon Press, 1979).

[3] The 'retail' side dealt direct with businesses that needed to buy insurance.

Adrian Gregory, which one. After a quick conversation with one of my colleagues, I said San Francisco, and I could tell by Gregory's face that was not what he had in mind, but he agreed. It seems incredible today that I was then allowed to take my three weeks' holiday at the same time, so that I had a week's holiday followed by a week's work in New York, a week travelling around, and a week's work followed by a week's holiday in San Francisco.

As this was my first ever trip to the US I immediately went round the family to see if anyone knew anyone I could stay with. My uncle Lyon Bergne-Coupland had a great friend, Lloyd Swift, with whom he had shared a cabin travelling out to the Galapagos Islands on the *Linblad Explorer* in 1968. The Swifts were only too pleased to repay some of the Bergne-Coupland hospitality by having me to stay at their spectacular home on Lake Barcroft in northern Virginia. Equally keen to repay Bergne-Coupland hospitality was Peg Ailes, who had stayed with Lyon and Pam at the same time as Rose Swift. Peg kindly hosted a dinner at Fort McNair Officer's Club in Washington, and persuaded her daughter, Anne, to come along as well. I can still see the face of the violinist who came and played at our table. At the end of dinner, Anne and I crashed a midshipmen's dance, and had our first dance. Other memorable moments on that trip were hearing on the car radio on the way to Flagstaff that Mrs Thatcher had won the General Election, and taking the helicopter ride over the Grand Canyon. Thinking that I might never come to the US again, I was determined to make the most of it. In San Francisco I was befriended by Charlie Bates and his family, and invited to Janaca, their spectacular ranch outside Gilroy. But in addition to having an incredible holiday, I came away hugely impressed with Johnson & Higgins and all their people.

That morning at the photocopier my rather bluff main-board director, Tommy Thomson, came out of his office and said, 'I want a word with you.' Gathering up my photocopying, I followed him back into his office, wondering what was going to come next. 'How would you like to go out and work with J&H in New York for three years?' he said. 'I would like to very much,' I replied. 'Don't be so bloody silly – go away and think about it.' 'I don't need to think about it,' I said. 'The answer's yes.' Very slowly and deliberately, Thomson banged out his pipe on the glass ashtray on his desk. 'Got any dependants?' Thus it was that at the beginning of June 1980 I moved to New York for three and a half years.

Everyone should go to America. It is the ultimate 'can-do' society, and Americans have that wonderful sense of optimism and a seemingly boundless energy to succeed. This coupled with a directness and genuine friendliness makes it a great country in which to do business. I quickly discovered that Americans liked their Brits to be caricatures, and being a natural extrovert, I was determined not to disappoint them. Addressing my first production meeting in pinstriped suit, blue and white striped shirt, old school tie and red braces, I announced that I had a sense of humour, a hide like a rhinoceros, and was not nearly as stupid as I looked. They loved it. The timing of my secondment was very fortuitous because it coincided with an ever-increasing wave of British investment going into the USA. I fitted perfectly into the role of the resident representative of the British partner in the head office of their American counterpart – the only Brit in an office of a thousand Americans. I loved the people, the country, the culture and the work, and in consequence my secondment from Willis Faber's point of view was a great success. Not only did it open my eyes to an entirely different way of life, but it set me on course for the next stage of my business career. This was to be heavily involved with UNISON, the global network put together by J&H, Willis Faber and the leading independent insurance brokers in Europe.

J&H was the foremost marine insurance broker in the USA and had always remained a private company owned by the working partners. In the early 1950s it had expanded into South America by opening offices in first Brazil, then Argentina, Venezuela and Colombia. Not only did these prove to be very profitable, but they gave J&H the opportunity to reverse themselves into the much more lucrative domestic business of the American parent companies of many of their South American clients. When some of their US clients started expanding into Europe at the end of the 1950s, the partners quickly realised that to maintain the relationship they needed to follow their clients and provide local service in Europe. But the solution of opening up J&H offices that had proved so successful in South America would not work because there were many well-established and very experienced European insurance brokers against which a fledgling J&H office would prove ineffective. As a private company J&H did not have access to the capital to buy one of these brokers, let alone one in every European country. So a strategy was developed of forming an exclusive relationship with the leading independent broker in every country to service the J&H-introduced business in that country. As J&H had very limited contacts throughout most of Europe they turned for advice to Willis Faber in London, with whom they had had an exclusive relationship on marine business for almost seventy years. As a result an informal network was set up consisting initially of Jauch & Hübener in Germany, Boels & Bégault in Belgium, SGCA (later Gras Savoye) in France, Mees & zoonen in the Netherlands, Gil y Carvajal in Spain, Costa Duarte in Portugal and Willis Faber in the UK. There were no insurance brokers in Italy, so J&H opened their own office in Milan. In time this network would expand to provide a correspondent company or subsidiary of an existing network member in almost every country of the world.

As the flow of US business continued to increase, so did the efficiency and cohesion of the informal network and strong friendships developed between the international staff of the various members. Then, at the beginning of the 1970s, European investment started to flow into the US that resulted in a reversed flow of introduced business back to J&H. It was this reciprocal business flow among the main network partners that really bound the network together. By the beginning of the 1980s it was clear that a more united face would be presented to prospective clients if the network operated under a common brand name (the concept of independently owned networks is notoriously difficult to sell), so UNISON was adopted in 1982. It would go on to become the most successful and professional servicing network that the financial services industry has yet seen and, quite simply, the envy of its competitors.

Over the almost hundred years that J&H and Willis Faber had an exclusive working relationship there had been a number of attempts to combine the two firms, often thwarted by poor personal relationships between the respective chairmen. A final attempt was made at the end of the 1980s, but there were staunch objectors on either side and Willis realised that the discussions were going nowhere. In almost undue haste, discussions were opened with a second-tier US broker, Corroon & Black, resulting in the formation of Willis Corroon in June 1990. J&H had no idea about this, and the announcement came as a great shock to the entire UNISON network; it led in effect to the expulsion of Willis. Business managed to continue without Willis, but by the middle of the 1990s, UNISON was in danger of being overtaken by wholly owned rival networks. Part of the problem was that J&H itself was running out of steam. The very laudable practice of always appointing partners from within had taken its toll and, with one or two notable exceptions, the quality of the partners had declined. Although the global business environment was healthy and J&H's short-term future was strong, the longer term did not look so encouraging. Faced with industry consolidation and enormous requirements for capital to fund both technology and expansion, J&H's private ownership presented formidable constraints. To the shock of employees around the world, the board of J&H announced that it was selling to arch rival Marsh & McLennan in 1997, making all the partners multi-millionaires in the process. Within twelve months all the other independent UNISON partner firms had done deals with one or other of the three major global brokers and J&H, once the world's largest privately owned insurance broker and one of the oldest and proudest names in the insurance broking business, had ceased to exist. Its people were swallowed up by the survivors in the business, and its records, like its art collection, disappeared without trace. The tale of all this has been told elsewhere.[4]

One of the many advantages of having an American girlfriend whose family were unbelievably kind and welcoming was that I was able to see small-town America – something that the normal business visitor or tourist from overseas would rarely encounter. What really made the country great was the millions of nameless people in small towns up and down the country who go happily about their daily business: the barber, the gas-pump attendant, the man who runs the hardware store. Many are immigrants, or children or grandchildren of immigrants, but all are now part of the American Dream. For in the can-do society, everything is possible, and the man collecting your trash today knows that tomorrow he might be doing something entirely different.

[4] Ian Macalpine-Leny, *UNISON – the Envy of its Competitors. The Origins, Rise and Eventual Decline of the UNISON Network* (Haggerston Press, 2004).

Anne Ailes' mother Margaret, always known as Peg or Peggy, had been born in Minnesota. In 1939, while in her second year of home economics at the University of Minnesota, she applied to work at the Pentagon in Washington. Her mother was not best pleased, but to a girl raised on a farm in the depths of Minnesota, the prospect of going to work in Washington must have seemed like a dream come true. She went with a couple of university friends and they lived in a rooming house under strict supervision. Starting off in the typing pool, she would end up in the office of the Chairman of Joint Chiefs of Staff, working directly for General Omar Bradley, the last serving Five-Star General. Ever on the look-out for new challenges, Peggy then applied to go out to Japan as part of the Office of Reconstruction under General Douglas Macarthur. She left from San Francisco in a hospital ship with five or six girl friends from the Pentagon and had a fascinating eighteen months in Tokyo. On returning to Washington, she worked for Tom Gates after he became Under Secretary of the Navy in 1953.[5]

I never knew Peggy's husband, Rear Admiral John W. Ailes III, because he had died when Anne was seventeen, leaving Peggy with the problem of bringing up a rebellious and determined teenage daughter on her own. The admiral had very clear ideas about privilege and how everyone should make their own way in the world, so she was never allowed to go to a private school. Instead she went to Laurel High School and then, after an unsuccessful attempt to read medicine, majored in psychology at George Washington University.

After his own wife died, Peg married Rear Admiral Carlton R. Adams, a Naval Academy classmate of John Ailes and old family friend. He retired to Charlottesville, Virginia in 1968. He was a kind man with a wonderful sense of humour, but was very different from his old friend John Ailes.

The first any of Carlton's friends knew that anything was going on was when he was seen driving his 1965 Ford Mustang very slowly through Charlottesville with a blonde in the passenger seat. He and Peg were married in 1982 and had eight very happy years together. Carlton had a nice

---

[5] Thomas S Gates, Jr, would go on to become Secretary of Defense from 1959 to 1961 under President Eisenhower.

house in Meadowbrook Hills and a lot of old Charlottesville friends, and Peg as always was a superb hostess.

Not having been brought up in a military environment, I was hugely impressed with the US Navy, its traditions, its manners, and the members of the Naval Academy class of 1930 that I met. It was just the football games that took a bit of getting used to. So when our engagement was finally announced in *The Times* and the *Washington Post*, I felt immensely proud to be marrying an American from a US naval family.

Peg lived on in Charlottesville after Carlton died in 1990, ever the accomplished hostess, at one point even dating her third admiral. She made annual trips over to London to see her grandchildren[6] and was always very supportive of her British son-in-law, even though he had taken her only daughter 3,600 miles away. She was a class act in every sense of the word.

[6] William was born on 13 August 1989 and Jamie on 20 June 1992.

15 With Rod and Gun

If you have followed the story thus far, you cannot have helped noticing that the Macalpine-Lenys have been preoccupied by hunting and killing things, and that excludes, for political correctness, countless Germans, Boers and Turks, not to mention the occasional Arab. This warrants further discussion. It is not difficult to appreciate some of the finer points of fly-fishing, even if you don't fish. Beautiful countryside, a constant battle of wits between fisherman and fish, and at the end of the day, something delicious to eat. We cannot, after all, say the same about golf. Game shooting on the other hand is more difficult to appreciate unless you do it, but we will at least try to put it into perspective.

There is something idyllic about an English chalk stream flowing through the lush green meadows of southern England in late May or early June. Gin-clear water passing over strands of brilliant-green weed, waving in the current like a fine head of hair; sand martins swooping down just to kiss the water without seemingly pausing their flight; grey wagtails busily picking up flies as they search the stones along the side of the river, and a water vole suddenly appearing for a moment under the far bank.

In a little patch of dead water below an old fallen tree there is just the faintest indentation on the surface of the water. I freeze, and drop down on one knee. My eyes are straining – transfixed by that little patch of water as the seconds tick by. Perhaps I was mistaken, perhaps I was imagining it, perhaps . . . There it is again. This time I distinctly see the dorsal fin of a large trout. I look at my fly – a Hawthorn – I don't think that will do – too small and too dark. I hurriedly open my fly box and take out a Grey Wulff – always a good bet when there's a hatch of fly on but you're not entirely sure what the fish are feeding on. There it is again – further out into the current this time. I cut off the Hawthorn and tie on the Grey Wulff. It would be quite a long cast from here, so, bending double, I move slowly upstream towards the fish. That should be far enough, but it has not risen for a bit – don't tell me I've put it down. Oh, there it is again, back into the slack water. If only I could cast just above it and bring the fly slowly round. With mounting excitement I start to cast. Out goes the line as I take more off the reel until I can see the end of my fly line just covering that patch of slack water, and then with a final push I let it drop. It all lands in a heap. I can't believe it. No fish will take that. I try again, and this time the fly lands perfectly, just where I want it. It comes round and swims over the spot as I take up the slack line to keep in contact with the fly. Any second now . . . Nothing. I try again. Not nearly such a good cast this time – too far out into the current; I had better retrieve and . . . bang! There is a large swirl on the surface and the line instantly tightens. The rod bends in a graceful arc as the fish starts to take line off the reel with that wonderful sound so dear to all fishermen. It stops as the fish turns and comes towards me. Reel in quickly to keep in contact. Off it goes again. I still haven't seen it – it must be at least 3 pounds. After several strong runs the fish eventually begins to tire. Slowly, slowly it comes to the surface. Look at that tail and those beautiful markings. It could be $3\frac{1}{2}$ pounds – perhaps even 4. I begin to imagine the conversation when I get back to the Rod Room. 'Where did you get it? What did it take?' I have my net out now . . . Take it slowly . . . this could be my largest brown trout ever . . . Not too much pressure as I pull it towards the net . . . It's gone. The line hangs limply and so do I. One minute the prospect of an incredible tale, repeated and expanded as the years go by; the next, nothing. The river moves ever onward, the sand martins still swoop down and kiss the surface, but the pool is quiet. That small corner of still water out of the current looks just as it did before, but I am left reliving those minutes of intense excitement coupled with extreme disappointment over and over again. The walk back to the Rod Room seems to take for ever . . .

Then there are the salmon. Why is it that fishermen will spend hundreds of pounds to stand up to their armpits in freezing water just to have the chance of catching a salmon? What is it about this king of all fish that makes people lay down their lives just to catch one? Of course they are usually fishing amidst the most amazing scenery; but that's not it. When you first connect with a very large, strong fish, it is something completely different. Often, it is like getting caught on the bottom. Then all of a sudden, the bottom begins to move and in a millisecond something large and heavy is streaking for freedom. And you are attached to it, and feel every jerk and change of direction through a 15-foot carbon fibre fly rod bent almost double. Once a salmon knows that it is hooked, the world changes. As it sets off for the horizon, the reel gives line in a never-ending scream. This is the sound that every salmon fisherman wants to hear. The fun has just begun.

I have been lucky enough to catch quite a few salmon over the last forty years, but I will never forget the first. I had gone with my uncle Gerald Moyers to Donegal in April 1971 to fish on the River Lackagh, something he had done every year for the previous thirty years. He kept a car outside Belfast's Aldergrove airport, and we drove from there through London-derry and Strabane and then across the border into the Republic. This was pretty interesting because the Troubles were at their height, and London-derry in 1971 was the nearest I have yet been to a war zone. Hardly surprisingly, all my uncle's usual fishing guests, many of whom were retired army, had got cold feet. But Uncle Gerald wasn't going to let the IRA get in the way of his annual fishing holiday, so he asked me. I had never fished with a double-handed rod, much less possessed one, so he lent me a $12\frac{1}{2}$-foot cane rod (which we used to use in those days), and gave me a professional casting lesson before we left London.

The Lackagh flows due north out of Glen Lough, over the falls and then down through the long rapids to the fishable part of the river below. It can be no more than $2\frac{1}{2}$ miles from the Lough to where it flows into Sheep-haven Bay on the north Donegal coast. In consequence many of the fish are straight out of the sea and incredibly strong. My uncle being a somewhat old-fashioned fisherman, it was plus-fours and meet the ghillie[1] at ten o'clock; we were not even allowed to carry our rods down to the river. And however good the fishing, we always packed up at four o'clock so Uncle Gerald could get back to the lodge for tea. Our ghillie, Eddie Gallagher, had been on the river all his life, was now in his mid-sixties, and was the most excellent fisher. He lived in a little whitewashed stone cottage by the Lackagh Bridge that carries the road from Carraigairt to Creeslough. And he was always dressed the same: old cap, faded pinstriped jacket, non-matching trousers, and gumboots. If it was wet, an old full-length raincoat

[1] A local assistant on a fly fishing expedition, who would be an expert fisher who knows the river intimately.

appeared from somewhere. As I was the beginner, and my uncle knew the river like the back of his hand, Eddie stayed with me. He proved to be an excellent teacher, the most wonderful company, and to have a very dry sense of humour. We arrived to find the river very low and a large number of fish in the Eel Weir, the big pool in front of the fishing hut. There was a little wooden bridge across the stone weir separating the Eel Weir from the Garden Pool above, and this was where we crossed the river. April is a wonderful time of year in Donegal, with the gorse in flower and all the hills decked out in yellow. 'I love to hear the sound of the river,' I said to Eddie. 'I'd rather hear the sound of the reel,' came the reply.

As so often when fish have been trapped by low water for a long time, they had become stale and simply would not look at anything, although this did give me a tremendous amount of casting practice. Then at the end of the first week we had three days of rain followed by a flood, and the river rose 2 feet. All the fish took the opportunity and ran up into the Lough. The next day, Eddie knew that the only chance was to go above the rapids, and took me right up to the New Pool at the top of them where there was one place where you could cast nicely across the pool from the left bank. Perhaps there was just one fish that had not made it into the Lough. There was a strategically placed ash tree fairly close by, which I succeeded in hooking on the first cast. Ever the perfect ghillie, Eddie climbed the tree to retrieve my fly – a Garry Dog that he had tied himself using the hair from his own collie dog. With fly recovered I started to cast again. This time I made a much better job of it, and the fly swung obligingly back across the tail of the pool and then stopped – I was hooked up on something. A couple of seconds later it started to move and I was into a fish.

I had caught a lot of trout on the Gravel Pit in Lincolnshire over the years, but to have a salmon on the end of the line was a totally different experience. The heart raced, the reel screamed, and I knew this was it. 'It might be a bloody kelt,'[2] muttered Eddie, but it was soon clear to both of us that it was a fresh fish. Finally, after what seemed like an age, I managed to get it into the bank and Eddie scooped it out with a net that would easily have handled a 40-pounder. A fresh hen fish of $9\frac{1}{2}$ pounds. Eddie searched

[2] A spent fish that is returning to the sea after spawning.

for a suitable stone and swiftly hit in on the head.[3] Then we shook hands and I lay back on the grass, completely exhausted from sheer excitement. My first salmon – I couldn't believe it. It turned out to be the only fish caught in the fortnight. I didn't sleep a wink – I was catching salmon the entire night.

Brown trout live out their lives in English chalk streams, so a large fish seen in a certain spot one day could well be in the exact same spot the next. The Atlantic salmon on the other hand is migratory, feeding out in the sea off the coasts of Greenland and returning to fresh water to spawn, typically to the same river in which it hatched. So when you go salmon fishing, there might not be any fish in the river and you are happily fishing over nothing. But there is an equally fundamental difference between trout and salmon. Trout hunt by sight, feeding predominantly on insects either in their free-swimming larval (immature) stage, or emerging as adult insects. The whole skill of trout fishing is discovering what they are feeding on at any particular time, and deceiving them into believing that the artificial fly that you have placed in front of them is equally good to eat. And their eye-sight is very good. Salmon on the other hand cease to feed when they come into fresh water, and why they take a salmon fly is not fully understood despite years of dedicated research by both fishermen and scientists.

Clearly aggression plays a significant part, particularly with cock fish, but that is not the entire story. A salmon pool stuffed with showing fish can be fished all the way down, but only one will take the fly. As often as not, nothing does. Then, just as if someone has flicked a switch, a fish will take hold, then another, and then fishers up and down the river will be into fish around the same time. The producers of watches showing the atmospheric pressure did a roaring trade for a time when it was supposed that a change in pressure brought the fish on, but this was soon shown not to be the case. To quote old Eddie Gallagher, 'When the fish are taking, they'll take the button off your coat.' It is when they are not that you have a problem. One thing is certain: if you are fishing a river stuffed with fish and there is not a taker among them, you should try something new: the size of the fly, the weight and hence the depth you are fishing, the speed and the angle of

[3] This was forty years ago; today any salmon that I am lucky enough to catch is put back – I derive so much pleasure from seeing them swim away.

presentation of the fly. The one thing that salmon fishers spend more time deliberating on than anything else, the pattern of fly, probably makes very little difference. Two of the best salmon fishermen I know never change fly patterns they use all through the season, but use different sizes and weights depending on the conditions. When completely exasperated, I have even resorted to changing caps, sometimes with dramatic results. The longer I do it, despite all its great excitement and fascination, I become more and more convinced that salmon fishing is a mug's game.

Game shooting is more difficult to understand for those who have never done it. I once had a secretary who said that she did not agree with killing any of God's creatures. It is difficult to know how to answer that and equally difficult to understand how someone can marvel at the sight of a roding woodcock,[4] or a cock grouse perched atop a drystone wall one minute, and happily shoot either the next. But however much those that disapprove of the pastime are loath to accept it, the fact remains that we owe a large part of the incredible biodiversity that we have on this over-crowded island of ours to previous generations reserving vast tracts of the countryside for the pursuit of field sports. The urge to hunt and kill is deeply ingrained in some of us. As I sit here at my desk in the bay window of the old dining room at Doddington, my eye catches a pigeon far out over the farmyard. For some reason, it suddenly changes direction and heads straight over the house. The muscles across my back instinctively tighten and that imaginary gun comes up.

A shooting day is not just about killing things; the people, the place, the occasion, oh, and the lunch, all play their part. But of course, the actual shooting plays a key part too. Our American friends find it hard to understand the *raison d'être* of driven game shooting. So unsporting; you do not even have to search out the birds for yourself. They do not realise that the whole point is to make the actual shot as difficult as possible. And when the partridges are coming over the guns in a never-ending stream helped by a good old Lincolnshire east wind, such niceties are furthest from your mind: unless you are concentrating wholeheartedly on the business in hand, you will miss.

Duck flighting, sitting partially concealed on the edge of a duck pond as

[4] The display flight performed by the male woodcock.

the light fades waiting for wild ducks to return to spend the night on the pond, is in complete contrast to a day's driven game shooting. As the minutes tick by, the sights and sounds of early evening take over: pigeons flighting back to the woods behind; the call of a cock pheasant as it goes up to roost; a barn owl floating ghost-like along a hedgerow, and a woodcock flying directly over the pond. Eyes and ears strain for the first sign of a duck. Finally there is the unmistakable sound of a couple of mallard. They come in very high, circle the pond twice and then disappear in the direction of the nearby river. What put them off? Did they spot something unusual? Back to waiting. Another two sneak in low over the fields and by the time they are spotted it is not safe to shoot, so down they go on the pond with a lot of splashing and quacking. Oh well, two good decoys. Then as the light begins to go, the air suddenly seems full of ducks; wait until they are right over the pond, aim for the feet and then off go both barrels in quick succession. Immediately all the ducks lift, giving the two guns on the other side of the pond a chance, and each shot is followed by a reassuring splash as a duck hits the water. Like aircraft, ducks have to land into the wind, so you have some idea of the direction they will come from, but there are always surprises. As the light fades still further, teal join the mallard and widgeon coming in. They are much smaller, and sometimes seem to come down almost vertically, so that by the time you have put your gun up they are on the water. Finally it is almost pitch dark and time to pack up and let the dogs hunt for the downed ducks. Many will be actually on the pond, especially any that have been wounded, and more lie out on the surrounding field. A careful count is made to ensure every duck is accounted for, and a further search will always be made the following morning at first light. It is very different, but in its own way, every bit as exciting as a day's driven shooting.

However often I go fishing or have a day's shooting, the anticipation and the excitement never diminishes. I suppose there is a small boy or girl in all of us. Checking the river reports and the weather, so vital for any fly-fishing expedition, and then that moment when you first see the river; waiting on the side of a Welsh valley for the first pheasant to appear over the top of the pine trees high above. Here it comes, well wide at first but suddenly it catches the wind and, still climbing, swings straight towards you. Wait for the moment and up goes the gun, swinging straight through and beyond the still-climbing bird. And further down the line of guns, your host is watching, shot counter in hand . . .

If horse-racing is the sport of kings, driven bird shooting is the sport of gentlemen. Today there are many new entrants to that sport – good luck to them, provided they can embrace its spirit. But at the end of the day, when all the scientific and other explanations have been put forward, the bottom line remains the same for any field sport. To quote the last letter to *The Times* on a whole letters page devoted to the hunting debate: 'The only reason people hunt foxes with dogs is for the fun of it.'

16 Aftermath

It is not until you embark on a project like this that you realise the importance of writing things down. 'The faintest of pencils is better than the best of memories,' goes the old proverb. We know so much more of the Macalpine-Leny story because many of James Macalpine's letters to his uncle Dr Robert Leny have survived, and Agnes Macalpine-Leny and her eldest son Bob both kept a diary. In Agnes's case this ran from 1869, the year she married, until 1916, the year she died. It is pretty dull stuff because it is purely factual, but in consequence provides a very complete picture of the life they lived. What a pity that Robert Downie did not write a journal of some sort. Perhaps he did, and it all went up in smoke on that Appin House bonfire.

In an age when the letter was the only form of long-distance communication, everything had to be written down. But it then has to be kept. After two house fires in Kenya and all the moves associated with military careers, it is amazing that so much has survived. Now we live in ever smaller houses, and keeping things becomes an increasing problem. If it had not been for Betsey Seddon, all our great-grandmother's diaries would have been thrown away long ago.

Every time another member of the family decides to fold their tent and call it a day, so much dies with them. How I wish that my father was still here and I could ask him about his time at Trinity College Dublin, and in Australia. And what *is* the story about the model gun and limber in the drawing room at Doddington? And my mother – how many times did she refer to her experiences in the American Ambulance and I never wrote any of it down? The real answer for that ancient aunt whose memory is still crystal-clear about her time as a little girl is to get the tape recorder out. But when I finally came to record all Muttie Macalpine-Leny's stories about the early days in Kenya I had left it too late – she was past it and no longer wanted to talk about it.

So what of the future and the next generation? Who knows what lies ahead. Will William and Jamie be able to keep Doddington and all the large pictures and records that have survived for so many years? Only time will tell.

The sound of voices in the hall grows louder and louder until the door bursts open, and there is old William and his three sons, all in their dress uniforms (see frontispiece). 'What do you mean, you don't like my portrait, Bob' he roars. 'There I am in my prime. Actually, I think it's a damn good likeness.'

'Well, I didn't mean it quite like that, Dad', began Bob rather lamely. 'And I've always liked mother's portrait . . .'

'I wonder how many bottles of gin it took to design that hat,' chimed in Harley.

'Now don't you start, Harley. Come on, let's go and finish the port. I know I'm not allowed it now, but your mother will never find out.' With that they turn on their heels and close the door behind them with a crash.

I wake up with a start. It is twenty past midnight. The fire has gone out, the central heating has long since turned itself off, and I am cold and stiff. Tilly and Brownie have given up the idea of going up to bed and have cozed down for the night in their basket. With great difficulty I prise them up and persuade them to go out into the night for a moment. Once everyone is back in the house I lock the back door, and slowly and stiffly climb the stairs, saying goodnight to Robert Downie on the way.

And so to bed.

Books and Documents Consulted

A Brief History of the Halsey Family of Great Gaddesden (Gaddesden Estate, 2008)

Adam, Frank, revised by Sir Thomas Innes of Learney, *The Clans, Septs, and Regiments of the Scottish Highlands* (Johnston & Bacon, 1970)

Bainbridge, Agatha, unpublished reminiscences

Beckett, Ian F. W., *The Judgement of History: Sir Horace Smith-Dorrien, Lord French and 1914* (Tom Donovan Publishing, 1993)

Begg, Tom, *The Kingdom of Kippen* (John Donald, 2000)

Bergne, Richard C., *Rough Notes of a pleasant tour from West to East, 1859*, unpublished

Boyle, Capt. R. C., *A Record of the West Somerset Yeomanry 1914–1919* (St Catherine's Press, 1920)

Bridgland, Tony, *Field Gun Jack versus the Boers* (Osprey Publishing, 1998)

Burke's Landed Gentry, 18th Edition, Vol. III (Burke's Peerage, 1972)

Carlill, Vice-Admiral Sir Stephen, 'The Wreck of HMS *Raleigh*', *The Naval Review*, Vol. 70, No. 3, July 1982

Carlyle, Thomas and Jane Welsh, *The Collected Letters of Thomas and Jane Welsh Carlyle*, Vol. 27, 1852 (Duke, 1999)

Cole, Canon R. E. G., *History of the Manor and Township of Doddington* (James Williamson, 1897)

Creagh, O'Moore, *The Distinguished Service Order, 1886–1915* (J. B. Hayward, 1978)

Dalrymple, William, *White Mughals* (HarperCollins, 2002)

Dalswinton Barony Church Minute Book

Duncan, Andrew (ed.), *Medical Commentaries*, Vol. 8, 1793, pp. 301–6

Easterbrook, Charles, *The Chronicle of the Crichton Royal (1833–1936)* (Courier Press, 1940)

Edinburgh Philosophical Journal, July 1825 and July 1827

Ferns, P. N., Macalpine-Leny, I. H., and Goss-Custard, J. D., 'Telemetry of Heart Rate as a Possible Method of Estimating Energy Consumption in the Redshank *Tringa totanus*' in *A Handbook on Biomedical Telemetry and Radio Tracking*, ed. Amlaner, C. J. Jr, and Macdonald, D. W. (Pergamon Press, 1979)

Fieldsend, John, unpublished memoirs

Fisher, Dr David (ed.), *The History of Parliament: The Commons 1820–1832* (Cambridge University Press, 2009)

Fraser, William, *Memoirs of the Maxwells of Pollok* (Edinburgh, 1863)

Gardner, Brian, *Allenby* (Cassell, 1965)

Glover, William, *Journey through the Counties of Berwick, Roxburgh, Selkirk, Dumfries, Ayr, Lanark, East, West, & Mid Lothians, in the Year 1817* (privately printed, Edinburgh, 1818)

Halsey, Jean, Lady, unpublished memoir

Halsey, Lionel, unpublished letters from Ladysmith, 1899–1900

Hart-Davies, Duff (ed.), *The King's Counsellor: Abdication and War – The Diaries of 'Tommy' Lascelles* (Weidenfeld & Nicholson, 2006)

Hay, Doddy, *War under the Red Ensign – the Merchant Navy 1939–1945* (Jane's, 1982)

Herman, Arthur, *The Scottish Enlightenment* (Harper Perennial, 2006)

Hodson, V. C. P., *List of the Officers of the Bengal Army, 1758–1834* (Constable, 1928)

Hooley, Ray, web-based *Ruston & Hornsby Company History*

Huxley, Elspeth, *White Man's Country: Lord Delamere and the Making of Kenya* (Macmillan, 1935)

Innes, P. R., *The History of the Bengal Regiment, now the Royal Munster Fusiliers, and how it helped to win India* (Simpkin, Marshall & Co., 1885)

Jones, John, *Voluntary Aid Detachments in Norton sub Hamden during the First World War*, Somerset Archaeological and Natural History Newsletter No. 66, Autumn 2002

Judgements of Consistory Court, 29 March 1988, 15 April 1991 and 12 January 1993

Kirkmahoe Kirk Session Records, National Archives of Scotland

Macalpine-Downie, Roderick, unpublished final writings

Macalpine-Leny, Agnes, unpublished diaries, 1869–1916

Macalpine-Leny, Ian, *UNISON – the Envy of its Competitors. The Origins,*

Rise and Eventual Decline of the UNISON Network (Haggerston Press, 2004)

Macalpine-Leny, Kenneth, unpublished Family History

Macalpine-Leny, R. L., unpublished diaries, 1891–1902

MacKinnon, D. D., *Lapland Life, or Summer Adventures in Arctic Regions* (Kerby & Endean, 1878)

MacKinnon, D. D., *Memoirs of Clan Fingon* (Hepworth 1899)

Maxwell, Hon. Marmaduke C., *Religious Intolerance: or, a statement of facts, with reference to the appointment of a Matron to the Crichton Royal Institution, Dumfries* (Marsh & Beattie, 1859)

Maxwell-Irving, Alistair, *The Border Towers of Scotland, Their History and Architecture* (Creedon Publications, 2000)

Mellis, Capt. D. B. N., 'Mostly from the Bridge', *The Naval Review*, Vol. 64, Nos. 2, 3, and 4, 1976

Murphy, Sean J., *A Centenary Report on the Theft of the Irish Crown Jewels in 1907* (Centre for Irish Genealogical and Historical Studies, 2008)

National Archives, Ref. FO78 5319

Neeser, Robert, (ed.), *The Despatches of Molyneux Shuldham, January – July 1776* (The Naval History Society, New York, 1913)

New Statistical Account of Scotland, 1841

Paton, John G., *Missionary to the New Hebrides*, (Hodder & Stoughton, 1891)

Pelly, David, *Faster! Faster!* (Macmillan, 1984)

Pemble, John, *Britain's Ghurka War: The Invasion of Nepal, 1814–1816*, (Frontline Books, 2008)

Richardson, William, *A New Essay on Fiorin Grass* (J. Harding, 1814)

Smith, A. Cameron, papers in Ewart Library, Dumfries

Statistical Account of Scotland 1791–1799

Steele, Sarah, *Arthur MacMorrough Kavanagh* (Macmillan, 1891)

Stirling Council Archives, Ch. 2/390, Minutes of Kippen Kirk Session, 20 September 1778 *et seq.*

Sutherland, *Donald, Butt and Ben* (Blackwood, 1963)

Sweet, George, 'The Norton Fruit Farm', *The Nortonian*, No. 1, 1993

The Thin Red Line, Argyll and Sutherland Highlanders' regimental magazine, January 1930

Thorn, Sir Walter, *Memoir of Major General Sir R. R. Gillespie*, 1816

Ticehurst, N. F., *The Mute Swan in England* (Cleaver-Hume Press, 1957)

Weldon, Capt. L. B., *Hard Lying* (Herbert Jenkins, 1925)

Wilkinson, Theon, *Two Monsoons* (Duckworth, 1976)

Williams, Morag, *History of the Crichton Royal Hospital 1839–1989* (Dumfries and Galloway Health Board, 1989)

Windsor, HRH The Duke of, *A King's Story* (Cassell, 1951)

Yates, Keith, *Flawed Victory* (Naval Institute Press, New York, 2000)

Index